Modern
British Poetry,
1900–1939

Twayne's Critical History of Poetry Studies
ALAN SHUCARD, GENERAL EDITOR

•

Alan Shucard, Editor
University of Wisconsin–Parkside

Modern British Poetry, 1900–1939

James Persoon

Grand Valley State University

Twayne Publishers
New York

Modern British Poetry, 1900–1939

James Persoon

Copyright © 1999 by Twayne Publishers

Twayne Publishers
1633 Broadway
New York, NY 10019

Library of Congress Cataloging-in-Publication Data
Persoon, James.
    Modern British poetry, 1900–1939 / James Persoon.
        p.   cm. — (Twayne's critical history of poetry studies)
    Includes bibliographical references and index.
    ISBN 0-8057-1681-5 (alk. paper)
    1. English poetry—20th century—History and criticism.   I. Title.
    II. Series.
    PR610   .P43   1999
    821'.91209—dc21   99-29212
                                                                                        CIP

This paper meets the requirements of ANSI/NISO Z3948-1992 (Permanence of Paper).

10 9 8 7 6 5 4 3 2 1
Printed in the United States of America.

· *Contents* ·

· *Preface* ·

This study, as part of a series, is limited to the years 1900–1939 and to British authors. Ezra Pound and T. S. Eliot, as Americans, and W. B. Yeats, as an Irishman, are excluded. Thomas Hardy, as an important nineteenth-century figure, is likewise treated in detail in a different volume. This at first appeared to me to be a great problem. How does one write about modern British poetry without Hardy, Yeats, Pound, and Eliot?

Their necessary exclusion, however, has proved a great blessing. Their fatherly presences hover over this volume and allow some of their children to receive a fuller look. In that spirit, I have focused greater attention on lesser-known poets, sometimes not even very good poets, for what they tell us about this 40-year period. Poets behind Hardy, Yeats, and Eliot—in reputation more than in skill—have inherited much of the attention: Wilfrid Owen, Edward Thomas, Robert Graves, D. H. Lawrence, H. D., Edith Sitwell, Stevie Smith, W. H. Auden, Dylan Thomas, Edwin Muir, Louis MacNeice. Poets with damaged reputations occupy more space than they would normally receive in a more canonical survey: Alfred Austin and Henry Newbolt, Arthur Symons and Rudyard Kipling, Rupert Brooke and Frances Cornford, Wilfrid Gibson and W. H. Davies, Siegfried Sassoon and Richard Aldington, Osbert Sitwell and Charlotte Mew, Eleanor Farjeon and Anna Wickham, David Jones and Vernon Watkins, Basil Bunting and Hugh MacDiarmid.

The awareness of war in British life over these decades has been used as a metaphor throughout this volume. First, there were four bloody military conflicts in these four decades: the Boer War, the First World War, the Spanish Civil War, and the Second World War. The period also witnessed a class war, which saw the founding of the Labour Party and the first General Strike; there was a war between the sexes, which issued in greater rights for women, including the vote; there was violent agitation in Ireland for Home Rule, which was eventually won; there were the wars in the arts, on all fronts, pit-

ting tradition against Modernism; there was a war between generations, young against old, that found its most bitter expression in the
poetry of young men in the trenches, sent there, they felt, by old men
to die.

This book is dedicated to the memory of Friedrich Ernst Eckhard
(1898–1972), my wife's grandfather, who went into the trenches a
sensitive, artistic boy and returned a silent, angry man. He won the
Iron Cross in 1918, volunteering for a reconnaissance patrol to locate
British troops in the Ardennes, because the weather that morning
was nice. He spent the day out of the trenches in the woods collect-
ing butterflies and sketching them; on his way back in the evening,
he ran into the British and was wounded. It was for this encounter
that he won his medal, which he refused with an obscenity; it was
sent home to his mother and was found in his toolbox after his death.
As an automotive engineer in 1936, he observed the re-arming of
Germany and left for America in August 1937, settling in Detroit. He
refused to speak of war but retained a lifelong passion for butterflies.
It is on his drafting table that this book was written.

· *Acknowledgments* ·

I am indebted to many scholars for their insights into this period, but I want to mention two in particular, both, coincidentally, infantry soldiers in the Second World War, Paul Fussell and Samuel Hynes. They, and many others, I kept finding, had written the books I wished I had written. I also wish to thank the postgraduate students I taught and friends I met in England, who unsystematically but profoundly gave me lessons about class and regional differences.

I owe many particular debts of thanks: to my editor, Alan Shucard, for his good judgment and sharp green pencil; to Wendy Wenner and David McGee, for their support of released time, which has made possible this book's completion; to Mack Smith and Forrest Armstrong, for travel funds, which gave this book its beginning; to Laurel Balkema and Yvonne Williams of Inter-Library Loan, for their cheerful patience with my floods of requests; to Michelle Kovacs of Macmillan Reference and Mary Jo Heck and Mary Boss of Impressions for seeing this book through to publication; to John McCully, Karl Gwiasda, and Peter Casagrande, for starting me on this path; to Justin, Cathy, Julia, Margaret, Andy, and Tom, first, for turning out so well and thus relieving me of parenting duties, and second, for not complaining when I commandeered most of the house for piles of books; to my brothers, for helping me through a couple of tough patches; and to Christl Reges, a disciple of Emerson, who has taught me that contentment is less important than doing useful work, which brings contentment.

Acknowledgment for permission to use lines of poetry is gratefully made to the following:

Herbert Asquith, "The Volunteer," from Poems 1912–1938 (London: Sidgwick and Jackson, 1934). Reprinted by permission of Macmillan Publishers, Ltd.

Excerpt from "The German Auden: Six Early Poems," trans. David Constantine, in *W. H. Auden: "The Map of All My Youth,"* ed. Kather-

Acknowledgments

ine Bucknell and Nicholas Jenkins. Copyright ©1990 by Clarendon Press. Reprinted by permission of Oxford University Press.

Excerpts from various poems by Basil Bunting, from *Complete Poems*. Copyright ©1994 by Oxford University Press. Reprinted by permission of Oxford University Press.

Excerpt from various poems by Frances Cornford, from *Collected Poems*. Copyright ©1954 by Cresset. Reprinted by permission of the Trustees of Mrs. F. C. Cornford Estate.

From Elizabeth Daryush, "War Poem," in *Collected Poems* (Manchester, England: Carcanet, 1976). Reprinted by permission of Carcanet Press.

Excerpts from various poems by H. D., from *Collected Poems: 1912–1944*. Copyright ©1982 by the Estate of Hilda Doolittle. Reprinted by permission of New Directions Publishing Corp.

Eleanor Farjeon, "In Memoriam," from *First and Second Love* (London: Michael Joseph, 1947). Reprinted by permission of David Higham Associates.

Robert Graves, "The Cool Web" and "The Face in the Mirror," from *Complete Poems*, 2 vols., ed. Beryl Graves and Dunstan Ward (Manchester, England: Carcanet, 1997). Reprinted by permission of Carcanet Press.

From John Heath-Stubbs, "The Poet of Bray," in *The New Oxford Book of Light Verse*, ed. Kingsley Amis. Copyright ©1978, 1992 by Oxford University Press. Reprinted by permission of Oxford University Press.

Excerpts from various poems by Stevie Smith, from *Collected Poems of Stevie Smith*. Copyright ©1972 by Stevie Smith. Reprinted by permission of New Directions Publishing Corp.

Excerpt from "A poem about Poems About Vietnam," in *The Anzac Sonata: New and Selected Poems* by Jon Stallworthy. Copyright ©1986 by Jon Stallworthy. Reprinted by permission of W. W. Norton & Company, Inc.

Acknowledgments

Excerpts from various poems by Dylan Thomas, from *The Poems of Dylan Thomas*. Copyright ©1939 by New Directions Publishing Corp. Reprinted by permission of New Directions Publishing Corp.

Anna Wickham, "Multiplication," in *The Writings of Anna Wickham: Free Woman and Poet*, ed. R. D. Smith (London: Virago, 1984). Reprinted by permission of George Hepburn and Margaret Hepburn.

We are Making a New World, by Paul Nash. Used with the permission of The Imperial War Museum, London.

· *Chronology* ·

1840 Thomas Hardy born.

1844 Gerard Manley Hopkins born. J. M. W. Turner's *Rain, Steam, and Speed.*

1850 William Wordsworth dies; *The Prelude* published posthumously. Alfred Tennyson's *In Memoriam.* Tennyson becomes poet laureate.

1855 Walt Whitman's *Leaves of Grass.*

1859 Charles Darwin's *On the Origin of Species.*

1865 William Butler Yeats born. Rudyard Kipling born. Arthur Symons born.

1870 Education Act guarantees a primary school education for both boys and girls.

1874 Robert Frost born. Winston Churchill born.

1885 D. H. Lawrence born. Ezra Pound born. Coventry Patmore's *The Angel in the House.*

1886 Siegfried Sassoon born. Hilda Doolittle born.

1887 Edith Sitwell born. Rupert Brooke born.

1888 T. S. Eliot born. Vincent Van Gogh's *Sunflowers.*

1889 Robert Browning dies. G. M. Hopkins dies.

1892 Alfred, Lord Tennyson dies. Rudyard Kipling's *Barrack Room Ballads.* Richard Aldington born.

1893 Wilfrid Owen born. Edvard Munch's *The Scream.*

1895 Robert Graves born. David Jones born.

1896 A. E. Housman's *A Shropshire Lad.* William Morris dies. Coventry Patmore dies. *Daily Mail* founded, beginning mass circulation journalism. Alfred Austin becomes poet laureate.

1898 Thomas Hardy's *Wessex Poems.* Oscar Wilde's *Ballad of Reading Gaol.* Lewis Carroll dies.

Chronology

1899   Arthur Symons's *The Symbolist Movement in Literature*. W. B. Yeats's *The Wind Among the Reeds*. Sigmund Freud's *The Interpretation of Dreams*. The Boer War begins.

1900   Oscar Wilde dies. Friedrich Nietzsche dies.

1901   Queen Victoria dies. Edward VII becomes king. Thomas Hardy's *Poems of the Past and Present*.

1902   Stevie Smith born. John Masefield's *Saltwater Ballads*. The Boer War ends.

1907   Mary Elizabeth Coleridge dies; *Poems Old and New* published posthumously by Henry Newbolt. W. H. Auden born. Louis MacNeice born.

1908   Ezra Pound arrives in London.

1910   Edward VII dies. George V becomes king. Roger Fry's Postimpressionist show in London of Cezanne. E. M. Forster's *Howard's End*.

1912   Ezra Pound makes H. D. and Richard Aldington the first Imagists. Robert Frost arrives in London. Edward Marsh's anthology *Georgian Poetry*.

1913   Robert Bridges becomes poet laureate. Igor Stravinsky's *The Rite of Spring*. Robert Frost's *A Boy's Will;* meets Edward Thomas.

1914   The Great War begins. T. S. Eliot comes to Oxbridge to study; meets Ezra Pound. James Joyce's *Dubliners*. W. B. Yeats's *Responsibilities*. Thomas Hardy's *Satires of Circumstance*. Dylan Thomas born.

1915   Rupert Brooke dies on troop ship, eulogized by Winston Churchill. Germans use poison gas at Ypres. D. H. Lawrence's *The Rainbow*.

1916   Heavy losses at the Somme and at Verdun. David Lloyd George replaces Herbert Asquith as prime minister. Charlotte Mew's *The Farmer's Bride*.

1917   Edward Thomas dies in combat, after publishing *Poems*. Wilfrid Owen meets Siegfried Sassoon at Craiglockhart War Hospital. T. S. Eliot's *Prufrock*. Thomas Hardy's *Moments of Vision*. D. H. Lawrence's *Look! We Have Come Through!* Paul Nash's "Ypres Salient" Exhibition.

Chronology

1918   Wilfrid Owen and Isaac Rosenberg die in combat. The Great War ends. Gerard Manley Hopkins's *Poems* published posthumously by Robert Bridges. Franchise Bill gives vote to women.

1919   Siegfried Sassoon's *War Poems*. First German Expressionist film, *The Cabinet of Dr. Caligari*. W. B. Yeats's *Wild Swans at Coole*.

1920   Keith Douglas born. Wilfrid Owen's *Poems* published posthumously by Siegfried Sassoon.

1922   T. S. Eliot's *The Waste Land*. Edith Sitwell's *Facade*. Thomas Hardy's *Late Lyrics and Earlier*. C. M. Grieve publishes poems in Scots under name Hugh MacDiarmid. Alice Meynell dies. Philip Larkin born. David Lloyd George replaced as prime minister by Ramsay MacDonald and first Labour government.

1923   W. B. Yeats wins Nobel Prize for literature. D. H. Lawrence's *Birds, Beasts, and Flowers*. Rainer Maria Rilke's *Sonnets to Orpheus* and *Duino Elegies*.

1925   W. B. Yeats's *A Vision*. Adolph Hitler's *Mein Kampf*. Edwin Muir's *First Poems*.

1927   Robert Graves's and Laura Riding's *A Survey of Modernist Poetry*.

1928   Thomas Hardy dies; *Winter Words* published posthumously. Charlotte Mew dies. W. B. Yeats's *The Tower*. Stephen Spender hand-publishes Auden's pamphlet *Poems*. Walt Disney's first Mickey Mouse cartoon, *Steamboat Willie*.

1929   The Great Depression begins in America. Robert Graves's *Good-bye to All That*. D. H. Lawrence's *Pansies*. Virginia Woolf's *A Room of One's Own*.

1930   The Depression hits England. D. H. Lawrence dies. Rudyard Kipling dies. Robert Bridges dies. John Masefield becomes poet laureate. William Empson's *Seven Types of Ambiguity*. W. H. Auden's *Poems*. Stephen Spender's *Twenty Poems*. T. S. Eliot's *Ash Wednesday*. Derek Walcott born. Ted Hughes born.

1931   Wilfrid Owen's *Collected Poems*, edited by Edmund Blunden.

1932   D. H. Lawrence's *Last Poems* published posthumously by Richard Aldington. Sylvia Plath born.

Chronology

1933 Hitler becomes *Reichskanzellor*. T. S. Eliot delivers anti-Semitic lectures *After Strange Gods*. Vera Brittain's *Testament of Youth*. George Barker's first book, *Thirty Preliminary Poems*. Geoffrey Grigson founds *New Verse*.

1934 Dylan Thomas's first book, *18 Poems*. David Gascoyne's first book, *Man's Life Is This Meat*. Nancy Cunard's anthology *Negro*.

1935 William Empson's *Poems*. T. S. Eliot's *Murder in the Cathedral* and *Burnt Norton*.

1936 George V dies. Edward VIII becomes king, abdicates to marry American divorcée Wallis Simpson. George VI becomes king. A. E. Housman dies; *More Poems* published posthumously. Dylan Thomas's *Twenty-five Poems*. W. H. Auden's *Look, Stranger!* Surrealist exhibition in London. Spanish Civil War begins.

1937 Pablo Picasso's *Guernica*. Stevie Smith's first book, *A Good Time Was Had By All*. David Jones's *In Parenthesis*.

1938 *Kristallnacht*. Sudetenland Crisis. Prime Minister Chamberlain signs Munich Pact. Louis MacNeice's *Autumn Journal*.

1939 W. H. Auden leaves for America. W. B. Yeats dies; *Last Poems and Two Plays* published posthumously. Sigmund Freud dies. Auden writes elegies for Yeats and Freud. Henry Treece and J. P. Hendry edit anthology, *The New Apocalypse*. Seamus Heaney born. World War II begins.

· ONE ·

"Make It New":
Edwardians, Georgians,
Impressionists, and Imagists,
1900–1912

The Great War of 1914 to 1918 so affected every aspect of European life that literary history, too, almost immediately used it as a touchstone. In Britain, everyone who fought and also wrote poetry during the war, no matter how different the work, was a War Poet. Following the war, and especially with the publication in 1922 of both James Joyce's *Ulysses* and T. S. Eliot's *The Waste Land*, the Modernist revolution dominated literature and criticism. For a population devastated not only economically but emotionally, the title of Eliot's poem provided a metaphor for the postwar world. The War Poets had by 1916 lost any sense of the possibilities of heroism, and soon after the war, in the face of continued high unemployment, the general population, too, began to ask what the war had been for. It seemed a tragic waste. David Lloyd-George, the victorious war leader, was suddenly ousted from power in January 1922, and the job of the first Labour government became economic revival. The job of the poet became cultural and spiritual revival—to *Make It New*, in the simple phrase that Ezra Pound used for a collection of his essays. From hindsight, the period before the war looked naive. Its innocent virtues seemed to come from an unforgivable complacency and blindness toward what was about to happen. Edwardians and Georgians, those poets who wrote during the reigns of Edward VII (1901–1910) and George V (1910–1926), were likewise increasingly dismissed, and their reputations have still hardly recovered.

The Edwardians

The Edwardian decade passed quickly enough that it had little time to denote more than a style, and that style reflected the love of lavish parties and of dressing up in uniforms exhibited by the new king. John Osborne's groundbreaking 1957 play *Look Back In Anger* refers to the period with disdain, though one can also detect the powerful image that Edwardian England was to project deep into the century: "The old Edwardian brigade do make their brief little world look pretty tempting. All home-made cakes and croquet, bright ideas, bright uniforms. Always the same picture: high summer, the long days in the sun, slim volumes of verse, crisp linen, the smell of starch. What a romantic picture. Phoney too, of course. It must have rained sometimes."[1] Queen Victoria had always intended for her eldest son, when king, to become Albert the First, memorializing the austere and earnest virtues of her German husband, but on her death Bertie instead assumed the name of Edward VII. He created around himself exactly the sort of life his father and mother had always disapproved of, a world of courtiers and card tables, horse races and shooting parties. The poet and aristocrat Osbert Sitwell described the time, in which he had been a participant, as a profusion of exotic fruits: "Never had Europe seen such mounds of peaches, figs, nectarines and strawberries at all seasons, brought from their steamy tents of glass.... And to the rich, the show was free."[2] *Edwardian* came to imply an expensive, excessive, exquisite surface, maintained by and for the rich. The decade seemed to lack seriousness, as if it were one long country house party, a criticism carried over to the Georgians as well, who were charged with having a weekend-picnic view of the world which issued in poems in "Ye Olde Teashoppe Style," as Roy Campbell satirized in *The Georgiad* (1931). Reading the criticism that the Modernists, led by Pound and Eliot, aimed at the Edwardians and Georgians, one finds colorful and reductive epithets: the poetry of rainbows and wood-smoke, cottages and ducks, happy brook and cuckoo's song. And certainly there was a willful innocence and nostalgia in the first decade of the twentieth century. In *The Condition of England* (1909), Charles Masterman (at the time a sitting Liberal member of Parliament and during the war the nation's first propaganda minister) laments the loss of a rural world of "little red-roofed towns and hamlets, the labourer in the fields at noontide or evening, the old English service in the old English village church," a world irrevocably passing for the majority of Britons, four-fifths of whom, Masterman notes, now lived in cities.³ Though indulging in nostalgia, Masterman is aware both of the passing of this yeoman's world and of problematic new conditions underlying the pleasant aristocratic surface.

The Poet Laureate Alfred Austin wrote the official verse for the newly urban and suburban nation, verse that took no account of the new realities, though it betrayed some anxiety that the Victorian achievement could be maintained by the Edwardians. Austin's verse was backward-looking, to his great predecessors in office, William Wordsworth and Alfred, Lord Tennyson. While he was as aware as his contemporaries that there was a considerable falling off in his selection as Tennyson's successor, he dutifully strove to preserve the accomplishments of the past, as in these lines from "Why England is Conservative," a poem addressed to "our dear Mother, the fair Past":

> Mother of happy homes and Empire vast,
> Of hamlets meek, and many a proud desmesne,
> Blue spires of cottage smoke 'mong woodlands green,
> And comely altars where no stone is cast.⁴

What Austin fears is political change, which may bring about the collapse of social order and perhaps even natural order:

> And shall we barter these for gaping Throne,
> Dismantled towers, mean plots without a tree,
> A herd of hinds too equal to be free,
> Greedy of other's, jealous of their own,
> And, where sweet Order now breathes cadenced tone,
> Envy, and hate, and all uncharity?

In the poem's next section, Austin immediately upbraids himself for having so little faith in England's ability to "stem the tide" which England had periodically "routed in the field." How far this is from Percy Bysshe Shelley's response to the Peterloo Massacre in "A Song: 'Men of England,'" which did become, as Shelley wished, a hymn of the British labor movement. Despite the bravado, or evident in its forced heartiness, doubt and fear are visible. Even more striking, however, is the denial of reality. England has already lost its "woodlands green" and, for four-fifths of the nation, its "hamlets meek" and "cottage smoke." Throughout the industrial Midlands, people have already been herded into "mean plots without a tree." Whether the "comely altars" can long maintain a peaceful and cadenced harmony in the nation (and indeed whether poetry will long be peaceful and cadenced) is open to debate.

In Samuel Hynes's phrasing, the "essential Edwardian mood is sombre—a feeling of nostalgia for what has gone, and of apprehension for what is to come."[5] This Hynes traces to two large unanswered questions: "how to live in a scientific universe, and how to live with industrialism." Though Edwardian poets did not directly address the issue of how science undermined one's confident assumption of a central place in the universe or the growing problem of the transformed economic and social basis of people's lives, they did not revert simply to nostalgia. If the Edwardians seemed to live in a land of Sunday picnics and weekend walks, their poets certainly knew of ants at the picnic and brambles on the walk, and of much else beyond. They were extremely conscious of social issues, perhaps in reaction to the "art-for-art's-sake" aesthetic of the 1890s (itself a reaction to a Victorian sensibility that preferred "art for morality's sake"). Women's rights, the unfairness of social Darwinism, the poor condition of the cities and of workers, Irish nationalism, and international belligerances all found their expression, especially in the novel and drama, but also in the poetry, initially through the realism of the phenomenally popular Rudyard Kipling (1865–1936).

Kipling lived his first six years in India, then returned there at the age of 18 as a journalist for the Lahore *Civil and Military Gazette*. He published some stories and verses on India and the military, and when he returned to England at age 24, quickly produced a series of works, among them the two *Jungle Books* (1894–1895) and *Barrack Room Ballads* (1892), that made him the literary phenomenon of the day. In an 1897 review, William Dean Howells, the dean of American realism, called Kipling the "Laureate of the Larger England."[6] He meant by this that Kipling was the poet and defender of empire, and he made sure to note that Americans were unstirred by such poetry. But by the end of his review, Howells has succumbed to the "beauty" and "sincerity" of Kipling and claims for him a larger empire still, one that includes even America, for Kipling is the laureate "wherever the English tongue is written or spoken." It is in part Kipling's reinvigoration of the narrative poem, and the creation of an audience for reading it, that led that venerable Victorian Thomas Hardy (1840–1928) in his first volume of poetry to concentrate so heavily on Napoleonic ballads. Even that Celtic mystic William Butler Yeats (1865–1939) turned, in the first decade of the next century, to a more embodied, realistic, and popular focus by concentrating on the theater. Yeats and Hardy, better poets than Kipling, would inspire alternate traditions that would have little to do with him. Kipling must be credited, however, with the resuscitation and expansion of the audience that Robert Browning aimed for, an audience wider than the genteel British middle class. Whatever political and social influence poetry would have in the remainder of the century owes its debt to the power of Kipling to attract readers, even when those readers, such as C. S. Lewis, were unsure of whether they loved or hated him.

Kipling is most often damned as the poet of empire. His celebration of imperialism, however, has a darker undertone of realism than was later commonly acknowledged. His contribution to Victoria's Jubilee celebration of 1897 was "Recessional," a warning against chauvinistic boasting that recalls the fate of all empires, to "melt away."[7] At the same time, he wrote approvingly of men who could boast of their hard-won accomplishments in building up their merchant empires. One such character is Sir Anthony Gloster, who in a long death-bed narrative ("The 'Mary Gloster'") tells his success story to his son. The father recognizes that his son, Dickie, will probably let the family fortune melt away, as Dickie's interests are not mercantile, nor is he a hardy soul: "For you muddled with books and pictures, an' china an' etchin's an' fans, / And your rooms at college were beastly—more like a whore's than a man's" (*Kipling,* 132). One can almost hear Kipling as the disapproving Victorian parent looking upon the interior decoration interests of Oscar Wilde and James McNeill Whistler. George Orwell, no friend of imperialism, faulted Kipling for his lack of awareness of class—"Kipling is almost unconscious of the class war that goes on in an army"—but defended him politically, arguing that Kipling aligns himself with those in power, who actually must and do decide things, and that this has the advantage of giving him a "certain grip on reality," compared with the armchair intelligentsia.[8] Kipling most often wrote of ordinary people, often soldiers, in their own dialect, though the Cockney slang he puts in their mouths sometimes makes them cardboard cutouts rather than real people. He was also unafraid of conventional thoughts and common truths. Thus Kipling alone among serious poets could not only accept but praise clichés and conventional wisdoms, the kind young children would be required to write in their copybooks, calling them the "Gods of the Copybook Headings" (*Kipling*, 793–95). These "Gods" teach such truths as "if you don't work you die," and such inevitabilities as, in this "brave new world," "terror and slaughter return." This poem from 1919 was of course commenting on the Great War, but Kipling's verse had already turned darker in writing about the soldier's experience of the Boer War, or the empire's recessional. He valued highly the ordinary realities, especially when faced vigorously with duty, energy, and heart.

Kipling's ordinary people are most typically soldiers, just as John Masefield's are sailors, but Kipling also added to that mythic figure the "Englishman" in his creation of Hobden the Hedger. Hobden is a relative of Thomas Hardy's Wessex farm laborer, Hodge, and of Edward Thomas's Lob. Kipling locates Hobden in a past that predates the Norman Conquest:

> His dead are in the churchyard—thirty generations laid.
> Their names were old in history when Domesday Book was made;
> And the passion and the piety and the prowess of his line
> Have seeded, rooted, fruited in some land the Law calls mine.
>
> (*Kipling*, 603)

Here are Kipling's booming rhythms, alliterations, and rhymes, which made his verse both memorable and popular; here also is picked up the new concern with "Englishness" that came to dominate Edwardian and Georgian poetry, betraying an anxiety about the empire that elsewhere Kipling celebrated. Can little England long sit on top of a world empire? And while England is bringing Englishness to India and Hong Kong, what are those places bringing to England? What is England? The subtext of this concern with creating a solid Anglo-Saxon English past is overtly stated at the end of the twentieth century by the Jamaican poet Louise Bennett, who wonders how England, "de motherlan," will like what is happening— "de tunabout" of colonial immigrants changing the face of England in the "Colonisation in Reverse."[9]

The old century ended with the illness and death of the queen, whose name had become synonymous with the age over which she had presided for so long. The country was in the middle of a disastrous war against the Boers in South Africa and in a growing armaments competition with Germany. The cultural poses of nineties decadence seemed to signal the end of a stable society built on the high Victorian values of duty, sobriety, and moral earnestness. It was a time of mixed anxiety and hopefulness, as the ends of centuries tend to be, evoking images of death and rebirth. At the end of the eighteenth century, for example, despite the political excesses and failures of the French Revolution, William Wordsworth and Samuel Taylor Coleridge in *Lyrical Ballads* (1798) could optimistically argue for a new poetry in a new language, and in 1799 the German poet Novalis could exclaim that "the world must be romanticized, that the original meaning may be rediscovered!"[10] Likewise, at the end of the nineteenth century, it was natural for poets to look back at the past in reevaluation and forward to the future in anticipation.

On the last day of the century, one of its great novelists, Thomas Hardy, who had recently turned his back on the novel to make a new reputation as a poet, composed a short lyric which itself looks backward and forward. The poem is "The Darkling Thrush," which is both an epitaph for the nineteenth century, whose corpse appears in the poem, and a look forward to the possibilities of the new century, heralded by the thrush's song. The poem ends with the auditor of the song unsure of its meaning: "I could think there trembled through / His happy good-night air / Some blessed Hope, whereof he knew / And I was unaware."[11] The poem is a famous anthology piece and the hopefulness or doubt of its last lines often debated; it contains both contrary emotions. The importance for Hardy of facts and exact dates, as it had been for his earliest poetic mentor Wordsworth, means that he quite correctly dated the end of the century as December 31, 1900, but in the popular imagination it was the approach of the year 1900 that seemed like the new beginning. Yeats, in his introduction to *The Oxford Book of Modern Verse* (1936), recalled the year 1900 as the date when things changed, when "everybody got down off his stilts," when "nobody drank absinthe with his black coffee."[12]

Yeats's stilts are metaphorical, but the absinthe controversy was real, the source of a great public debate, similar to the debate about drug use at the end of the twentieth century. In mid-century, in France, absinthe moved from a working-class drink to one immensely popular with all classes. But unlike beer and wine, which were considered healthy drinks, absinthe soon became associated with addiction. Pale-green in color and counting the poison wormwood among its ingredients, it seemed to have a frightening but enticing, almost hallucinogenic quality. In the words of the painter Alfred Delvau in

1862, "it sticks immense wings on your shoulders and you leave for a country without horizon and without frontier, but also, without poetry and without sun."[13] Arthur Symons's "The Absinthe-Drinker" described the experience as an attractive but confusing dream:

> Far off, I hear a roar, afar yet near,
> Far off and strange, a voice is in my ear,
> And is the voice my own? the words I say
> Fall strangely, like a dream, across the day;
> And the dim sunshine is a dream.[14]

When Yeats says that in 1900 everyone suddenly stopped drinking absinthe, he is signaling a deeply felt cultural change as well as a change in literary style, the end of Wilde's "dicky-dongs" decade and of his own Celtic Twilight and symbolist periods, and, cold turkey, he is entering a new place for poetry, in the sun. Smokey cafés certainly remained a favorite and fertile haunt for poets, but Yeats is recalling the striking reemergence in poetry of light, air, health, sanity, the ordinary, even the out-of-doors—in short, all the favorite locations of Edwardian and Georgian poetry. Orpheus has come up from the underworld, and moral earnestness is no longer banished.

Impressionism

Born the same year as Yeats and Kipling, the poet and critic Arthur Symons (1865–1945) is most responsible for bringing French Symbolism and Impressionism across the channel to England. The French poet Jean Moréas in 1886 proposed the terms *symboliste* and *symbolisme* to describe Charles Baudelaire's *Les Fleurs du Mal* (1857), and the terms soon were used to describe the work of Stephane Mallarmé, Paul Verlaine, Arthur Rimbaud, and others who attempted to write of a world of abstract feelings and metaphysical realities in terms of metaphor and symbol, usually in free verse. Symons's *Symbolist Movement in Literature* (1899) famously fueled the development of Yeats, but his own poetry in the 1890s had already popularized French practice. His poems often had the effect of Impressionist painting: Just as Claude Monet painted and repainted a succession of haystacks or cathedral facades in the changing light of dawn, midmorning, noon, early afternoon, and so on, Symons wrote poems in series, revisiting a scene to study its changing moods. One such series, titled "Colour Studies At Dieppe," from *London Nights* (1895), includes poems subtitled "Rain on the Down," "After Sunset," "On the Beach," and "Grey and Green." This last poem carries the same title as a painting by the English Impressionist Walter Richard Sickert (1860–1942), who lived in Dieppe from 1885 to 1905. Sickert, who studied first with Whistler and then Edgar Degas, performed the same service for English painting that Symons did for English literature, as the main conduit of the ideas of the French avant-garde. Symons's poem uses Sickert's subtleties of scene and color and adds subtleties of sound to translate the painting into a poem, creating an effect of sharply delineated listlessness:

> The grey-green stretch of sandy grass,
> Indefinitely desolate;
> A sea of lead, a sky of slate:
> Already autumn in the air, alas!
>
> One stark monotony of stone,
> The long hotel, acutely white,
> Against the after-sunset light
> Withers grey-green, and takes the grass's tone.
>
> Listless and endless it outlies,
> And means, to you and me, no more
> Than any pebble on the shore,
> Or this indifferent moment as it dies.
> (*Symons*, 42–43)

Oscar Wilde had even earlier than Symons attempted similar painterly translations, reacting to Impressionism and especially to the American expatriate in London, James McNeill Whistler. Whistler's paintings were often given musical titles, such as "Symphony in White" or "Nocturne in Black and Gold," which Wilde appropriated in such poems as "Symphony in Yellow." Symons's Impressionism would issue in the early poems of T. S. Eliot (1888–1965) and lead Ezra Pound (1885–1972), who once said he regarded Symons as a personal god, to Imagism.

The movement he brought to England even reached the elder Hardy, as one can observe in "Neutral Tones," published in 1898.

The poem's opening line establishes an action and a scene, which the rest of the stanza then fills out with almost total reliance on visual elements, here primarily color and objects, to establish mood:

> We stood by a pond that winter day,
> And the sun was white, as though chidden of God,
> And a few leaves lay on the starving sod;
> —They had fallen from an ash, and were gray.
>
> (*Hardy*, 12)

The scene's limited palette of white and gray suggests both a stark intensity of feeling and a constriction in expression of that feeling. The yoking of "sun" and "God" with the unusual word "chidden" works on the semantic level to suggest the Fall, of which fallen leaves are a remote reminder; the starving earth, too, suggests the life-and-death seriousness of the human situation. The painful limits of expression are suggested by the spare and minimalist nature of the scene: a few leaves, starvation, sod without vegetable growth or covering, an ash tree with its evocation of a burned-out fire, helped along by the nearness of "gray." The poem returns to this scene in its ending, but in this second time around those images have risen to the level of symbol: "Your face, and the God-curst sun, and a tree / And a pond edged with grayish leaves." Face, tree, pond, leaves, and sun are now disembodied objects which themselves can create for the speaker (and reader) the emotions surrounding the ending of love. For Hardy to nod to French Impressionism and Symbolism in this way shows their power.

France seemed in the 1890s to be the source of new directions in the arts. After the Impressionists, the new influence to emerge at century's end was Paul Cézanne, from whom one can trace a line directly to Picasso and Cubism and from thence to Modernism. It is Cézanne who stands behind the attempt of another British writer, younger than Hardy and Yeats, to pinpoint the end of the nineteenth century and the beginning of something new. Virginia Woolf (1882–1941) claimed December 1910 as the date when human nature changed. Woolf was probably referring to the first Postimpressionist exhibition that had just opened at the Grafton Galleries, for which her fellow Bloomsburian Roger Fry had cowritten the catalog, inventing along the way the name "postimpressionist" for Cézanne. Fry championed Cézanne as the artist who had finally given structure to Impressionism, and it was this structure that gave Woolf the direction she was looking for in creating a new kind of fiction, different from the Edwardian masters she disliked, Wells, Galsworthy, and Bennett.

What Woolf did for the novel, Pound did for poetry. If one were to pause at the heights of Modernism and look back, Ezra Pound might appear to be the father of twentieth-century British poetry. His mentoring of Eliot, among other willing and unwilling young poets, and his tireless reviewing and editing and manifesto-writing and opinionating provided a vast wave of energy upon which many poets and several movements rode. Pound's Imagism and then Vorticism and then Modernism followed in a line of "isms" popular in succession at the turn of the century—Symbolism, Unanism, Futurism. But something different happened with poetry in Britain after the ascendancy of Pound's ideas. While Modernism certainly continued to exert a strong influence, especially on the novel, British poets, by and large, turned to a style that had more in common with what the Georgians were doing before so many of them were killed in the Great War. And those poets, when looking for a tradition and a poetic forefather, came increasingly to fasten not on Pound or Eliot or Yeats, but on Thomas Hardy.

Hardy seems at first an unlikely choice. He does not have the fierceness, erudition, or energy of Pound, a self-appointed leader of the arts who admired another strong leader, Benito Mussolini (who kept to the realm of politics and did not argue with Pound about poetry). He shows little of the innovativeness and scholarship of Eliot, who married French Symbolism to metaphysical poetry and ransacked the world for images. He displays none of the brilliance and technical skill of Yeats, probably a consensus choice for best poet of the century. Hardy was self-taught and sensitive to the frequent charge that he wrote too roughly, awkwardly inserting dialect words and unlikely situations into his work. But to a younger generation reacting against the self-consciousness and refinements of Aestheticism and Symbolism, Hardy seemed to possess a deeper authenticity than more polished artists. The generation of the Georgians adopted him as mentor and father, even though by the end of his life he was so private as almost to be inaccessible. The trail of twentieth-century writers who made a pilgrimage to his house on the outskirts of Dorchester included W. B. Yeats, Virginia Woolf, Robert Graves, T. E. Lawrence, and Siegfried Sassoon. More important are the poetic responses of the most important British poets of the next several generations, from the Georgians Edward Thomas, D. H. Lawrence, and Robert Graves to the following generations of W. H. Auden, Dylan Thomas, and Philip Larkin.

Graves in his autobiography *Good-bye to All That* (1929) records Hardy saying that "all we can do is to write on the old themes in the old styles, but try to do a little better than those who went before us."[15] With this modest, or perhaps immodest, aesthetic, Hardy's influence seems to come not from any innovation in style or method, but from his perseverance and endurance as an artist, his determination to not be stopped by criticism, old age, or programmatic movements from being a poet. Acceptance as a poet came late for Hardy; when his attempts to publish poetry in the 1860s were unsuccessful, he turned to novel-writing as a career to support himself and his new wife. He was by the 1890s, however, becoming frustrated at the limitations of writing serially for magazines and their audience, and when he was financially secure turned to poetry where he could finally be an artist. He did not receive his first recognition as a poet until 1898, with the publication of *Wessex Poems*, which needed, Hardy felt, the allusion to his popular Wessex novels to convince his publisher, Harper's, to take a chance on it. Even while Modernism dominated the 1920s and 1930s, poets such as Graves, and later Auden and Dylan Thomas, found themselves attracted to formal verse. Hardy's persistence and solitariness in the face of Victorian and then Modernist prescriptions and proscriptions seemed not only admirable but useful. Hardy, as a link to the past, became the old father reclaimed by British poets after a rebellious Modernist interlude.

Modernism was in part rejected because it lost the national audience that Browning, Tennyson, and Kipling had created for poetry. It was the same in the art world; the styles that issued from Impressionist painting never became widely popular. Cubism, Constructivism, Dadaism, Surrealism, and Abstract Expressionism took artists and insiders by storm, but the popular audience did not follow. Later in the twentieth century, Impressionism became the darling of the people, a guaranteed moneymaker at exhibitions and retrospectives, and of course for ancillary uses such as images for advertising, tea towels, note cards, calendars, and souvenirs. The critic Robert Herbert argues, without condescension, that this was so because the Impressionists were the last to envision a harmonious world not yet completely violated by industrialization, urbanization, world wars, mass torture, and extermination (Herbert, 306). Images of leisure and of the country, such as boating, walking, eating at picnics or in cafés, or simply enjoying a landscape, allowed people to construct a desirable history for themselves in the face of change. In the same way, poetry in Britain moved closer to a popular audience in mid-century, especially through the efforts of W. H. Auden, Dylan Thomas, and Philip Larkin, who did not ignore Modernist advances but chose to subordinate Modernist principles to writing on the "old themes in the old styles." Thus Auden went on American television's *Tonight Show* to recite limericks, Thomas made his boozy but entertaining circuit of American colleges, and Larkin, though a very complex and private man, through the simplicity and earthiness of his language and his themes became the people's laureate.

It was not clear in 1900 that this is how things would play out in British poetry. The most popular poet at that moment was undoubtedly Kipling; the most promising, Yeats; the most revered but ignored, Hardy, a ghostly visitant from another century. Gerard Manley Hopkins was as yet unknown. The Americans had not yet arrived. Any who literally set foot in Britain did so to pay homage to a superior culture, not to challenge it. No school of poets dominated. Some, like John Masefield, faithfully attended Yeats at the Monday night meetings in his flat in London. Some, like William Watson and the current laureate Alfred Austin, were holdovers from the Victorian past who sought to sustain its virtues. There were classical scholars such as Robert Bridges and A. E. Housman who wrote an academic poetry imitating Greek and Latin rhythms. There were followers of the worst of Kipling, such as the apologist for imperialism Henry Newbolt, and others, like G. K. Chesterton (and Yeats and Masefield), who wanted to write of Kipling's "manly" world of contemporary realism and vigorous action. There were crafters of the beautiful, such as Walter de la Mare, who could reproduce the music of Tennyson and Swinburne. There were the unabashed entertainers, such as Alfred Noyes, who commanded a large audience by self-confidently writing romantic ballads in the style of Robert Louis Stevenson's novels. There was a generation of younger writers, such as Robert Graves and D. H. Lawrence, who would emerge as Georgians and later profoundly affect the new directions poetry would take. In a plebiscite held by the *Journal of Education* in 1913 to determine the country's favorite poet, the top vote-getters were Kipling, the winner by two to one over Watson, followed by Bridges (who became Poet Laureate that year, succeeding Austin), and Noyes.

The Georgians

Some crucial changes were already underway, however, which would lead to the emergence of a new poetry from the transitional Edwardian years. Virginia Woolf's pegging of 1910 as the beginning of the time of change, coinciding with the beginning of the reign of George V, gives us her sense of the Edwardian period as a stagnant time. There is more justice in noting the unsettled variousness of the Edwardian years. Metaphorically, those years are fallow but fertile ground from which the new would spring.

The first new buds were announced in a brief preface written in October 1912 by Edward Marsh for the anthology *Georgian Poetry, 1911–1912:* "This volume is issued in the belief that English poetry is now once again putting on a new strength and beauty ... [which] may if it is fortunate help the lovers of poetry to realize that we are at the beginning of another 'Georgian Period' which may take rank in due time with the several great poetic ages of the past."[16] Marsh edited four more anthologies of "Georgian" poetry, the last in 1922, and his term for the period stuck, as well as the practice of introducing new poets by way of an anthology. Marsh included some Edwardian stalwarts to signal the seriousness of the book—Chesterton, Masefield, de la Mare—but he introduced what he considered the best of the new—D. H. Lawrence, Gordon Bottomley, Wilfrid Gibson, W. H. Davies, Lascelles Abercrombie, and Rupert Brooke (1887–1915).

Brooke, a friend of both Marsh and the anthology's publisher, Harold Monro, the founder of the Poetry Bookshop in London (where Brooke gave the inaugural reading), became the essential Georgian in the public's eye after his early death in the Great War. His poem "Grantchester" from the first anthology became the quintessential Georgian lyric. It is a witty, urbane poem celebrating, ironically, simple country village life, made all the more piquant to the poet by his sojourn in Berlin in 1912, where the poem was composed. The freedom of English meadows, where, unkempt, blows an "English unofficial rose," is contrasted in the poem to the regulated and stuffy life in Germany, where "tulips bloom as they are told."[17]

Brooke's broad patriotism then turns in the poem to an increasingly specific love of place—not just England but Cambridgeshire, not just Cambridgeshire but Grantchester, and finally not just Grantchester but the specific elm-clumps and bathing pool by Brooke's residence, the Old Vicarage. Here Brooke and his circle of Cambridge friends achieved a reputation for challenging Victorian social strictures by indulging in nude bathing, for which they were named "Neo-pagans" by Brooke's friend Virginia Woolf. Brooke includes himself and the Neo-pagans in the poem in a gently deflating way: "In Grantchester their skins are white; / They bathe by day, they bathe by night." The paradisal Grantchester is such a garden of youth and high spirits that even aging and death are treated cleanly, bravely, and with an attitude of fun by the inhabitants, who "when they get to feeling old, / They up and shoot themselves, I'm told." "I'm told" is a broad irony here, because these free-living, day-and-night bathers are none other than Brooke and friends.

Other ironies are more subtle and uncertain. The poem ends by asking a series of questions:

> Say, is there Beauty yet to find?
> And Certainty? and Quiet kind?
> Deep meadows yet, for to forget
> The lies, and truths, and pain?
> (*Brooke*, 97)

Is there still such a haven, such an England, Brooke asks? In this haven, lies and pain would be forgotten, but so, significantly, would truths. What a price to pay for "Quiet" and "Certainty." Those qualities, and "Beauty," are opposed to "truths," uncapitalized and plural and thus brought into doubt. Grantchester is not only an idealized England but also an idealized Childhood and Youth, the last and fast-fading certainty of a young man on the brink of adulthood. The concluding couplet repeats the questionings of the penultimate couplets in more grounded language: "Stands the Church clock at ten to three? / And is there honey still for tea?" These lines attempt to change the abstractions of the previous lines into a final image of an English summer afternoon stopped at its honey-golden moment of perfection. The clock stands at its specific time, and "still," in another of its denotations, freeze-frames the picture. Read in context, the last line is both wistful and intentionally ironic; read alone, it easily lends itself to parody.

This has been a problem for Brooke with critics. That he could call war "fun," as if it were a cricket match, has given him a reputation ever after for an optimistic, upper-class nonchalance, even though that plucky pose was quite commonly struck by everyone from the First Lord of the Admiralty Winston Churchill on down. Read in context, Brooke's more outrageous lines are purposely flippant, ironic in a self-mocking way. A small poem written in praise of him, by his close friend Frances Cornford (1886–1960), came after the war to stand for the inadequacy of Georgian poetics:

> A Young Apollo, golden-haired
> Stands dreaming on the verge of strife,
> Magnificently unprepared
> For the long littleness of life.[18]

Cornford, a granddaughter of Charles Darwin, wrote the quatrain in 1908 while rehearsing with Brooke for his production of *Comus*, being staged at Cambridge in honor of the birth of its most famous poet, John Milton, in 1608. For her, Brooke's curse would be that such magnificence as he possessed would not be able to find a satisfying outlet in the ordinary world, that like the hero of his favorite play, *Peter Pan*, he could not sustain his supernatural self in the mundanity of life. The strife to come would be the battle between his great self and the little world. She could not forsee that Brooke would be blessed with the great event a golden-haired god needs, the Great War.

That war did make his reputation. Churchill gave his funeral eulogy. The dean of St. Paul's preached a sermon from one of his sonnets. That sonnet, "The Soldier," came to stand for England's war aims when those aims were increasingly unclear. One fought, not for any cause in particular, but out of a love of England, because one was "a body of England's, breathing English air, / Washed by the rivers, blest by the suns of home" (*Brooke*, 148). The war also unmade Brooke's reputation. The poets who lived long enough to turn against it, such as Siegfried Sassoon and Wilfrid Owen, became popular after the war, as War Poets, precisely because of the audience created for them by Brooke. Their antiwar stance soon won the day, amid the general disillusionment with the war and its aftermath. What Orwell called "Rupert Brookeish emotions," meaning a sense of patriotism and a willingness for self-sacrifice, were seen as the cause of the war, rather than as virtues needed to pursue a cause. Brooke thus became a victim of his success. His small poem, large enough to temporarily fill the vacuum left by unarticulated British war aims, was made responsible for the war. Even his own death became trivialized when it was noted that, after all, he did not even die in battle, but only on the way to battle. Cornford's lines took on new meaning, with Brooke now an impractical dreamer standing only "on the verge of strife," unprepared, as was an entire generation, for what was to come.

Imagism

The year 1912 was a momentous one for poetry for many reasons besides the first Georgian anthology. It was the year Ezra Pound invented Imagism. Pound had been in England since 1908, absorbing the influences that were to become part of his program to reform modern poetry. David Perkins, in his extended two-volume history of modern poetry, succinctly lists those influences: "impressionist exact notation; interest in Japanese and Chinese poetry, in which poets now remarked a spare, suggestive, visual imagery in terse forms such as haiku; the orientation of poetry in the 1890s to painting, sculpture, and other 'spatial' arts; the special attention symbolist poetry directed to imagery; Hulme's plea that poetry must be precisely phrased and that the essential means to precision is metaphor; the development of free verse; the rejection of poetic diction and 'rhetoric'; the cultivation of the idiomatic and the colloquial."[19] Much was in the air for Pound to absorb, it is clear; no movement springs full-blown from a poet's brain without precursors. But in the case of Imagism, despite the groundwork laid by T. E. Hulme and others, a movement started because Ezra Pound announced to two young poets in a London teashop, Richard Aldington and H. D. (Hilda Doolittle), that they were *imagistes*. He communicated his new term to Harriet Monroe, who used it in her November 1912 issue of *Poetry*, and Imagism was instantly transplanted to America. Its adherents quickly grew from H. D. and Aldington to include Amy Lowell, John Gould Fletcher, and William Carlos Williams in America and Herbert Read and F. S. Flint in England. Flint's "interview" with an *imagiste* in the March 1913 issue of *Poetry* (the interview was actually written by Pound, who was also the interviewee) defined Imagism as the "direct treatment of the 'thing,'" using "absolutely no word that did not contribute" to the poem, and written in free verse, not according to the beat of a metronome (Perkins, 333).

Pound intimated in later years that it was for Hilda Doolittle (1886–1961) that he founded and promoted his new movement. Pound had befriended her while at the University of Pennsylvania (where he also met William Carlos Williams, a medical student ahead of him by two years) and for a short time had been engaged to her. When she visited England in 1911 for a summer's stay that turned into a 50-year sojourn, she looked up Pound, who immediately championed her poetry to Harriet Monroe as "objective—no slither; direct—no excessive use of adjectives, no metaphors that won't permit examination."[20] The poems he sent to Monroe were signed only "H. D. Imagiste." In 1912 she and Pound and a young English poet named Richard Aldington (1892–1962), whom she married the next year, made almost daily visits to the British Museum, followed by teashop discussions. It was thus that Pound in the British Museum tearoom or in "some infernal bun-shop in Kensington," as conflictingly reported by H. D. and Aldington, found two devotees willing to be discovered and mentored.[21]

The draw between the younger pair was a devotion to everything Hellenic. Hulme had predicted that a "period of dry, hard, classical verse is coming."[22] H. D.'s spare images, written in what Flint called "unrimed cadence," became the model Imagist poems, as in the second section of "Garden," from 1916:

O wind, rend open the heat,
cut apart the heat,
rend it to tatters.

Fruit cannot drop
through this thick air—
fruit cannot fall into heat
that presses up and blunts
the points of pears
and rounds of grapes.

Cut the heat—
plough through it,
turning it on either side
of your path.[23]

Forceful and direct, almost stripped of adjectives, the poem relies on images of roundness and pointedness, and on the implied metaphors of "tatters," "blunts," and "ploughs" to create in a few words a striking and fresh description of heat as a substance having body, weight, and force. But even H. D. was not simply an Imagist, as a cursory glance at "Eurydice," from 1917, will show. This poem is 135 lines long, a complex reimagining of a Greek myth rich in historical overlay. The poem is Eurydice's monologue, the passive object of Orpheus's love given a voice, with which she reproaches him:

> So for your arrogance
> and your ruthlessness
> I have lost the earth
> and the flowers of the earth,
> and the live souls above the earth.
> (51–55)

She refers to him as "you who have your own light," suggesting the very great power not just of life lived literally above the earth, in the sun, but of life lived openly, spaciously, assertively, "in the sun," which males could do. The "arrogance" and "ruthlessness" of male hegemony over poetry, the earth, and living above the earth is indicated here, subtly but directly. As a modern woman in a society that offered very little room in the sun, H. D.'s take on Greek myth focused on the women in the story. For poems such as "Eurydice" and "Pursuit," H. D. has received increasing attention from feminist critics. Traditionally, Apollo or Orpheus are the poets; women are pursued objects, silent, often muses for males. H. D., in the words of Mary Loeffelholz, "finds ways of making the ancient stories speak in women's voices."[24]

Aldington, too, wrote poems held up as models of the new style, but early on his subject matter allowed for an urban realism, containing chimneys, the underground, cripples, the cinema, iron and smoke, everything including the kitchen sink, literally, as in "Evening," a seven-line poem that ends with the poet looking at the moon, prosaically, "over the kitchen sink."[25] In the poem "Childhood" from the 1915 volume *Images* published by the Poetry Bookshop, he comes close to both Eliot and Lawrence in subject matter and tone, if not in control of cadence:

"Make It New"

> The long street we lived in
> Was duller than a drain
> And nearly as dingy.
> There were the big College
> And the pseudo-Gothic town-hall.
> There were the sordid provincial shops—
> The grocer's, and the shops for women,
> The shop where I bought transfers,
> And the piano and grammophone shop
> (Aldington, *Collected*, 42)

In "Church Walk, Kensington," a poem whose title suggests the preoccupation of a Thomas Hardy or an Edward Thomas with observations on an ordinary walk, Aldington begins as either of those poets might, except in free verse:

> The cripples are going to church.
> Their crutches beat upon the stones,
> And they have clumsy iron boots.
>
> (31)

The description continues into a second stanza: Their clothes "are black"; their legs are "withered / Like dried bean pods"; their eyes are "stupid as frogs." Then with his third stanza Aldington suddenly shifts to an overt classical allusion. It is evidently autumn, because "the god September" is pausing here garlanded in "crimson leaves," smiling "like Hermes the beautiful / Cut in marble." That arresting final image of classically perfected male beauty, permanently cut into marble, is set in high relief against the image of the cripples. Where Hermes is swift and athletic, they are clumsy and withered. Where he is crimson and garlanded in glory, they are dried and blackened, beating upon the stones like slaves. The suggestion is that the classical ideal, blazing at its height like an English autumn at its prime in September, will turn withered, dried, browned and blackened, and find itself in a permanent and ironclad, unhealable state of falling off. The effect is almost too blunt to call ironic. Greece had Hermes; modern England has cripples.

The self-promotional Pound and his followers were quickly skewered by more traditional critics and poets, including Eliot's friend at Harvard, Conrad Aiken, who composed a newspaper ballad (reprinted in the New York *Sun* on May 9, 1915) that begins

"Make It New"

> Ezra Pound, Dick Aldington,
>   Fletcher and Flint and sweet H. D.,
> Whether you chirp in Kensington
>   or Hampstead Heath, or Bloomsbury

and asks them "Where in a score years will you be" (qtd. in Hughes, 50)? The reinvigoration of language that the movement generated swept the field, although the movement itself did not, and in the 20 years Aiken allots, all had moved in a new direction or disappeared. The new direction was Modernism; Pound had first modernized himself and then English poetry.

Other events in 1912 were less immediately electrifying than Imagism but ultimately as profound. In that year Herbert Grierson published an edition of the poems of John Donne, further encouraging the already reviving interest in seventeenth-century metaphysical poetry. It should be remembered that Rupert Brooke, dead by 1915, had been part of that revival. The rebellious note he initially struck owed much to his study of metaphysical wit and rigor. He wrote his dissertation on John Webster and shared with Eliot, whom he knew slightly, a keen interest in that dramatist.

Both a public event and a private one in 1912 moved the 72-year-old Thomas Hardy to some of the most powerful poetic achievements of the decade. The public event was the sinking of the *Titanic*, which resulted in Hardy's "The Covergence of the Twain." The impact of the sinking on the public mind was as monumental as the ship itself. The epitome of modern achievement felled in a single blow by a primitive creation of Nature, an iceberg, seemed a commentary on human pride, a new tower of Babel, another working out of the old theme the vanity of human wishes. The private event was the death of his wife, Emma, which shocked the old poet into a series of elegies published as "The Poems of 1912–1913." In those poems the seemingly isolated Hardy wrote lines revealing that even for him Imagism and Modernism were in the air. The first poem in the series, "The Going," mixes an older poetic diction with lines as pure, spare, and conversational as anything Pound or Robert Frost could write: "Why did you give no hint that night?" "Why do you make me leave the house?" "Why, then, latterly did we not speak?" Rather than receiving answers, the poet wakes each morning to see "morning harden upon the wall" (*Hardy*, 338). Hulme's prediction of a coming day of dry, hard verse arrived for Hardy on the day of this personal dry, hard event.

"Make It New"

The year 1912 also saw an exit and an entrance in British poetry. The exit was by D. H. Lawrence (1885–1930), a promising young writer who was included in the Georgian anthologies but also seen as an Imagist. Lawrence ran off with the married Frieda von Richthofen Weekley to begin a new life in Germany, setting a pattern of exile and uneasy relationships with the world that would soon issue in his poetry. The entrance was by Robert Frost (1874–1963), frustrated and desperate at his lack of poetic success in America, gambling all on uprooting his family to London, arriving with his wife and four children in September 1912 after school had started. Frost's coming of age poetically in England at age 39, and his friendship with another frustrated writer, Edward Thomas (1878–1917), resulted in an intense outpouring of poetry by them both, laying down an alternative track for poets who did not wish to follow the Modernist high road.

· TWO ·

"The Land of Lost Content": From the Georgian Countryside to the War's Trenches, 1913–1915

The American poet Robert Bly, who grew up on a farm in Minnesota, once remarked on the difficulty of becoming an artist from the rural Midwest. The difficulty came, he said, from the need for writerly support, absent in the wide spaces and utilitarian ethos of America's center, but more easily found in cities, where groups of writers often emerged together. In the nineteenth century in Britain, there were certainly rural backwaters. Thomas Hardy's Dorset, before the railway came in the 1840s, was such a place, and Hardy found it necessary to go to London to make his fortune, much as Robert Burns left Dumfries for Edinburgh and Thomas Carlyle left an even smaller village in the area of Dumfries, Ecclefechan, for Edinburgh and then London. After a half-century of railway improvements, all roads led to London, and quickly. Even the most famous rural voices, such as Hardy, spent the winter season in the city, attending plays, parties, and concerts, and mixing frequently with other artists. Isolation such as Yeats achieved for a while in Ireland's west country was self-imposed, difficult to find, and short-lived, not the previously unavoidable result of geographical distance or cultural insularity. As Hardy noted, whatever was popular in London was popular everywhere, driving out the local ballads and traditional tunes. Local culture was increasingly replaced by a national one.

The cultural insularity of the countryside which Hardy, Burns, and Carlyle shed for the bright lights of the big city was as much conditioned by class as by geography. Burns's father was a poor farmer, while Hardy and Carlyle were the sons of the village stonemason. In contrast, the Brontë sisters, though they appeared to visitors to live in isolation in their father's parsonage in Haworth on the very edge of the Yorkshire moors, were firmly situated in the middle class, and within reach of middle-class culture; in the 1830s the family subscribed to three newspapers and two quarterlies, *Blackwood's* and *Fraser's*, and their father, who wrote out his sermons and had published religious verse, could model the life of writing in a way that was impossible for the fathers of Hardy, Burns, and Carlyle.[1] Thus Charlotte Brontë was able to conceive of sending the sisters' verses to the poet laureate Robert Southey for a critiquing, a move beyond the imagination and daring of a working-class youth. The sisters' novels, though set in great country houses in windswept locations, show almost no interest in the life of the local rural inhabitants. Emily Brontë's most localized characters are servants, whose speech she renders in Yorkshire dialect, while at the same time caricaturing them as overly religious, superstitious, and certainly incapable of literary abilities themselves; there is no young Thomas Hardy or Robbie Burns sitting in the kitchen.

For middle-class readers (and writers, it seems), rural life meant the goings-on of their class, in the country house. John Galsworthy (1867–1933) parodied this attitude in his 1907 novel *The Country House* with this credo of conservatism:

I believe in my father, and his father, and his father's father, the makers and keepers of my estate; and I believe that we have made the country, and shall keep the country what it is. And I believe in the Public Schools, and especially the Public School that I was at. And I believe in my social equals, and the country house, and in things as they are, for ever and ever. Amen.[2]

"Country," in English, carries the dual meanings of "rural place" and "national entity," as the second sentence of Raymond Williams's influential study *The Country and the City* (1973) points out. Elizabeth Helsinger advances the argument further in her study of how land, especially in Britain, became a sign for the nation in the nineteenth century (15). That century in particular saw the bulk of the population change from a rural community tied together by family relationships, local customs, and shared knowledge of local life to city dwellers whose community had to be constructed on new grounds. One way the newly urban country developed a national cohesiveness was through the literary representation of the "country," in the sense of nation, by images of the "country," in the sense of rural places. One might no longer till fields to make one's living, or even be able to see anyone who does so once the suburbs have their suburbs, but the ancient images of oak and elm, thrush and nightingale, and ploughman and milkmaid provide a national identity, an "Englishness," to replace the lost identity of home in the countryside.

In the first dozen years of the twentieth century, rural themes were so common in British poetry that the Edwardians and Georgians are still usually treated as agreeable and minor nature poets, nostalgically visiting the countryside in their work the way city clerks visited it on weekend walks and picnics. There is some truth to this caricature. Gordon Bottomley (1874–1948), a better poet than the following lines from *To Iron-founders and Others* indicate, could reduce the industrialization of England to the moral equivalent of walking on the grass:

> When you destroy a blade of grass
> You poison England at her roots:
> Remember no man's foot can pass
> Where evermore no green life shoots.[3]

England is the land. More accurately, England is the green life, with its roots in the land. It is Shakespeare's emerald jewel, the garden of *Richard II*. As John Lucas points out, as soon as the First World War broke out in 1914, John of Gaunt's famous speech and that of the gardeners in Act III of that play were endlessly appealed to as embodying the essence of England.[4] Kipling's 1911 poem "The Glory of the Garden" opens with the same representation of the nation by the cultivated rural: "Our England is a garden" (*Kipling*, 732). Kipling, like Shakespeare, is aware of the workers in the garden, "the men and 'prentice boys" who "do as they are bid and do it without noise." This is reminiscent of his praise for that mythical British soldier, Tommy Atkins, as the unsung hero who holds the empire together. What Kipling does not acknowledge is the thorough industrialization of England by 1911. Shakespeare, at least, had the advantage of a greater correspondence to the real work of his day when he imaged the gardeners in Richard's kingdom.

The great center for producing, and consuming, this literature of the countryside was, ironically enough, London. The Poetry Bookshop in London was an important literary meetingplace, and its founder, Harold Monro (1879–1932), himself a poet, produced a series of "Week-End Sonnets" which show in the opening lines of the first sonnet the city's valuation of the country at this time:

> The train! The twelve o'clock for paradise.
> Hurry, or it will try to creep away.
> Out in the country everyone is wise:
> We can be only wise on Saturday.[5]

Two rural Americans were attracted to London as the center of literary culture in English, the place where a man could make his mark. One, Ezra Pound of Idaho, came in 1908 to shed American provincialism for the superior culture of the Old World, and the other, Robert Frost of New Hampshire, took passage with his family in September 1912 in hopes that his unpublished poetry of the rural locales north of Boston might find a more favorable audience in England.

Pound soon established himself as a literary leader in London. In March 1913 he famously helped the older Frost finally achieve a reputation and an audience, walking with him an hour through London, from Pound's flat near Kensington Gardens to Frost's Bloomsbury Street publisher, Nutt's. There Pound grabbed the only advance copy of *A Boy's Will* and that very day wrote a review, followed by an enthusiastic letter to Harriet Monroe at *Poetry* in Chicago that he had found a new and original American voice. Pound later put Frost in touch with Yeats, but the writers whom Frost found most congenial in 1913 were the Georgians—Bottomley, Monro, Brooke, Wilfrid Gibson (1878–1962), William Davies (1870–1940), Lascelles Abercrombie (1881–1938), Ralph Hodgson (1871–1962), and Edward Thomas (1878–1917).

The freshness of the Georgians just before World War I had more to do with a deflation of Victorian rhetoric than with a change in subject matter, though some of Rupert Brooke's poems were shocking at the time for their perceived crudity of both language and subject. Brooke's "A Channel Passage" (*Brooke*, 85), for example, deals in vomit; it is hardly shocking, however, in the traditional canon of poetry. It is an updated version of Lord Byron's *Don Juan*, including the original's linking of serious thought with humor. In Byron's poem, the young hero, while on board ship, swears he can think of nothing but his beloved, at which point the ship lurches and he thinks immediately of his stomach. So much for the primacy of idealism and romantic love. Brooke, whose retching hero has a "sea-sick body" and a "you-sick soul," similarly concludes " 'Tis hard, I tell ye, / To choose 'twixt love and nausea, heart and belly." That this was considered shocking, and that Brooke was strongly advised by his editor Edward Marsh to remove "Lust" as the title of another poem, shows the extent to which middle-class Victorian high-mindedness had captured the public market for poetry. It also reminds us that the Georgians were out to create something new and different.

Wilfrid Gibson

One of the most popular of the early Georgians was Wilfrid Gibson. He was at first admired by Frost, who contrived to move to the Gloucestershire countryside to be in his presence. But Frost soon realized he had more in common with a friend of Gibson's, Edward Thomas. Gibson is now remembered mainly for his connection to these two better poets, Frost and Thomas, but his contribution to a new direction in British poetry is genuine. Thomas, as a reviewer, was at the forefront of the push for something new. He was quick to praise Gibson for dispensing with false poetical rhetoric (although he took him to task for the narrowness of his subject matter, complaining that Gibson was trying to write as if there were no such thing as a Tube or Grape Nuts).[6] When he was asked years later for his recollections of Frost and Thomas, the shy Gibson said he had no memories, but he copied out a poem, "Reunion," written in 1928 but still very much in his prewar Georgian mode. The poem is dedicated to Frost in honor of his return visit to England that year, but its emotional force lies in recalling the long glorious summer of 1913 when the small circle of poets lived near each other in the Gloucestershire countryside:

> now we sit at peace
> Talking once more together, as we talked
> With Abercrombie, Brooke, and Thomas then
> Of the old craft of words.[7]

This prosaic poem achieves whatever effect it has by the nostalgic power inherent in naming Brooke and Thomas, killed in the war. The instinct is the same as the famous St. Crispin's day battle speech of

"The Land of Lost Content"

Henry V—we few poets, we happy few, we band of brothers. The poem shows why Gibson is mostly unremembered. In it one can see what Frost and Thomas both initially admired, the lack of rhetoric; in it one also sees what led them away from Gibson, the lack of music. What initially seemed refreshing did not contain the crafted music of the subtly altered speaking voice that Frost, and then Thomas, was striving for.

Gibson was, however, included in *The Oxford Book of Modern Verse*, selected by Yeats in 1936, and selected again by Philip Larkin in 1973 for *The Oxford Book of Twentieth Century English Verse*. He received the more generous treatment from Larkin, who included one of Gibson's longer narrative poems, "The Drove-Road." It was Gibson's abandonment of a youthful romantic poetry about knights and ladies in favor of narratives of simple country life that led to the initially high evaluation he received from Frost in early 1913. Yeats included no Gibson narratives, but both he and Larkin agreed upon the value of a World War I lyric, cast almost in the form of a triolet, "Breakfast":

> We ate our breakfast lying on our backs
> Because the shells were screeching overhead.
> I bet a rasher to a loaf of bread
> That Hull United would beat Halifax
> When Jimmy Sainthorpe played full-back instead
> Of Billy Bradford. Ginger raised his head
> And cursed, and took the bet, and dropt back dead.
> We ate our breakfast lying on our backs
> Because the shells were screeching overhead.[8]

This is not quite the Tube or Grape Nuts, but the three lines devoted to an upcoming football match do show Gibson's attempt to invest ordinary things with poetic power, as a modern-day Wordsworthian might aim to do (and as the Imagists were also just then attempting).

A short lyric that Larkin includes, "Ice" (137), achieves this aim more successfully. An old woman, "decent and precise," on her day out from the workhouse stands "among the other children by the stall, / And with grave relish eats a penny ice." The young men standing around her jeer at her "wizened toothless gums" and "quaking hands," but she is happy, Gibson tells us in the concluding line, for while her tormenters will grow old, "she, who's been old, is now a child again." From its focus on a penny ice cream cone the poem builds to a final line extraordinary in its simplicity and clarity, redeeming the overwritten surface of adjectives that cloy the earlier description of the woman and the situation. Those adjectives, vivid but close to bathos, are themselves "precise" and meant for a reader who with "relish eats." As we consume the poem, tasting its language, especially in the mouth-twisting array of its consonants, we enact the woman's experience. We end in simplicity, the accidents of age, health, occupation, and clothing made unimportant in re-achieving the full-bodied experience of pleasure that, in a Wordsworthian view, childhood offers.

One more lyric deserves mention, "Lament," which shows Georgian sensibilities coming up against the Great War:

> We who are left, how shall we look again
> Happily on the sun or feel the rain,
> Without remembering how they who went
> Ungrudgingly, and spent
> Their all for us, loved too the sun and rain?
>
> A bird among the rain-wet lilac sings—
> But we, how shall we turn to little things,
> And listen to the birds and winds and streams
> Made holy by their dreams,
> Nor feel the heart-break in the heart of things?
> (Larkin, 142)

As a war poem, this is unreconstructed Rupert Brooke, England made holy by its dead. But the poem is not a simple panegyric to the dead. It is rife with tensions. It opens with those "who are left" having some difficulty enjoying sun, and later rain, bird-song, wind, and streams. The poem wishes to claim that these things have been saved by the sacrifice of the dead, even sanctified by them. But what is left has not been saved; it is tarnished past its easier, original enjoyment by the very sacrifice that attempted to preserve it. The speaker's memory of "they who went," and how they went, and why, impinges on and forever modifies the present. England's rapid urbanization could be ignored by Georgians for a time, as long as one could catch the Saturday train for the country and be wise for a day, but this new blow, the Great War of 1914 to 1918, has rendered nature psychologically ineffective and permanently changed.

Gibson's second stanza counters the uneasiness of the first by opening with an image rich in traditional associations. "A bird among the rain-wet lilac sings" suggests growth, health, life, the beauty of nature, renewed hope, reinvigoration, fruitfulness, joy, wisdom. This line asserting a romantic view of Nature is powerful in its compactness, suggestive of haiku, but it is followed immediately by a negating "but" and the repetition of the first stanza's question, this time summed up as "But we, how shall we turn to little things"? These ordinary and little things are, however, the very things upon which Gibson has built his poetic practice. How does one now not feel the "heart-break in the heart of things"? At its heart, nature is broken; at its core, nature poetry is heart-sick. This lament is for the war dead, but it is also for those left behind and for the breaking of certainties that made life an experience of loving—for when they were with us they "loved too the sun and rain." Now that experience of loving seems to be consigned to dreams and, in fact, to the dreams of the dead, not the living. The sun remains, the rain remains. What is lost is the power to look upon them happily, lovingly, whole-heartedly, and ungrudgingly. The poem's argument is that nature (and thus nature poetry) is finished as a source for life (and for writing), yet it insists upon using nature imagery to make its argument, even in its last line. Which is the stronger, the message of the argument or the message of the poem's practice? That the two are at odds shows the difficulty that Georgian poetic practice would face in describing the experiences of the Great War.

A. E. Housman and Thomas Hardy

In the Georgians' push for a new direction, two older poets began to receive greater attention, Thomas Hardy (1840–1928) and Alfred Edward Housman (1859–1936). Both poets are difficult to categorize. Hardy is difficult because he lived two literary careers, that of a Victorian novelist in the age of Realism and that of a twentieth-century poet drawn to the Romanticism of Shelley and Swinburne but open as well to the new influences around him. Housman conspicuously rejected categorization, refusing to be included in Symons's *A Book of Nineties Verse* or in Marsh's Georgian anthologies. He saw himself, in the words of his biographer Norman Page, as "a professional scholar who occasionally strayed into writing English verse."[9]

He was one of the renowned classical scholars of his day, a Professor of Latin at University College, London, and then at Cambridge for a combined 44 years. In 1895, he attempted to publish a collection of lyrics that he called *Poems by Terence Hearsay,* an irreverent reference to the Latin comic dramatist Terence. When the poems were rejected, Housman changed the title of the collection to *A Shropshire Lad,* whereupon it was accepted and published in 1896. But it was only in 1914 that it quickly achieved great popularity. Its pessimism was brash, jaunty, and militant, an attitude useful for viewing the war.

Some of Housman's most famous lyrics are easily assimilated to the war experience; it is not much of a stretch to feel in "To An Athlete Dying Young" the admiration of virtues the public would see in Rupert Brooke in 1915, both in his poetry and in his person. Even that permanently anthologized chestnut that begins "Loveliest of trees, the cherry now / Is hung with bloom along the bough" has its note of mortality, a mortality faced, however, with a plucky persistence:

> And since to look at things in bloom
> Fifty springs are little room,
> About the woodlands I will go
> To see the cherry hung with snow.[10]

Housman's poems typically use a pastoral landscape without the comfort that the pastoral tradition offers. Mortality seeps into the stanzas, and the traditional associations of the nature imagery are blunted toward that end. In "With Rue My Heart Is Laden," for example, the rose moves from its traditional significations of Petrarchan love and Dantean heavenliness to almost take on the role of a poppy:

> With rue my heart is laden
>   For golden friends I had,
> For many a rose-lipt maiden
>   And many a lightfoot lad.
>
> By brooks too broad for leaping
>   The lightfoot boys are laid;
> The rose-lipt girls are sleeping
>   In fields where roses fade.
>   (*Housman,* 80)

Roses and rue are the flowers of this prewar pastoral, which may be lamenting the loss of confidence in the pastoral as much as the loss of friends. The "lightfoot" boys are strangely prescient of the boys on the front, organized as light infantry, or foot soldiers, and the "brooks too broad for leaping" are suggestive, to a 1914 audience and to readers ever since, of literal distances and barriers that did not exist in 1896. The fields "where roses fade," likewise, are easy to identify explicitly with battlefields and graveyards. These fields of fading roses in Housman's poem disturb the peace of the pastoral; used in the most popular poem of the war, "In Flanders Fields," the image, in contrast, borrows some of the comfort of the pastoral, euphemizing mass sections of perfunctorily marked graves as a flower-filled field where dancing and courting might have taken place. Housman's lyrics become, in this way, funereal pieces with which to comfort the living and honor the dead.

In contrast, Thomas Hardy's "In Time of 'The Breaking of Nations' " is both more stoical and more positive. Its initial image is often seen, inaccurately, as a ploughman laboriously working his field: "Only a man harrowing clods / In a slow silent walk" (*Hardy,* 543). But harrowing, of course, is not the same as ploughing; it is the breaking up of chunks of clotted soil after ploughing and prior to planting, and as such, an image finely attuned to the "breaking of nations" going on in 1914, especially as the rest of Hardy's famous poem offers an assurance of continuation. The agricultural cycles and sexual-courting cycles of life will continue despite any war and despite any dynastic quarrel ("Yet this will go onward the same / Though Dynasties pass"). Hardy was a loyal subject who answered the king's call for poems to help the war effort. One, "A Call to National Service," begins with a phrase appropriate for a recruiting poster: "Up and be doing, all who have a hand / To lift, a back to bend" (546). Another's title tells its quite overt purpose—"An Appeal to America on Behalf of the Belgian Destitute" (541). The use of "Dynasties" in "In Time of 'The Breaking of Nations,' " however, comes subversively close to suggesting that World War I makes no sense in terms of the lives and purposes of common men and women, because war is in the province of great Dynasties, which, as any lover of Shelley would know from "Ozymandias," means the overproud and very temporary arbiters of things.

Hardy's favorite Housman poem was "Is My Team Ploughing." Housman's poem begins with an agricultural setting similar to that of Hardy's "In Time of 'The Breaking of Nations,' " but it is closer in theme to Hardy's "Ah, Are You Digging On My Grave?" in its depiction of the forgotten dead. In Hardy's poem a woman hears scratching on her grave and imagines first that it is her lover, then her kin, then her enemy, and finally her dog who is disturbing her sleep, each time to be disappointed that none remembers her, not even her dog. Hardy is here explicitly reversing a Victorian commonplace of dog as man's best friend, brought to its apotheosis in Edwin Landseer's painting of a sheepdog sitting by his dead master's coffin, "The Old Shepherd's Chief Mourner" (1837); even that cynic Byron, in "Darkness," leaves as the single positive image in that poem a dog waiting, again, by its dead master. In Housman's poem, a dead youth asks a similar series of questions of the living: "Is my team ploughing"? "Is football playing"? "Is my girl happy"? Each time, he is answered in the affirmative, until the last question:

> "Is my friend hearty,
>   Now I am thin and pine;
> And has he found to sleep in
>   A better bed than mine?"
>
> Aye, lad, I lie easy,
>   I lie as lads would choose;
> I cheer a dead man's sweetheart.
>   Never ask me whose.
>   (*Housman*, 42–43)

The poem's clever wordplay is pure Housman. The youth who pines is in a pine coffin, and the friend who lies easy in bed also lies easily to the pining youth. The poem would appeal to Hardy's sense of humor as a satire of circumstance. Its reversal of genders from Hardy's, however, makes it, for a 1914 audience, even grimmer than it already is, for it raises a common fear for a soldier, that while he is away, his sweetheart will not be true.

These resonances with the war experience perhaps explain some of the sudden popularity of *A Shropshire Lad* in 1914. Rupert Brooke recommended it during an address to the boys in Rugby's literary society. George Orwell, while at Eton, learned it by heart. Auden averred that to his generation, the one at school during the Great War, no other poet so perfectly appealed to their sensibilities.

A second reason for its swift rise might be the route it gave for Georgian poets to approach the war. The often cited influence on the trench poets was Thomas Hardy. He was respected by them even when they bitterly regarded the rest of the home front as incapable of understanding what was really happening. Siegfried Sassoon (1886–1967) and Robert Graves (1895–1985) especially sought him out. His long-standing feud with God, religion, conventional morality, Victorian optimism, and any sort of phony boosterism did not seem to them unwarranted gloom and pessimism. After life in the trenches, they could agree with Hardy that he was just being a realist, not a pessimist. In addition, Hardy had taken a strong stance against the Boer War, writing a series of poems that sympathized with the sufferings of combatants and civilians alike. Housman did not receive that level of affection; he was not sought out and adopted as a poetic godfather. But he did show how the English tradition in nature poetry could be pitched in an almost subversive lower key, in a way that seemed true to the times, focused as they were on maintaining the values of a mythic rural England while trying at the same time to recognize twentieth-century realities.

One of those realities was the disappearance of any real knowledge of English country life. It is significant that Shropshire is not where Housman was a lad. He was a Worcestershire lad, for whom Shropshire was a "province just out of sight over the Malvern Hills."[11] He invented personal associations for those habitations—what his brother called the "romantic falsification of local history" (Millard, 98)—as in the poem "Hughley Steeple":

> The vane on Hughley steeple
>   Veers bright, a far-known sign,
> And there lie Hughley people,
>   And there lie friends of mine.
>   (*Housman*, 87)

Kenneth Millard points out that in a letter from 1925 Housman admits that he has never seen the steeple. Housman's Shropshire is, in John Lucas's phrase, a "tourist's landscape, one to walk through rather than to know."[12]

It is Housman's personal absence from the landscape, rather than his knowledge of it, that imparts the powerful tone of loss in the poems. The absence, in larger terms, is England's loss:

"The Land of Lost Content"

Into my heart an air that kills
From yon far country blows:
What are those blue remembered hills,
What spires, what farms are those?

That is the land of lost content,
I see it shining plain,
The happy highway where I went
And cannot come again.

(*Housman*, 58)

This land of "lost content," which requires a highway for the poet-tourist to reach, is a place marked by hills appearing blue from lying on the horizon. The spires are visible, as are generic farms. If the "blue remembered hills" are a construction of a Shropshire that Housman has not actually visited, what is being remembered? What earlier known contentment is now lost? Childhood? Pre-Victorian religious certainty? An emotional Eden or heroic age? There are scant clues in the poem; only a "shining plain" is perhaps suggestive of anything grander, biblical or Homeric. Housman's language stays fixed in a plain rural imagery, but only of the most abstract and generic type. The loss is not the loss of a memory of what was, but the loss of never even being allowed to form the memory. We are excluded from the place with the certainty of the last line's assertion that we "cannot" come there. The poem adds that we cannot come there "again," but the vagueness of its recollections, indicative of not only an absence of knowledge but perhaps the absence of the place, makes the "again" seem final and forever, rather than causing us to cast our eyes back on what we once might have known.

Compare this with Hardy's "Let Me Enjoy," whose cheerful-seeming title is bolstered by its position as the first in "A Set of Country Songs." This song lists, in fact, reasons not to be happy, but it stubbornly insists that despite those reasons one can assert happiness. Its last stanza directly images Paradise:

And some day hence, towards Paradise
And all its blest—if such should be—
I will lift glad, afar-off eyes,
Though it contain no place for me.

(*Hardy*, 238)

The poem's argument is that one must enjoy the earth because there is no other paradise. Or, if there is a Paradise, the speaker is sure it contains no place for him (though he intends to will himself to lift his eyes, glad we're not quite sure why). Paradise is imaged as a container, a delineated space, such as a box or enclosed land. Its boundaries are certain, and Hardy's exclusion is certain. Hardy is a poet who actually has knowledge of rural life, who knows the difference between harrowing and ploughing, or what the enclosure movement did to farm laborers, excluding them from the use of land held in common by a village since the Middle Ages, now fenced off for the large landowner's profit. That knowledge, however, is not put to the traditional romantic use of comforting us. Rural life, even in a "country song," is no pastoral retreat. Paradise is not a country setting. Paradise is bounded, enclosed, excluding, not organic, agricultural, or unifying. Housman uses the absence of rural experience to suggest loss; Hardy uses the presence of rural experience to suggest the same loss, as modern life has become alienated from the country, and to be rural is now to be living in a lost world. The modern and even the paradisal (in this poem at least) are of the bounded city.

W. H. Davies

This point is underlined in considering the popularity of William Henry Davies (1870–1940). Davies was discovered to the literary world by George Bernard Shaw, who received in the post one day a small book of poems that Davies had had printed, along with a letter asking Shaw to return to the author either the book or a half-crown. Shaw recounted the story the next year in his preface to Davies's *The Autobiography of A Super-Tramp* (1906): "Here, I saw, was a genuine innocent, writing odds and ends of verse about odds and ends of things; living quite out of the world in which such things are usually done, and knowing no better (or rather no worse) than to get his book made by the appropriate craftsman and hawk it round like any other ware" (Untermeyer, 173). Shaw adds that the verse "was not in the least strenuous or modern; there was indeed no sign of his ever having read anything otherwise than as a child reads." The American poet Louis Untermeyer's remarks on Davies follow Shaw's closely and are typical of the comments Davies inspired. Untermeyer edited an anthology called *Modern British Poetry* in 1920, revised every five or six years (it was extremely popular as a textbook for the next half-century), which began with Thomas Hardy and acknowledged Hardy's personal advice in choosing selections. About Davies he writes that "one can no more imagine Davies self-critical than one can imagine him in the labor of creation, his 'labor' being about as arduous as a bird's and his song being no less recreational" (Untermeyer, 174). Untermeyer takes his analogy seriously, claiming that no poetry has ever been more birdlike, and then asks the obvious next question: What bird is Davies like? Not the lark (that is Shelley's music), not the nightingale (that is Keats's song), not even the hermit thrush, but the English robin, who, though limited to only three or four notes, produces always "fresh" songs of "crisp spontaneity." This insistence on Davies's spontaneity, that his authenticity comes from an untutored, unread, uncorrupted childlike innocence, betrays a fear that any more normal person would not be able to throw off modern life enough to be in touch with the robin's song.

Davies is the robin. Thus his poetry can be trusted, although one must be willing to overlook what in other poets would be seen as simplistic or maudlin sentiments. This is all rather curious, given that Davies's life, for which he was perhaps more famous than his poetry, is not markedly rural or natural or childlike. He was born in a tavern in Newport, Monmouthshire, apprenticed to a picture framer, crossed the Atlantic on cattle boats to ride the rails in America and Canada, where he lost a foot trying to hop a train to the Klondike, and back in England was making an uncertain living as a peddler and a street singer when Shaw received his verses. Poems such as "Jenny Wren," "Sheep," "Leaves," and "The Dog" suggest by their titles that his customary focus is upon the country. In fact, "Sheep" takes place in Baltimore and on shipboard; the dog in "The Dog" (that is the extent of its description) belongs to a prostitute named Molly. In "A Great Time," the great time is had by seeing and hearing at the same moment a rainbow and a cuckoo, but the poem also indicates that Davies's real residence is the town, not the country ("Sweet Chance, that led my steps abroad, / Beyond the town, where wild flowers grow").[13] In his poem "The Rat," it is that urban animal that displaces the sheep, making the poem an antipastoral; the rat waits in a cottage gnawing on a bedridden woman while the husband, son, and daughter are in a tavern. The notion of the great moral purity of the rural naif goes back in English poetry at least as far as Chaucer's parson, who uses as earthy a language as his brother the ploughman to express himself ("And shame it is, if a preest take keep, / A shiten shepherde and a clene sheep," ["General Prologue" to *The Canterbury Tales*, lines 505–506]). Davies is closer to the tradition of the wise fool of Shakespeare's comedies than to that of the innocent rustic, but the times required him to be both, as if it took a double dose of these two traditions to convince an English audience that the countryside was still alive and well.

After an appointment to the Civil List, the government list of artists deserving of an annual pension, Davies retired to the country to write poetry for the rest of his life. He was linked to the circle of poets then beginning to be called Georgian simply because their subject was the country and their aim a greater simplicity.

Edward Thomas

Edward Thomas, up to that point a writer of prose only, chose Davies as his first confidante. It is a mark of Thomas's reticence and insecurity that he showed his first poems to Davies, though Thomas must have known even then that his was a talent far superior to Davies's. That is perhaps what made Davies a safer choice than the more accomplished members of the circle. But Thomas was crushed when Davies offered that the poems must be by the new arrival, Robert Frost. For Thomas this was confirmation that he did not possess a distinctive voice.

This was only a temporary setback, however, for Thomas was becoming a poet and there was no turning back. Two things turned Thomas from prose to poetry. The first, in 1913, was Robert Frost's friendship and encouragement. The second was the outbreak of war in 1914.

When Thomas met Frost, he had been employed for years as a professional writer, churning out the equivalent of coffee-table books commissioned by publishers on topics they calculated would sell. In the three years previous to their meeting, besides his prodigious output of essays and reviews, he had written 13 books, mostly pleasant if undistinguished appreciations of other writers or of various regions of the British Isles. Thomas had wanted to be a writer since childhood. After a disagreement with his father and an early marriage, he set about earning a living in journalism, but by the time he met Frost the pace of what he considered hackwork was killing him, and he despaired of ever being able to do his own work. Literary friends such as the poet Gordon Bottomley had long been encouraging him to trust in his gifts, especially for poetry. But Thomas continued to write only salable prose works and to review poetry. He protested, despite his poetic prose style, that he had never written a poem and knew nothing about how to do it.[14]

Meeting the equally despairing and desperate Robert Frost changed all that. Thomas, of course, knew a great deal about poetry after writing hundreds of articles and reviews; his was a respected voice, and his three incisive reviews of Frost's first book helped greatly to establish Frost's reputation as a skilled poet, not the unartful but sincere country bumpkin Ezra Pound portrayed him to be. In Frost, Thomas finally found a poet who was already writing the kind of verse that Thomas was urging his contemporaries to write.

In Thomas, Frost found the first appreciative audience that mattered to him. Thomas's high reputation as a reviewer, his obvious intelligence, and strong opinions (though he was mild and unassuming in person, so that Pound dismissed him as someone who had no vinegar in him), meant to Frost that he was finally being seen by someone who knew poetry. What Frost gave to Thomas was to return the gift of recognition. Frost saw the poet in him before Thomas had ever written a line. Having Frost, a *bona fide* published and reviewed poet, accept him as a fellow poet without any pressure to write or perform freed Thomas to finally overcome the powerful resistance that had prevented him from even attempting verse. Frost's acceptance quieted Thomas's highly developed critical faculties and simply allowed him to write. They were each other's best audience. They wrote poems for each other, and in that sense each functioned as a muse for the other.

Just as Thomas, oddly, is sometimes not included as a Georgian, he is sometimes not discussed as a War Poet. For the first year of the war he wrestled with what he should do. One option was to accompany Frost to America, an idea he continued to toy with even after his decision to enlist. In 1915 he enlisted, in early 1916 he became an officer, and by April 1917 he was dead from an artillery shell at Arras. Thomas spent only 40 days out of England, so it is not surprising that his subject matter is less the experience of France and the trenches than it is the country and countryside for which he was willing to fight. He is not as famous a War Poet as Rupert Brooke or Wilfrid Owen. A friend who sometimes accompanied Frost and Thomas on their walks in Gloucestershire in August 1914, J. W. Haines, later wrote that Thomas, being far older than most new enlistees, had a different attitude toward the war. He did not "embrace it passionately like Rupert Brooke, nor revolt from it as passionately as did Wilfrid Owen" (Motion, 92). His poetry, though written almost entirely during the war, does not overtly address the war. And yet the war lies unavoidably behind it and is woven within it.

Significantly, the moment that helped Thomas end his personal indecision about his role in the war (he was notoriously indecisive about most things) was tied to his love of the English countryside. In an essay he wrote in September 1914 for *The Nation* (titled "This England," recalling that most patriotic of plays by that most patriotic of Englishmen concerning its greatest warrior king, Shakespeare's *Henry V*), Thomas describes walking out with Frost one evening and, looking at the new moon, beginning to wonder what things that new moon was seeing along the Meuse, in France: "[I]t seemed to me that either I had never loved England, or I had loved it foolishly, aesthetically, like a slave, not having realised that it was not mine unless I were willing and prepared to die rather than leave it."[15] This famous sentence fit well with the public attitude toward the war; the less often quoted sentences following, however, reveal more of Thomas's particular character: "Something, I felt, had to be done before I could look again composedly at English landscape, at the elms and poplars about the houses, at the purple-headed wood-betony with two pairs of leaves on a stiff stem, who stood sentinel among the grasses and bracken by hedge-side or wood's edge. What he stood sentinel for I did not know, any more than what I had got to do." There is no political argument here. As the wood-betony stands sentinel by the wood, so will Thomas, with no more requirement for a justification than the plant demands. In another famous incident, when his close friend the poet and children's author Eleanor Farjeon (1881–1965) asked him if he knew what he was fighting for, he simply bent down, picked up a handful of earth, and replied "Literally, for this" (Motion, 26–27).

The soil of England was a powerful rallying cry. Rupert Brooke's last and most famous sonnet, "The Soldier," begins:

> If I should die, think only this of me:
>   That there's some corner of a foreign field
>   That is forever England.

> (*Brooke*, 148)

Brooke makes this claim literally, for he is "a dust whom England bore," fed by English air and washed by English rivers, who, when he returns to dust, returns English dust to the earth. Thomas Hardy, in the Boer War poem "Drummer Hodge," used the same literal understanding, but with a much less sanguine outlook. Poor Hodge is also dust on a foreign field, but that field does not then become England; instead, Hodge is condemned to forever look on unfamiliar constellations in the night sky, because he is now mixed with the earth of the Southern Hemisphere. Kipling, before the war, in 1910, had also proclaimed the earth of England sanctified by blood in a poem called "A Charm" (*Kipling*, 500) which begins with a command, one that Thomas can be seen as following:

> Take of English earth as much
> As either hand may rightly clutch.

After taking a handful of earth, one is to recall all those "who lie beneath," not the great, but "uncounted folk," whose toil and sacrifice make of the very earth a healing poultice:

> Lay that earth upon thy heart
> And thy sickness shall depart.

The war's appeal to defend literally the soil of England met in Thomas a lifetime's devotion to the countryside as the savior of his childhood. He now felt called to repay that debt. What that call to action released, however, was not initially soldiering, but poetry.

The first poem of his life, at age 36, he finally wrote on December 2, 1913, reworking a prose sketch, as Frost had suggested ("Up in the Wind"). On each of the next four days he produced another poem ("November," "March," "Old Man," "The Sign-Post"), and this first sustained output gave him enough confidence to reveal to Frost the next week that he was "in it and no mistake" (Marsh, 121). "Up in the Wind" is taken, like an exercise, from a sketch, though it is no amateurish work; the next poem, "November," describes the month just ended and celebrates its least celebrated feature, mud; the third poem of his life shows Thomas already rifling the years of his rich reading and reviewing, as he responds to November by imagining "March."

"March" melds Thomas's detailed knowledge of the countryside with his equally deep awareness of literary history:

> Now I know that Spring will come again,
> Perhaps to-morrow: however late I've patience
> After this night following on such a day.[16]

The poem opens with an assertion of knowledge, "Now I know that Spring will come again." This confident knowing is tempered by the phrase dropped to the second line, "Perhaps to-morrow." Then "tomorrow" is immediately doubted by the phrase "however late." However late spring is, the speaker claims he has patience, because the beautiful December day that has just passed has given him intimations of what will surely come around again in March.

In a similarly vacillating way, the poem at first seems to insist that it is grounded in the actual rather than the reconstructed particulars of the immediate day's experience, for the feeling being argued occurs after "this" night following hard on "such a day." The poem's next line also suggests an immediacy of experience, as the cold seems literally impressed "still," in the present moment of writing, upon the temples of the speaker:

> While still my temples ached from the cold burning
> Of hail and wind, and still the primroses
> Torn by the hail were covered up in it,
> The sun filled earth and heaven with a great light
> And a tenderness, almost warmth, where the hail dripped,
> As if the mighty sun wept tears of joy.

But this line has switched us into the past tense, and as we finish the long sentence that it begins, we find ourselves receding from the presumed immediacy of the sun and the cold; we begin to realize that the moment of composition is, after all, after the night after the day of the experience.

Thomas's descriptions in this section are highly romantic. Heaven is filled with a great light. Hail drips, almost warm. Hail, in fact, is really the sun's tears. At its moment of highest rhetoric, personifying the "mighty sun" who "wept tears," Thomas suddenly retreats to a more realistic description of the scene:

> But 'twas too late for warmth. The sunset piled
> Mountains on mountains of snow and ice in the west:

Somewhere among their folds the wind was lost,
And yet 'twas cold, and though I knew that Spring
Would come again, I knew it had not come,
That it was lost too in those mountains chill.

The first half of the poem thus ends with the opening line almost perfectly reversed—"I knew it had not come, / That it was lost too in those mountains chill." Present and future tense certainty and hopefulness are burdened by the past, as the speaker's *knowing* that spring *will* come is turned into "I knew it had not." If one were given to psychobiological interpretation, the poem would seem to mimic Thomas's depressive nature: an initial moment of hope and confidence quickly undercut by doubts which take on the longer and greater reality, though the poet battles them.

The second half of the poem then begins with an unprepared-for new set of characters, some thrushes:

What did the thrushes know? Rain, snow, sleet, hail,
Had kept them quiet as the primroses.
They had but an hour to sing. On boughs they sang,
On gates, on ground; they sang while they changed
    perches
And while they fought, if they remembered to fight:
So earnest were they to pack into that hour
Their unwilling hoard of song before the moon
Grew brighter than the clouds. Then 'twas no time
for singing merely.

The thrushes seem to be integrated realistically into the setting, as earlier description, such as that of the primroses, is repeated. But the line echoes a long history of thrush poems in which the bird is connected to hoped-for knowledge, from Milton, Keats, Shelley, and Hardy to Thomas's friend the author and naturalist W. H. Hudson (1841–1922) to his older contemporary Alice Meynell (1847–1922).

Meynell's intense Catholicism expressed itself in intensely religious lyrics. "A Thrush Before Dawn" uses the thrush's voice, single, darkling, and deliberate, to communicate the sweetest sweetnesses of earth, such as "first first-loves" (Untermeyer, 64). She asks what the note means; it is "wilder" than song, "sweeter" than youth, "clearer" than Greece, "dearer" than Italy, yet a "remoter mystery" than these "all-natural things":

"The Land of Lost Content"

> How do these starry notes proclaim
> A graver still divinity?
> This hope, this sanctity of fear?
> *O innocent throat! O human ear!*

Hardy's "A Darkling Thrush" is probably a direct reaction to Meynell's poem, and Thomas knew both. For him, there is no thrush-spokesman, but thrushes. They do not communicate Meynell's ecstatic vision or Hardy's broad doubt; they sing. And sing. And sing. "On boughs they sang, / On gates, on ground; they sang while they changed perches / And while they fought, if they remembered to fight." They sing so fiercely because they have "but an hour to sing" and must "pack into that hour" all their song, and more than "merely" song:

> So they could keep off silence
> And night, they cared not what they sang or screamed;
> Whether 'twas hoarse or sweet or fierce or soft;
> And to me all was sweet: they could do no wrong.
> Something they knew—I also, while they sang
> And after. Not till night had half its stars
> And never a cloud, was I aware of silence
> Saying that Spring returns, perhaps to-morrow.
>
> *(Works, 124–125)*

Meynell's "starry notes" are for Thomas just sounds—some of them screams, some hoarse—and stars are stars. And, unlike any of his predecessors, Thomas credits the silence after the cacophony of thrush noise with saying that spring returns.

In traditionally romantic poetry, Nature speaks to the poet in the form of bird-song or perhaps in the notes of an aeolian harp played by the wind. But bird-song is not the primary voice speaking to Thomas. What is this silence that speaks? Is it, too, a part of nature? A denial of nature? Separate from and beyond nature? Frost's "The Need of Being Versed in Country Things" turns on the point that deep knowledge of nature, or country things, leads one *not* to anthropomorphize phoebes or any other creature, a post-Darwinian and anti-Romantic stance. Hardy, too, is a great doubter of his thrush. But all of them, Hardy, Frost, and Thomas, are situated in a late romantic ethos, still wanting to believe in something beyond what their physical senses can tell them. For them, Meynell's (and later T. S. Eliot's) turn to religious belief is no solution. Neither is the simple Romanticism of Davies, a solution that the Victorians had already worn out. Neither is the dark self-sufficiency of Charles Baudelaire or Oscar Wilde's art for art's sake; or W. B. Yeats's mysticism; or Robert Graves's eventual mythic path; or the nihilism, existentialism, and indeterminacy that some of the Modernists moved toward. They are stuck with Romanticism as their way to meaning, but they are also committed to the skepticism that modern experience seems to be teaching. They want to be hopeful but not foolish. As the countryside continues to recede in the early years of the century, it is ever more powerfully invested by the Georgians with a myth of an older, rural, merry old England of ordered and benign social relations. Yet at the same time even the most popular and hopeful of them, such as Gibson, take uneasy account of the realities—the more so do Frost and Thomas (and before them, Hardy).

As late Romantics, Hardy, Frost, and Thomas are dealing with the very old question of how the natural world and the transcendant are related as sources of meaning. The two deepest traditions in the West that attempt to answer this question are the Hebraic and the Hellenic, commonly thought of as religion and philosophy. Religion, whether Judaic, Christian, or Islamic, was characterized by revelation, from an authority outside the individual, revealed in a sacred text. The Greek heritage which it replaced but did not want to totally abandon valued philosophy, a search initiated by and arising from within an individual. Science was Natural Philosophy, a study of the world (the world amenable to the senses) arising from that inner desire to know. The Middle Ages and the Renaissance, from Augustine through Milton, attempted to reconcile the competing claims of religion and philosophy in one way, the Christian one, of subordinating both metaphysical and natural philosophy to religion. Thus in Book III of *Paradise Lost*, John Milton accepts that one path to wisdom is Nature—the Book of Nature—and that another is Revelation. But these two paths are really the same, for both are books and thus both have authors—and that author is the same, God. The eighteenth and nineteenth centuries, from Hume through Darwin, saw the reconciliation go the other way, with the scientists and philosophers sometimes atheist but more often subordinating religion to philosophy by defining God as Nature. This was the solution begun by Enlightenment poets and seized upon by the Romantics, who posited a clouded Force or Unity or Truth (or by the time of Thomas Hardy, an It) which could occasionally be glimpsed by the power of the imagination acting upon Nature. In a high Romantic poem such as Shelley's "Ode to the West Wind," the wind can be addressed directly, asked for knowledge: "O Wind, / If Winter comes, can Spring be far behind?" Or in John Keats's "Ode to a Nightingale," the poet, solitary, darkling, wishing to fling his soul outward toward the bird, can also, in formal language, make a familiar address: "thou, light-winged Dryad of the trees." Wind or bird is a path toward knowing.

Thomas's capitalized "Spring," like Shelley's, stands for more than the season, but he has no capitalized "Wind" to reveal its meaning. His thrushes are not Keats's "immortal Bird." His "Spring" poem uses all the romantic machinery but in lowercase. The grand pronouncement of Shelley's "O Wind, / If Winter comes, can Spring be far behind?" becomes the private, colloquial voice of "now I know." Shelley's rhetorical question's certainty becomes "perhaps" in Thomas. And yet for all the undercutting of the high Romantic mode, in its quiet way this poem is just as self-assured and insistent in its belief as anything Keats or Shelley wrote. By its end, there is "never a cloud," nothing to fog things up. We are "aware," not wondering. And the poem's opening line is repeated, this time shortened and more definite (translated from future tense to the present), and the last two undercutting words placed this time on the same line, comfortably and stably: "Spring returns, perhaps to-morrow." The silence that speaks to Thomas is reminiscent of Hardy's favorite biblical passage, marked in his *Book of Common Prayer* with the date of every year he attended church just to hear it read—"and after the wind, a still small voice." After the Romantics' godlike Birds and great Wind, it is the silence that allows the simple truth "Spring returns" to emerge and be heard.

Is this silence, then, a marker of religious belief, an echo of the Bible? In this reading, Thomas's thrushes are reduced from the Romantics' treatment of them because they are subordinated to religion. Or are the thrushes essentially undiminished, leaving Thomas still a romantic, but a lowercase one, not quite up to the faith of Keats? The line from the poem "they could do no wrong" argues this, being much too close to Keats's immortal bird. Or are the thrushes, like Frost's phoebes, solidly thrushes, not carriers of human meaning, exploding that tenet of Romanticism? Their cacophony of sound argues this. The evidence in the poem is mixed.

Perhaps a more powerful way to read the poem, especially given its place as the middle poem written in the first week of his life as a poet, is to see all its attention to the thrushes' voices as Thomas's attention to his own voice. Whether his newfound voice is "hoarse or sweet or fierce or soft" it is all beautiful to him. At age 36, feeling until that week that he would always be a hack writer and never a poet, and with the war already underway, he also must surely have felt that he "had but an hour to sing" and felt also the earnest necessity to "pack into that hour" his "unwilling hoard of song," poetry unwillingly stored in him because, as he told Eleanor Farjeon as late as just the year before, 1913, "I couldn't write a poem to save my life" (Marsh, 113). And yet what fear there must have been that the gift of this expression, this springing out of poetry, would be, like that just-experienced warm December day giving promise of spring, as quickly chilled and lost. By the completion of the poem, however, that fear is calmed with a quiet certainty. Poetry will return, "perhaps to-morrow." What did the thrushes know? What does Thomas know now, as well? The answer does not lie in the song but in the singing. Thomas, as thrush, singing what he elsewhere calls "a pure thrush word" (*Works*, 154), is less concerned with the meaning of things than the experiencing of things. This newfound poetry is spring, a new life rising from his dry-as-dust prose writing, and just the singing ("they cared not what they sang or screamed") is what keeps off the previous, unvoiced state. That state is imaged as silence and night, which the thrushes are fighting. But by poem's end even those are made his muses. He is "in it, and no mistake"—in voice, in life, and in the natural world, a part of it like the thrushes, rather than a tourist wandering its landscape.

As a marker of Thomas's discovery of his voice, this poem is very clear, but as a document in the history of poetry, its tangled and mixed Romanticism makes for problematic readings. That very fact is a sign of the coming shifts in poetic belief and poetic practice. The Georgians want to be new—in Edward Marsh's gardening metaphor, "putting on a new strength and beauty." Pound wants to "make it new." Virginia Woolf proclaims that human character is beginning anew. These notions of newness imply that what currently is, is old. The ground is already prepared for Modernism, as a break with the old. But there is also a middle way, which Thomas and the Georgians are groping toward. It is implicit in Marsh's metaphor. The old branches of the tree of poetry are not dead, just dormant, and ready now to put on new buds. Whether these buds will have the strength to withstand what comes next is the question.

· THREE ·

"Brother Lead and Sister Steel": Poetry and the Great War, 1916–1918

The poetry of the Great War has achieved a canonical status in British literature, almost precisely in the sense of the church councils that decided which specific scriptural works were inspired and which were not. For British schoolchildren, the poetry of the war is a common classroom and examination topic. Anthologies such as *Men Who March Away: Poems of the First World War* appear as hardbound textbooks in even the poorest innercity comprehensive schools. The most widely used American anthology of British literature, published by Norton, abandons its usual arrangement in this one instance; its chronological listing of twentieth-century authors is interrupted in order to group together poets as different as Rupert Brooke (1887–1915), dead seven years before *The Waste Land* and *Ulysses* appeared, and David Jones (1895–1974), a Modernist writing into the 1970s. Their shared experience of the war, though unarguably powerful, cannot claim to be more influential on their poetry, however, than gender, class, and nationality, a Depression, a Second World War, a Holocaust, or even the more personal events of life—loss of a parent, exile, depression, or, in the case of Robert Graves, the arrival of a Laura Riding as muse.

The holiest poem of the war is "Dulce et Decorum Est" by Wilfrid Owen (1893–1918); it is the standard text by which poetry not as passionately opposed to the war is judged and found wanting. The poem enacts a moment central to another famous work of the Great War, Erich Maria Remarque's novel from the German soldier's point of view, *All Quiet on the Western Front* (1929). In the widely known film version from 1930, a soldier named Paul, home on leave from the front, revisits the school where as a boy he learned lessons of patriotism. He sees in the faces of the boys there the same naive idealism that led him and his classmates to eagerly enlist in 1914. Rather than address them with inspiring words of heroism, as his old teacher wishes, he scolds them all for teaching and believing in such dreams. He cuts his leave short to return to the front, the only place where there are no lies, no illusions about what the whole enterprise entails. Owen's poem, after a vivid description of a man's death by poison gas and his own tormenting dreams that replay the horrible vision, ends with the famous lines that indict classic notions of patriotism. He says that if, in our dreams, we too could see and hear what his dreams contain, then we

> would not tell with such high zest
> To children ardent for some desperate glory,
> The old Lie: Dulce et decorum est
> Pro patria mori.[1]

The Latin phrase of Horace, exhorting that it is sweet and proper to die for one's country, was a part of the grammar school education of every upwardly mobile British boy. Remarque's novel and Owen's poem place the trench soldier outside the normative response of his society, giving British and German soldiers more in common with each other than with their civilian countrymen.

This single poem by Owen has obliterated Brooke's "The Soldier," making it appear silly, romantic, and naive, "the old lie," though Owen himself early in the war had been quite as capable as Brooke of writing romantically about it. As just one example of the power that Owen's poem projects deep into the century, one could read Miriam Cooke's introduction to her study of Arab women writers' responses to the Palestinian-Israeli conflicts and the Iraq-Iran War: "It is 1960, a dank afternoon in May when I, a twelve-year-old in the Tunbridge Wells County Grammar School for Girls, am asked to read out a poem. At first, haltingly because I have not had time to scan the text and then breathlessly as I tumble through the lines that from that day become part of my life."[2] The poem she is asked to read is, of course, "Dulce et Decorum Est."

The facts, as usual, are a bit more complicated than the legend, but the legend, as usual, presents a truth more powerful than can be accounted for merely by the facts. There are really two legends at work. The first is that the British upper and middle classes plunged with pluck and vigor into an adventure for which they were unprepared, thinking the fighting would soon be over, a little like the plantation aristocrats of the American Confederacy riding off to whip the Yankees and be home in time for the next ball. Common mottos in August 1914, before the Battle of the Marne, were "home before the leaves fall" and "home for the harvest." The hero of this story is Rupert Brooke, and the working-class soldiers who followed officers like him, who in the words of Kipling after the war "saved our heritage / And cast their own away" (*Kipling*, 805). The second legend is that trench warfare was so horrible that the soldiers who experienced it turned against the war, and, led by Wilfrid Owen and Siegfried Sassoon (1886–1967), those who wrote about it did so bitterly, convincing finally the British public that the whole enterprise was a huge mistake. In this story, Brooke was insensitive to the horrors of war through ignorance or blindness. As the most famous representative of the Georgian poets, he proves the inadequacy of Georgian poetry in general to respond truthfully to war, hence the low opinion of the Georgians ever after.

In truth, Brooke was far from that naive; he was admired by Owen, who carried with him Brooke's poems and a picture of his grave, and Brooke was defended after the war by Graves and Sassoon. Owen, until his death in 1918, and Graves and Sassoon after the war, all proudly called themselves Georgians. Edward Thomas, who died in the fighting the year before Owen, was never so passionately for the war as Brooke, nor against it as Owen. Ivor Gurney and Isaac Rosenberg, as enlisted men, felt estranged not just from Brooke but from officers such as Owen, Thomas, Sassoon, and Graves. All styles, Georgian, Imagist, Modernist, created important poems about the war, and the vast majority of the writing actually produced is conventional and patriotic, not experimental or pacifist. Owen's reputation as a pacifist and a poet was not made until well after the war; his poetry, not published until 1920, was never a force in turning public opinion during it. Many of the older Edwardians, including Kipling and Chesterton, feared a long, drawn-out conflict and did not smugly wish to send the young off to die; Kipling had the sad job of being on the Graves Commission, which oversaw the final resting place of the slain on foreign soil (including his own son, whose body, however, was never found). The list could go on.

Anthologies during the war purporting to show the patriotic things that the soldiers thought and felt were replaced after the war by anthologies showing the horrible things about the war that its soldiers thought and felt. The attitudes and the poets changed, but the anthologies continued to be made and continued to sell. One of the most popular of the former was E. B. Osborn's *The Muse in Arms: A Collection of War Poems, for the Most Part Written in the Field of Action, by Seamen, Soldiers, and Flying Men Who Are Serving, or Have Served, in the Great War.* First published in November 1917, it demonstrates in its preface at this late date in the war what a minority opinion Owen and Sassoon represented. The anthology undertakes to explain to Germany and to Britain's allies alike "why this stout old nation persists in thinking of war as a sport."[3] Along with a list of authors and their ranks (starred for those who died on duty), Osborn organizes his anthology into such sections as "The Mother Land," "The Sea Affair," "The Future Hope," "The Christian Soldier," "School and College," "Chivalry of Sport," "Songs," and "Loving and Living." Sassoon and Graves are included in the anthology, but they are represented by poems that are easily read as bravado rather than as satiric condemnations of war. For example, the penultimate poem is Graves's "Escape." In the summer of 1916, Graves was mistakenly reported dead. His response to that news is this poem, in which he imagines himself at the very gates of Hell, confronting its guardian, the three-headed Cerberus:

> "... Good Cerberus ... Good dog ... but stop!
> Stay! ... a great luminous thought ... I do believe
> There's still some morphia that I bought on leave."
> Then swiftly Cerberus' wide mouths I cram
> With Army biscuit smeared with Tickler's jam.
> (Osborn, 294)

As the hound of hell falls into a deep sleep, Graves makes his escape. Humor became his earliest escape from the war.

In an anthology from the last year of the war, Arthur St. John Adcock's *For Remembrance: Soldier Poets Who Have Fallen in the War,* one sees the conflicted attempt to reject heroic and romantic notions while at the same time to elevate the War Poets above civilian poets, as heroes:

There is a wide world of difference between those romantic old war lyrics that our patriotic civilians used to write and the grim realism or high spiritual significance of those that were written in the mud and squalor of the trenches, in dug-out or billet, just before going into action, just after coming out of it, in the quiet of a rest-camp or while the writers were lying wounded in hospital.[4]

The poems actually included in the anthology, the claim to "high spiritual significance," and the conventional reverence of the title argue that the realities of this war were not going to be fully faced. Public memorializing of the war dead also avoided too great a focus on the grim truths. Public schools, churches, and market squares commonly have memorials to the dead from this war, personalized in a way those from World War II seldom are. It is not unusual to find memorial side chapels dedicated to regiments or even to individuals. In the small Anglican parish church St. John Lee above Hexham in Northumberland, one can find the local squire's son honored by a marble tomb topped with the young man's effigy, laid out with all the iconography of a medieval crusader knight in one of England's great cathedrals. His head lies on his cavalryman's helmet, his sword unsheathed and displayed nakedly, indicating he died in battle while on his crusade in France in 1917.

Contemporary soldier-poets such as Walter de la Mare (1873–1956), T. Sturge Moore (1870–1944), Richard Aldington (1892–1962), and Edmund Blunden (1896–1974) have written on the War Poets, but the period has also consistently attracted the attention of the following generations of poets. The list of successive poet-editors of just Owen's poetry is a formidable collection: Edith Sitwell (1887–1964), Sassoon, Blunden, C. Day Lewis (1904–1972), and Jon Stallworthy. The same could be noted for Edward Thomas, with studies by de la Mare, Andrew Motion, Anthony Thwaite, Jon Silkin, and Desmond Graham. One reason for the fascination with this period may be that the second of the world wars, though vastly different in its immediate threat, clearer aims, and sometimes saner strategies, did not render obsolete the first's central conflicting legends but rather refought them. The "Rupert Brookeish" emotions that George Orwell complained about are not snuffed out by the Great War but survive in British consciousness well into World War II. The most highly regarded soldier-poet of that war, Keith Douglas (1920–1944), a tank officer in North Africa, in his frequently anthologized poem "Aristocrats," laments the strangely noble and useless chivalry of the World War II British officer class. And J. G. Ballard, whose experiences as a boy in a Japanese internment camp form the basis for *Empire of the Sun* (1984), indicates, like Douglas, that some of the Great War's essential mythologies are still operative. Years later in a column for the *Independent*, "The Worst of Times," Ballard selected as his own worst experience his family's return to England in 1946. Expecting a "sunlit, semi-rural land with beautiful rolling meadows and village greens and ivy-clad rectories," which he had read about in books, he found instead "a London that looked like Bucharest with a hangover."[5] Whatever victory the Modernists won over the Georgians in the literary wars of the 1920s, in the 1940s Ballard and Douglas are still fighting for a mythical rural landscape and against a public school aristocracy in ways that seem hardly changed from the time of the Great War.

Several reputations were made in the war, almost permanently, it seems. Brooke was first made and then unmade by it. Graves capitalized on it in an autobiography, *Good-bye to All That* (1929), which quite calculatingly strung together some family history, some travelogue, a meeting with Thomas Hardy, and some war stories, to create a best-seller that enabled him to move to Malta. But Graves, still revising his *Collected Poems* in 1975, was able to transcend the War Poet label with subsequent work. Sassoon, though he also survived and wrote long after the war, remains known chiefly for his bitterly angry protest voice. Faber & Faber keeps in print his *War Poems*, which outsells his *Collected Poems*, unlike the collected editions of Graves or Thomas, which is what they are known by. Owen is universally recognized as the most innovative and powerful of the War Poets but like Sassoon is totally identified with the war. Blunden and Thomas are still read as Georgian nature poets, having escaped the limiting label of War Poet, though perhaps at the cost of an equally limiting category. By one count, England produced 2,225 War Poets.[6] Out of this effluvia some are remembered for their representative stances more than the quality of their verses. Robert Nichols, Julian Grenfell, and Jessie Pope fit this category. A dozen others deserve mention—Charles Sorley, Edgell Rickword, Osbert and Sacheverell Sitwell, Ivor Gurney, Isaac Rosenberg, Herbert Read, David Jones, Leslie Coulson, Laurence Binyon, Ford Maddox Ford, and Richard Aldington. In addition, German, French, Italian, and Slavic voices are more likely to be heard, in recognition of the parallel experience of all sides, as seen by their inclusion in Jon Silkin's *The Penguin Book of First World War Poetry*.

The literature written by noncombatants is also vast. T. S. Eliot's *The Waste Land* is usually seen as a response to the postwar world;

D. H. Lawrence's novels *The Rainbow* and *Women in Love,* as well as the poetry in *Look! We Have Come Through!,* are war-based. In fact, it would be more difficult to find literature written during and in the decade after the war that ignores it. Children's literature is also not immune from the war's influence. *Bambi* (1922), by the Austrian Felix Salton, is arguably an allegory of the war, whose trench soldiers, like frightened deer, are ever on the watch for the most destructive enemy of all, "man" with his "thundersticks." Work by noncombatants, however, has often been judged less authentic than that of the participants, unless it conforms to the message that finally took hold with the popularity of Owen and Sassoon in the 1920s. There is a decidedly antifeminist slant in some of the poetry, and especially toward women poets, who are sometimes seen as the real jingoists who send the men off to slaughter. The first draft of "Dulce et Decorum est" has, beneath its title, "To Jessie Pope etc" cancelled out. Jessie Pope (d. 1941) was a competent versifier who played the role of cheerleader for the war, achieving immense popularity in the newspapers, which led to three slim editions of verse being published during the war. A defender of Owen might argue that the hostility toward Pope (and toward others represented by the "etc") is no different than the hostility toward any blithe supporter of the war, male or female. And certainly female participants, such as the poet and novelist Vera Brittain (1896–1970), who served as a nurse and deplored the casualties, pass muster. But "Woman" as the reason for the fighting crops up in more than one poem, perhaps a reaction against the wealth of government propaganda that used images of women to sell the war. Poster art especially appealed to images of motherhood and female purity as the reason to fight and sometimes solicited men with seductive appeals such as the poster showing a sultry blonde with the caption "I Want You—for the Navy."[7] A common theme in war posters was rape, with the enemy depicted as a giant, a gorilla, a barbarian, or a monster, with a fainting or screaming woman slung over his back. These posters have a perversely pornographic quality, attracting attention by the nudity of the female victims while at the same time overtly expecting that the viewer of the image will, once attracted by the rape scene, now be repelled by it, condemning the enemy. An adaptation of this theme is found in some of the war poetry, which projects a postwar life in which the wounded or disfigured male is now rejected by the girls back home in favor of a healthy-bodied man. In their rejection of the civilian world for not understanding the war experience, the trench poets found themselves in danger of rejecting the way females experienced the war. The front was largely an all-male world, and especially so for the officer class represented by Graves, Sassoon, Brooke, Grenfell, Sorley, Blunden, Thomas, Nichols, and the Sitwells (though not Owen) who had come from the single-gender public schools.

The public-school ethos had a profound influence on public attitudes in class-conscious wartime Britain. Public-school graduates were seen as the natural leaders of the country, in war as well as peace. They were usually commissioned as officers, even when they had little military training or aptitude. Most of the war poetry is by them. It is a literarily self-conscious poetry because of the educations they have had. The poetry of these officers is ironic, disillusioned. As Peter Parker points out, however, in *The Old Lie: The Great War and the Public School Ethos*, "to be disillusioned it is necessary to have illusions in the first place" (27). A major source of those illusions, according to Parker, is the English public-school system (the elite, private schools, such as Eton, Rugby, and Harrow). The game of cricket especially comes in for criticism. Cricket seems perhaps too insignificant to bear any weight of responsibility for wartime attitudes, but as a metaphor it was very powerful. It could be used to reproach slackers or to exhort boys to become heroes. The following lines by Jessie Pope, one of the purveyors of the Old Lie according to Owen, do both:

> Where are those hefty sporting lads
> Who donned the flannels, gloves and pads?
> They play a new and deadly game
> Where thunder bursts in crash and flame.
> Our cricketers have gone "on tour,"
> To make their country's triumph sure.
> They'll take the Kaiser's middle wicket
> And smash it by clean British cricket.[8]

Edwardians and the War

In Edwardian times, the game of cricket stood, along with the oak tree on the common and the sturdy swain laboring in the field, as a symbol of everything that was uniquely right about England. Cricket was rural, played on the village green; it was democratic, in that the whole village turned out to play and to watch; it was amateur sport, meaning fit for a gentleman, and played at the highest levels for honor, not profit; best of all, it was incomprehensible to foreigners, and thus uniquely English. In the public schools its place was even more special. In Wilkie Collins's novel *Tom Brown's Schooldays* (1857), the master of Rugby calls cricket "the birthright of British boys old and young," placing it alongside *habeas corpus* and trial by jury in importance (Parker, 78). In public-school culture, the boys best at games were given leadership positions in the school, so that physical skill soon became conflated with intellectual and moral prowess. Games at school, for the honor of the school, became invested with spiritual meaning, leading to the assumed moral and spiritual superiority of public-school graduates, and gentleman-athletes in particular.

One of the most popular Edwardian poets before and during the Great War, Henry Newbolt (1862–1938), is known today for a single poem, *"Vitai Lampada,"* from 1898, which is often trotted out as another example of the Old Lie. The poem uses a cricket match as a way to describe ideals of selflessness and proper behavior in the face of adversity. The poem begins a little like a well-known American sports poem, "Casey at the Bat," by setting a dramatic situation: "There's a breathless hush in the Close tonight" (Millard, 23). The team is down by ten, with an hour to play, and the last man in—the equivalent of bottom of the ninth, two on, two out. This insider language of cricket and baseball is not just for aficionados; it has become metaphorical language in England and America, respectively, for a tense situation when all the chips are on the line (another gaming metaphor, known in both countries). In cricket, the last man in is the weakest batsman; that the outcome of the match should ride on his shoulders makes this a different poem from the American one, in which mighty Casey is the best hope to have at the plate. Casey, of course, strikes out, the poem thus making a moralistic point about avoiding pride, and perhaps lack of effort (Casey blithely lets the first two strikes go by without even attempting to swing, so confident is he in his skills); ultimately, the outcome of the game determines success or failure; Casey is a failure because Mudville loses. The American poem is perfect for a capitalistic society honoring a Protestant work ethic and judging worth by the outcome of one's individual effort in the competitive marketplace.

"Brother Lead and Sister Steel"

Newbolt's poem reflects a different ethic:

> And it's not for the sake of a ribboned coat,
> Or the selfish hope of a season's fame,
> But his Captain's hand on his shoulder smote—
> 'Play up! play up! and play the game!'

This ritualistic last line becomes the refrain of the poem. Its sense is identical to these lines of the American sportswriter of the 1920s, Grantland Rice, which have moved into the status of cliché: "For when the one Great Scorer comes to write against your name, / He marks—not that you won or lost—but how you played the game."[9] Newbolt's poem inculcates the attitude that even the weakest must buck up and rise to the standard that the game itself sets. The Captain, biblical with his smiting hand, stands in for God, King, and Country in his command to the last batsman.

Newbolt's hearty Edwardian "play up!" comes at a time of real dangers, from the Boer War, the German naval build-up, and the approach of the First World War. His confidence is perhaps compensatory, as England's century-long military superiority is no longer unquestioned. Just as the Georgians made a religion of the countryside when it became clear the suburbs had put it in danger, so the belief in the God-given superiority of the English aristocrat, hardened on the playing fields of Eton, reached its height just when the outcome of actual military competition was no longer a foregone conclusion. "Play up!" becomes almost a sacred text; it is a credo of action, incumbent upon all players, informed by duty. Newbolt's cricket poem is fitting for a society moving toward a meritocracy but still preserving privilege, hierarchy, and tradition, and aware as well of its long feudal history of interlocking obligations between classes.

Newbolt's poem was extraordinarily influential. Even the young Basil Bunting (1900–1985), though a Quaker and soon to be a pacifist, wrote a spirited schoolboy imitation. Though he was clearly unhappy at Leighton Park School in Yorkshire, Bunting's "Keep Troth" is in Newbolt's patriotic, be-true-to-your-school manner:

> And while we're still at school, boys,
> The principle's the same;
> Stick to the golden rule, boys,
> Play up, and play the game.

"Brother Lead and Sister Steel"

> What do you do for England,
>   Who does so much for you?
> Keep troth, speak true for England,
>   Be straight, keep troth, speak true.[10]

The predominant attitude leading up to the war is probably best illustrated by J. M. Barrie's (1860–1937) classic Edwardian drama *Peter Pan* (1904) and its prose version *Peter and Wendy* (1911). Captain Hook, we learn in the latter, has actually "been at a famous public school" whose "traditions still clung to him like garments"; the school is Eton, and from his time there "above all he retained the passion for good form" (Parker, 91). John and Michael Darling are tempted to join him to become pirates but refuse when they discover that they would have to cry "Down with the King." John and Michael, like Rupert Brooke, are open to adventure, but their patriotism is unshakable. To disavow the king, why, it wouldn't be cricket. The Edwardian exhaltation of childhood, especially of the public-school boy, leads directly to the commissionings (and subsequent deaths) of so many of the boys from those schools.

Another powerful metaphor of the home front was chivalry. "The Volunteer" by the prime minister's son, Herbert Asquith (1881–1947), is perhaps the most famous poem on this theme. It addresses not the public-school boy destined to become an officer, but the wider audience of city clerks needed to make up the bulk of the army. By volunteering (Britain had no compulsory service in 1914 and 1915), an ordinary person could ennoble himself, joining that band of Englishmen who at Agincourt become the brothers of Henry V:

> Here lies a clerk who half his life had spent
> Toiling at ledgers in a city grey,
> Thinking that so his days would drift away
> With no lance broken in life's tournament.
> Yet even 'twixt the books and his bright eyes
> The gleaming eagles of the legions came,
> The horsemen, charging under phantom skies,
> Went thundering past beneath the oriflamme.
> And now those waiting dreams are satisfied;
> From twilight to the halls of dawn he went;
> His lance is broken; but he lies content
> With that high hour in which he lived and died.
> And falling thus he wants no recompense,

Who found his battle in the last resort;
Nor needs he any hearse to bear him hence,
Who goes to join the men of Agincourt.[11]

It is worth recalling that Rupert Brooke in death was extolled as a
knight, the poster boy for doing one's duty. Between them, cricket
and chivalry recruited an army.

The dissenter in all this, it comes as no surprise, was Thomas
Hardy. In a poem from April 1914, "Channel Firing," he anticipates
the war. This poem imagines the inhabitants of a graveyard suddenly being awakened one night by a great thundering that shakes
their coffins. They sit bolt upright thinking it must be the Judgment
Day, but it is only the British navy taking gunnery practice in the
English Channel. Before settling down after this false alarm, the
skeletons shake their heads and wonder if the world will ever be
saner, or whether, "mad as hatters," all nations will continue to strive
to make "red war yet redder." The poem's last stanza achieves a new
tone; from the comic situation of the awakened dead complaining
about all the noise out at sea, the stanza turns us back inland and
deeper into history:

> Again the guns disturbed the hour,
> Roaring their readiness to avenge,
> As far inland as Stourton Tower,
> And Camelot, and starlit Stonehenge.
> *(Hardy, 305–6)*

The three places that end the poem show an interesting progression.
We move from a Saxon and Norman stronghold to a pre-Saxon
British castle to a pre-British stone circle. The movement is from
more recent to more ancient; from the seacoast to further inland;
from actual and known to mythical and surmised; from secular warfare to Christian warfare to pagan blood sacrifice. Hardy places warfare in this deepening context, as all these eras of conflict (from pre-
historic times through 1914) and all these realms of conflict (racial,
political, military, spiritual) are confronted in the small space of
southwestern England and the small space of seven words. The single adjective in this string of place-names is attached to the final
site—"starlit Stonehenge." That adjective takes us back even farther
than the unknown builders of that monument, to the prehuman

world of Genesis or of astronomy, before the creation or origin of humans, when there were only the stars. "Channel Firing" thus presents both a comic denunciation of the madness of war and a recognition of war's deep roots in history, beyond even recorded history. It has an antiwar voice emerging from a mind filled with knowledge of war. It is a minority voice. But it is a voice that the trench poets found to be more authentic than the voices that compared war to cricket.

Hardy's voice was tolerated but not listened to. He became the famous pessimist. Frequently, he would send to the *Times* short lyrics on events of the day, as if he were the poet laureate speaking for the nation. He especially loved to commemorate Christmas, New Year's, and Easter. His lyric "Christmas: 1924" pithily displays the minority attitude that made him unthinkable for the laureateship:

> "Peace upon earth!" was said. We sing it,
> And pay a million priests to bring it.
> After two thousand years of mass
> We've got as far as poison-gas.
>
> (*Hardy*, 914)

This is not a Christmas morning poem destined to be beloved of a nation that preferred to see its soldiers as cricketers gone on tour. Though by 1924 public attitudes toward the war had moved closer to Hardy's, the vinegar in this lyric still smarted.

Georgians and the War

For the older poets included by Marsh in his Georgian anthologies, the war does not seem to be a defining moment. From his poetry, one would hardly know that Walter de la Mare had served in the war; it is only his letters that reveal the horrors he witnessed in the Ambulance Service. Wilfrid Gibson did produce a volume in 1915 entitled *Battle,* but he published volumes almost every year—*Fires* (1912), *Thoroughfares* (1914), *Borderlands* (1914), *Friends* (1916), *Livelihood* (1917), *Whin* (1918), *Home* (1920), *Neighbours* (1920), with poems as various as these volumes' titles; for him, war or no war, poetry just seemed to keep marching on. Laurence Binyon (1869–1943), for 50 years the head of the Department of Printed Books at the British

Museum, wrote nine books of poetry before the war, but is probably remembered today for the two beautiful elegies Philip Larkin selected for his Oxford anthology, "The Burning of the Leaves" and "For the Fallen." The latter, written at the very beginning of the war, in September 1914, was often quoted; one of its stanzas is inscribed in gold above the entrance to the British Musuem:

> They shall not grow old, as we that are left grow old:
> Age shall not weary them, nor the years condemn.
> At the going down of the sun and in the morning
> We will remember them.
>
> (Larkin, 102)

W. H. Davies is keenly aware of wasp, butterfly, and toad, but oblivious to the war. Ralph Hodgson, too, is more concerned with bulls and bats and goldfinches; when war's bugle does enter, it seems to come from Faeryland: "Castle-bells and Fare-ye-Wells, / And bugles sweet and shrill."[12] John Masefield published only one war poem, "August 1914," and then gave up trying to express in poetry the pain and suffering he observed in hospitals. He turned to prose for the war's duration; his book of poetry at war's end is *Reynard the Fox* (1919), which depicts traditional English village life through describing various characters, as Chaucer had done more than 500 years earlier. Edward Thomas is the only one of the older Georgians whose poetic noon was brought about by the war; his poetry is powerfully infused with a sense of loss by his coming service. Thomas, significantly, writes almost entirely while undergoing training; the trenches themselves seem to silence him.

The younger generation of Georgians saw the war as the great moment they were waiting for. They were led in this, famously, by Rupert Brooke. Those who survived beyond the first two years of the war, however, found the rhetoric of chivalry, heroism, and sport almost too painful to parody. Their classical educations appear in their poems in a conflicted way—part serious, part ironic. A brief example is the attitude of one of Brooke's fellow officers, sailing with him to the Dardanelles, Patrick Shaw-Stewart, who brought along a copy of Herodotus to use as a guidebook and the *Iliad* and *A Shropshire Lad* to use for inspiration. On a flyleaf of the latter he wrote a poem comparing himself with the hero of the former:

Achilles came to Troyland
And I to Chersonese
He turned from wrath to battle,
And I from three days' peace.
(Parker, 223)

The comparison with Achilles ennobles the venture and connects Shaw-Stewart to the classical past of his education, but the diminution of Homer's Troy to "Troyland" is unmistakable. The Trojan War becomes recognized as story, in the same realm as a medieval minstral's lay. Shaw-Stewart, unlike Achilles, is returning from a prosaic three-day leave and is far less confident of his storied place in history. But the fighting he will be called upon to do is just as prosaically real, not a dressed-up toyland of a war.

Charles Hamilton Sorley (1895–1915), like Rupert Brooke, showed great promise early in life but was killed in 1915. Sorley was only 20 years old. His father, a Cambridge professor, edited the poems in 1916 and the letters in 1919; as with John Keats, to whom Sorley is compared by Louis Untermeyer (378), the brilliance of the letters augments the poetry. In the generous selection of Sorley that E. B. Osborn included in his 1917 anthology, the young poet's classical education is evident. He often rhymes playfully on Greek words written, of course, in the Greek alphabet. "A Letter from the Trenches to a School Friend" begins "I have not brought my *Odyssey* / With me here across the sea" (Osborn, 178) and then launches into light-hearted comparisons to the Trojan War, in which Paris doesn't care for Helen, only stole her "to annoy her / He did it really, K. T. L." (179). Osborn does not gloss this for his audience, another mark of the assumed primacy of a classical education even for a book in general readership. The Greek letters are an abbreviation for *kai ta loipa,* meaning, roughly, *et cetera,* or "the rest of the things," which in this case is probably a sexual joke. Our need for a gloss owes some small part to the classically educated trench poets who wrote about the inadequacy of a public-school education to really prepare one for the realities of the twentieth century. They were so convincing that Greek is no longer standard equipage of an educated person.

It is Siegfried Sassoon who most completely turns from public-school attitudes to oppose the war. Sassoon, like Brooke, was the model young gentleman. He was a skilled cricketer, rode to hounds (his autobiography was called *Memoirs of a Fox-Hunting Man*), and, once the war broke out, enlisted in that most chivalric but useless of branches in modern warfare, the cavalry. Bored playing polo in camp, he sought a commission as an infantry officer. In France, he quickly established a reputation for courage. Robert Graves said he had "never seen such a fire-eater."[13] Graves took Sassoon's "The Kiss" straight, not in the ironic way it is often read today:

> To these I turn, in these I trust—
> Brother Lead and Sister Steel.
> To his blind power I make appeal,
> I guard her beauty clean from rust.[14]

The turning point in Sassoon's attitude toward the war seems to have been the death of a fellow officer, David Thomas (who had won his school's colors for cricket). In a little-known poem (published in the *Cambridge Magazine* in December 1916 but never collected in his lifetime), "The Poet as Hero," Sassoon describes his friend as Sir Galahad:

> But now I've said good-bye to Galahad,
>   And am no more the knight of dreams and show:
> For lust and senseless hatred make me glad,
>   And my killed friends are with me where I go.
>   (*War*, 61)

In March 1916 he had written a poem for David Thomas, "The Subaltern," which recalls summer days together in Cambridge playing cricket. Sassoon's memory could have been lifted directly from Henry Newbolt: "With twenty runs to make, and last man in" (*War*, 25). He contrasts those prewar summer days with the bad March weather, with Thomas, the stalwart cricket hero, complaining "he'd been having a bloody time / In trenches, crouching for the crumps to burst." Ten days later David Thomas was killed. Sassoon's long elegy for him, "The Last Meeting," is highly romanticized:

> Ah! but there was no need to call his name.
> He was beside me now, as swift as light.
> I knew him crushed to earth in scentless flowers,
> And lifted in the rapture of dark pines.
>   (*War*, 33)

This is not unusual for Sassoon even in 1916. From the beginning, he had a gift for realistically describing the sound and feel of the trenches—his onomatopoetic "clay-sucked boots" (16), "gun-thunder" that "thuds along the ridge" (42), "the long hiss of shells"and rifles that "rattled angrily" (43). This realism, however, he reserved for descriptions of the trenches. Satire was for generals, bishops, cowards, and braggarts. Soldiers who showed courage were romanticized. The phrase "Brother Officer" (49) was heartfelt. Even non-officers could receive this treatment. In "Conscripts" (from February 1917) he describes

> common ones that I despised
> (Hardly a man of them I'd count as friend),
> What stubborn-hearted virtues they disguised!
> (*War*, 69)

The "common ones" are contrasted with "many a sickly, slender lord" who "went home, because they couldn't stand the din." Sassoon, shockingly, switches sides in the class war here, declaring the decline of the aristocracy. At the same time, he inadvertently reveals how deep the class divisions run in Britain by the difficulty he has in allowing a common fellow to achieve the status of friend and equal, no matter how stout the heart. Rudyard Kipling's Tommy Atkins and Thomas Hardy's Hodge had been praised this way before, but Kipling and Hardy were self-made men, expected to stand up for talent and heart. They were not born with the social connections of any of the public-school officers.

After "The Poet as Hero," the elegies become cynical, almost flippant. In "To Any Dead Officer" (from June 1917), Sassoon begins offhandedly with "Well, how are things in Heaven?" and ends with "Good-bye, old lad! Remember me to God" and "Cheero! / I wish they'd killed you in a decent show" (*War*, 82–83). A hint of this new cynicism is already apparent in the summer of 1916. In "To His Dead Body," Sassoon's poem for Robert Graves upon hearing, falsely, of his death, Graves is sped on his way to Paradise to be with "Dear, red-faced father God" (44). The adjective "red-faced" brilliantly undermines the promise of the traditional elegy. God is painted as bellicose and blood-thirsty but also embarrassed at having killed off good men like Robert. He is further subject to embarrassment because of the hypocrisy of letting himself be addressed as "dear" and "father." Finally, the image recalls the out-of-breath old fathers who send their sons off to die, parodied so often by Sassoon ("The March-Past," " 'Blighters,' " "The General," "Editorial Impressions," "The Fathers"). In the often anthologized "Base Details," the multiple meanings of red are again invoked:

> If I were fierce, and bald, and short of breath,
> I'd live with scarlet Majors at the Base,
> And speed glum heroes up the line to death.
> *(War,* 71)

The image is expanded now by the detail that staff officers wore red shoulder tabs. By changing red to scarlet, the traditional color for harlotry, Sassoon declares the baseness of a staff officer's function. What should be a badge of honor (staff positions usually went to those with family connections) becomes a flagrant badge of shame— a scarlet letter, a base detail. To be detailed to the safety of the base is, literally, base.

Sassoon pushed the boundaries of tone, rivaling his fellow Georgian, D. H. Lawrence, as in the heavy sarcasm of "Does it Matter?" This poem was written in Craiglockhart War Hospital, where Sassoon was convalescing between July and November of 1917, under the care of Dr. W. H. Rivers, who was then developing new ideas on the treatment of psychological damage from war. Wilfrid Owen and Robert Graves were also patients of Rivers. The poem asks:

> Does it matter?—losing your legs? ...
> For people will always be kind,
> And you need not show that you mind
> When the others come in after hunting
> To gobble their muffins and eggs.
> *(War,* 91)

Like Lawrence, he found women complicit. The ironically titled "Glory of Women," also written at Craiglockhart, begins:

> You love us when we're heroes, home on leave,
> Or wounded in a mentionable place.
> You worship decorations; you believe
> That chivalry redeems war's disgrace.
> *(War,* 100)

The next line stops suddenly: "You make us shells." This is a richly evocative charge. Men are hollow because of women. Men are shell-shocked. Men are like artillery shells in that their toxic insides may explode at any moment. Men are "shills" in a shell-game their society plays with them. Men are vessels for the projections of women, who represent England. Glory and chivalry are what pass for "mentionable" back there.

Sassoon is a Georgian with a big topic and a loud voice. Unlike Lawrence, he never links his antiwar fervor to any larger pattern of issues. "Glory of Women" is not about the war between the sexes, as is *Women in Love,* for example. Women stand in, rather, for the home front, which encourages the prosecution of the war. In the 1920s, Sassoon continued to write essentially about the war, publishing poems, diaries, and several autobiographical fictions. In the 1930s, his fire waned. In 1935 he writes about war in a conflicted way. The poem "878–1935" compares King Alfred's conquest of the Danelaw in 878 to Sassoon's situation in the twentieth century:

> Then, it was quite correct to hack and hew the Dane,
> And to be levied for a war was life's event.
> Now in a world of books I try to live content,
> And hear uneasily the droning aeroplane.[15]

War is here described as "life's event," a curiously neutral phrase. The young Sassoon raged at the war, going so far as to invite court martial by writing a letter, read out in Parliament, that opposed its continuation. The Sassoon of 1935, who must "try" to live content in books, seems to miss something about those days. His "world of books" pales compared with the world of action. Yet he cannot bring himself to repudiate his fierce opposition to the Great War by now honoring it as an opportunity for greatness; it is only in the distant past, the "then" of King Alfred's time, that it is correct to hack and hew. But what is his attitude to the coming showdown with Germany? The uneasiness he feels at the droning of the planes is both ominous and ambiguous: uneasy that war is coming again? Uneasy that Britain will fight? Or not fight? Uneasy about his own stance this time around?

When the Second World War does break out, Sassoon seems to abdicate answering these questions. He writes little about that conflict, during it or after. Typical of the few poems is "A 1940 Memory" (1940 was the year of the Battle of Britain, the Luftwaffe's campaign to bomb British cities into surrender):

> One afternoon of war's worst troubles,
> Disconsolate on autumn stubbles,
> I marked what rarely rambles by—
> A Clouded Yellow butterfly.
>
> (*Collected*, 266)

There is perhaps a subtle optimism at work here, based on the kind of courage that refuses to notice the destruction the enemy is wreaking. The butterfly seems to indicate that Nature, in its traditional romantic function, is delivering a hopeful message, and that its cloudedness indicates the gray days now which will be replaced in the future by cheerful yellow sunniness.

If this is the message, however, Sassoon has chosen an odd messenger. The butterfly in the lexicon of the Great War stood for prewar innocence, easily and permanently destroyed. It was used to end the film of *All Quiet on the Western Front*, representing the idealism and romanticism of youth, which, if followed, would lead only to death. Sassoon would have blasted such a poem in 1916. Yet here he reverts to the kind of out-of-touch Georgian nature poetry he found irrelevant and then reviled during the First World War. The fault, perhaps, is not in the poetics, but in Sassoon's conflicted attitude. No longer as sure of his views as he was in the First World War—losing that single-minded clarity—he chooses to avoid dealing with the second.

Other Georgians, notably Edward Thomas, and to a lesser extent Ivor Gurney and Edmund Blunden, successfully adapted Georgian practice to the war experience, using images of the natural world to express the losses that war brought. They essentially linked two traditions, the pastoral and the elegiac, to achieve this end.

Their success was anticipated by Sergeant Leslie Coulson (1889–1916), who in a poem written a few days before his death on October 7, 1916, asked the question "Who made the Law that men should die in meadows?"[16] This poem (titled "Who Made the Law?") was not included by Osborn in his patriotic anthology of 1917. Osborn did include several poems of religious faith by Coulson, including "The Rainbow" from August 1916:

Where the parapet is low
And level with the eye
Poppies and cornflowers glow
And the corn sways to and fro
In a pattern against the sky.
The gold stalks hide
Bodies of men who died
Charging at dawn through the dew to be killed or to kill.
I thank the gods that the flowers are beautiful still.

(Osborn, 292)

The poem, however, is not as religiously orthodox as Osborn might have wished. Its title recalls a traditional religious image of hope. God shows Noah a rainbow as a sign that he will never again destroy the world by water. Coulson, however, after the heavy casualties of the Battle of the Somme in July 1916, is watching the world around him being destroyed by fire. His uncapitalized and plural "gods" is a departure for him as well, and shows a rough progression in belief from "God" to "gods" to "Who?"

The poem uses a motif common in religious and romantic verse—the beauty of cornflowers or dew or some other object in nature evidencing the existence of God, hope, rebirth, continuity, and so on. If the world looks dark now, be comforted; the sun will rise in the morning. If winter comes, can spring be far behind? Coulson presses this traditional claim with little energy and much doubt. Poppies are an obvious ambiguity. As well as being brilliantly beautiful summer flowers, they are traditionally associated with morphine, sleep, and death. The image of the corn swaying might suggest the swaying and falling of bodies, and the golden-ripe stalks ready for harvest certainly hint at the harvest of men in the full flush of their vigor. In this context, "stalks" is an ominous word, and that the flowers are "beautiful still" leaves lingering as the last word in the poem a description that could as well apply to a corpse.

Edward Thomas used the pastoral and the elegy with greater detachment than Coulson. In "Digging" (*Works*, 109) he describes burying two clay pipes and asks what difference it makes to his spade that one is his, just smoked, and the other is perhaps that of a soldier who fought at Blenheim, Ramillies, or some other continental battlefield. The answer lies in his observation that

> the dead man's immortality
> Lies represented lightly with my own,
> A yard or two nearer the living air.

The action of burying a just-smoked pipe in earth is the movement of ashes to dust. That the pipes are clay further links them to the Old Testament description of humankind's mortality. The only difference between the two men, Thomas and the unknown soldier, is about six feet of earth.

In one of his most often anthologized poems, "The Owl," Thomas subverts the traditional imagery of his Romantic forefathers by replacing their idealized nightingales, thrushes, and larks with the owl, a carnivorous night hunter. Resting in an inn, Thomas hears its "most melancholy cry"

> telling me plain what I escaped
> And others could not, that night.
> (*Works*, 26)

What does an owl's cry herald? Traditionally, death, and in a literal sense, possibly a meal caught. As Thomas salts his food, his repose is "salted and sobered, too." The bitterness of salt, its association with tears and wounds, and its use as a preservative and flavorer of meat grimly suggest that "all who lay under the stars, / Soldiers and poor," are not escaping what Thomas escapes in the inn—initially hunger, cold, and exhaustion, but more harrowingly sorrow, carnage, and death.

From the most ordinary sights, such as a pile of wood not used up over winter, Thomas constructs delicate insights. He imagines a blackbird or a robin nesting in the woodpile, because its familiarity will suggest to the bird that the pile will stand there forever—or "whatever is for ever to a bird" (*Works*, 46). But the wood will be used, perhaps soon:

> Before they are done
> The war will have ended, many other things
> Have ended, maybe, that I can no more
> Foresee or more control than robin and wren.

Here Thomas places himself in the larger context of nature, in which some things, such as wood, are being used up, while other things, such as birds, go about their lives, which will be ended in their turn.

Before the war, Thomas wrote of the countryside with a great love, longing to be connected to it in a deeper way than as an observer. In this poem, titled "Fifty Faggots," he comes closest to placing himself as a part of Nature and derives a strange comfort from it. The poem does not question the birds' knowledge or lack of it; it does not question whether Nature or God wishes us well or ill. Here he departs from his mentors Hardy and Frost (in, for example, "The Darkling Thrush" and "Design"). The image of the poem's title, suggestive of a roaring conflagration, is balanced in the last lines by a quiet acceptance of one's identity with robin and wren. That insight is without anger but also without a despondent passivity. It is acceptance, tinged with regret.

That same quiet acceptance Thomas applies even to considering his own death in "Lights Out." The simple command in barracks of "lights out" becomes the last words Thomas hears, for then he comes "to the borders of sleep," imaged as an "unfathomable deep / Forest" (*Works*, 92). Standing on the brink of this Dantean woods, he perceives that "here love ends, / Despair, ambition ends." Nothing may come with him on his Everyman-like journey. But surprisingly, he does not cringe from the journey as Dante and Everyman do:

> There is not any book
> Or face of dearest look
> That I would not turn from now
> To go into the unknown
> I must enter, and leave, alone,
> I know not how.

He contrasts himself implicitly to Orpheus, the poet who seeks to bring his beloved out of the underworld but at the last moment turns to look at her for fear she is not following. There is for Thomas a letting go of Orpheus's fear; that is because Orpheus's hope is pointless; one must enter and leave alone. He is in the place of the pagan Anglo-Saxons described in *Beowulf*, who at the ship-burial of Scyld Scefing cannot say who will receive that cargo. Literally, the front would not allow him to bring his wife or children along; symbolically, he is entering the unknown territory of death. The poem is not so heavy-handed as this description of it, however. In the plainest of words, broken by commas into slow, thoughtful pauses, Thomas expresses his quiet determination to go, not knowing where or how.

The first poem in Thomas's collected works, "The Trumpet," begins "Rise up, rise up" and ends "To the old wars; / Arise, arise!" (*Works*, 21). By its title and by its position leading off the volume, the poem appears to be an early call to arms, such as Robert Bridges and Jessie Pope wrote. It is from 1916, however, after the Battle of the Somme, with its 20,000 British casualties on the first day alone, July first—more than Britain had suffered in the entire three years of the Boer War from combat and sickness both. Its exhortations to arise are not directed at the Great War, but to the "old wars." As Fred Crawford notes in *British Poets of the Great War*, Thomas, who studied history at Oxford, is placing this war in the larger context of past wars. In his longest poem, "Lob," Thomas attempted to create a character who embodied the spirit of English patriotism. Lob "was seen dying at Waterloo, / Hastings, Agincourt"—and also "No Man's Land" (*Works*, 58). But Thomas's "old wars" go beyond even those famous British battles. The trumpet in the poem is the historical one of Henry V at Agincourt but also the mythical one of the Archangel Gabriel at Heaven's Gate, and it is also the ordinary trumpet of reveille. Its call is to awake, but to what? Not to the war, or to any war:

> While you are listening
> To the clear horn,
> Forget, men, everything
> On this earth new-born,
> Except that it is lovelier
> Than any mysteries.

Again, as in "Fifty Faggots," Thomas's love of country, which is inseparably both England and the countryside, is united with his calling as a soldier in a perfect balance. The earth, this life, is beyond even mysteries, such as images of heaven, used in much of the conventional war poetry. It is lovelier in its materiality than our abstractions. What are the old wars? Military conflicts, yes, but also that age-old attempt to find meaning in life and one's place in the universe. In this, his most optimistic poem (perhaps because it is a morning poem), Thomas faces that battle for meaning with renewed strength: "Open your eyes to the air," he exhorts, and "To the old wars; / Arise, arise!"

In more playful early poems, Thomas had used English placenames almost as incantations to call up memories of beauty. In "If I should ever by chance grow rich / I'll buy Codham, Cockridden, and Childerditch" (*Works*, 36), there is little description of the countryside or villages; the names themselves stand in for the description. This technique was already in general use before Thomas started to write poetry; it is a favorite of Kipling, Hardy, and Housman. Newbolt and Austin could hardly write a poem without invoking "England" or "Englishness." Two Georgians attacked this evocation of little England, Edmund Blunden and Siegfried Sassoon. Because the Georgians are so often accused of a simple pastoralism, these two antipastorals are worth examining briefly.

Sassoon, not surprisingly, parodied the technique, using it for opposite effect in a poem to Edward Marsh, "Stretcher Case." A confused soldier riding in a train is unsure if he is in England or on a "ride through death" (*War*, 50). He slowly turns to look out the carriage window and his heart leaps up at the sight of

> the blue serene, the prosperous land,
> Trees, cows and hedges; skipping these, he scanned
> Large, friendly names, that change not with the year,
> Lung Tonic, Mustard, Liver Pills and Beer.

The humorously flat trees and cows of the countryside do not heal this soldier, or even seem familiar to him. The signs that comfort him are not village names or signs of spring but literal signs, advertisements for the urban way of life—remedies for the ills of life, condiments to give life spice, and beer to make life pleasurable (or for many, bearable). The signs, of course, also vividly recall the horrors of the war—lungs poisoned by mustard gas, the pills and tonics of the hospitals and aid stations. Sassoon has here skipped over the Georgian landscape that Thomas finds so meaningful, showing its irrelevance to both the real life of the nation, which is urban, and the present life of those urban citizens, which is war and illness, not spiritual healing.

Edmund Blunden, a pastoral Georgian as much in love with the countryside as Thomas, makes the same charge against pastoralism as Sassoon. In "Vlamertinghe: Passing the Chateau, July 1917," even his title works ironically, implicitly contrasting the Romantic's standard walking tour of France with the soldier's slower crawl through the same terrain. The poem questions the sacrifice that soldiers are asked to make, and the easy honoring of the dead by the living, who strew flowers over soldiers' graves and over their own consciences.

Using the fact that flowers are inevitably brought to the wounded in hospital, Blunden asks a pair of pointed questions:

> Must those have flowers who are not yet gone West?
> May those have flowers who live with death and lice?
>
> (Silkin, 110)

As Jon Silkin argues in *Out of Battle* (110), the contrast between the decorous gift of flowers and actual life in the trenches implicates flowers, and through them the pastoral tradition, in a cover-up. The pastoral can too easily be used to foster a great unreality, obscuring the realities of war (and by extension, the realities of mechanized, industrial British urban life).

Blunden's poetry does not usually have that magical blend Thomas achieved of lyrical plainspeaking. His gnarled lines and fondness for archaic country words make his poetry seem a direct descendant of Thomas Hardy's often purposeful awkwardnesses. Blunden was criticized for his diction, but often those obscure words carry just the right meaning, as in his description of "stolchy plowlands hid in grief" (Untermeyer, 396). Robert Bridges glossed "stolchy" as a derivative of the Old English verb "stolch," meaning "to tread down in wet land or mud," but he argued that it was such a perfect onomatopoetic word that it hardly needed explanation. Like Thomas, Blunden sought detachment, acceptance, and balance in his poetry. A typical example of this effort at judiciousness and balance is the middle line of the middle stanza of a homely poem called "The Barn": "Use and disuse have come to terms" (Untermeyer, 397).

Ivor Gurney (1890–1937) also began the war as a conventional pastoral poet, but Edmund Blunden, his great champion, argues that there was always something unconventional in his attitudes, even then (Silkin, 120). An example might be "Strange Service," which combines an effusive expression of love for England with the oddly dislocating descriptions of the service that England requires in return as "strange," "dreadful," and "fearful":

> Little did I dream, England, that you bore me
> Under the Cotswold hills beside the water meadows
> To do you dreadful service, here, beyond your borders
> And your enfolding seas.
>
> (Osborn, 14)

In April 1917 he was wounded, recovering in time to be gassed at Ypres in July. In 1918 he read Robert Bridges's edition of Hopkins's poetry and was immediately taken with Hopkins's attempts to out-muscle language. His poetry became more vigorous and less romantic.

Whether due to the war or to conditions already in place and exacerbated by the war, for the rest of his life Gurney alternated between periods of sanity and confinement, which became then one of his topics. "Strange Hells," for example, refers to the overt "racket" of war: "One Hell the Gloucester soldiers they quite put out; / Their first bombardment, when in combined black shout / Of fury, guns aligned, they ducked low their heads" (Larkin, 246). But the title also refers to the soldiers' sanity: "There are strange Hells within the minds War made." Similarly, a poem not published until 1954, 17 years after Gurney's death, called "December 30th," describes the relationship between the weather, the year's end, and the poet's mind: "It is the year's end, the winds are blasting, and I / Write to keep madness and black torture away."[17] The linkage of blasting winds with madness is reminiscent of *King Lear*, which a dozen lines later is cited in the poem: "In such nights as this Lassington has been broken, / Severn flooded too high and banks overflown— / And the great words of *Lear* first tonight been spoken." Jon Silkin provides from manuscript some lines from Gurney's confinement that are even more direct and less crafted: "Why have you made life so intolerable / And set me between four walls, where I am able / Not to escape meals without prayer?" (Silkin, 128). The last lines of the fragment anticipate the confessional poetry of Robert Lowell (1917–1977) and Sylvia Plath (1932–1963): "I'm praying for death, death, death / And dreadful is the in-drawing and out-drawing of breath." It is difficult to judge Gurney's poetry, for it seems fragments of something greater. He joins that list of suffering English poets for whom nature was a bulwark against insanity—Christopher Smart (1722–1771), William Cowper (1731–1800), John Clare (1793–1864).

Like Gurney, who had been educated at the Royal College of Music, Isaac Rosenberg (1890–1918) had an artistic education behind him when he enlisted. Having grown up in the East End of London, the son of Russian-Jewish immigrants, he was apprenticed as an engraver (the profession of William Hogarth and William Blake), until three wealthy Jewish women sent him to the Slade School of Art. Before the war, he had privately published two volumes of poems, and he struggled with whether he was better suited to painting or poetry. He was not in contact with the Imagists but knew some of the Georgians through correspondence.

Edward Marsh functioned as a patron for Rosenberg but kept him at a distance and published only one of his poems, a section from *Moses,* in his Georgian anthologies. Rosenberg's letters to Marsh are moving revelations of his situation: enlisting out of desperate poverty in hopes his mother might get a separation allowance; standing so short he could only join the "Bantams"; awkward and forgetful, a bad thing in an army; ostracized by his fellow soldiers for his Jewishness and for his unsoldierliness; forgetting to take his gas mask to the front; bullied and sweared at by his "young pup" of an officer, he knows not why; marching frequently on extra tours of duty as punishment while his comrades rested; falling ill from lack of food and sleeping in the rain; forbidden by a censor from sending his poems home; assigned to wiring duty, during which the limbers (wagons) kept running over dead bodies; living eight straight months in the trenches "whispering" to his "old friend consumption"; writing during rest breaks while the others "squabble or gamble"; or expressing in his last letter, postmarked April 2, 1918, his great joy at being "lucky enough to bag an inch of candle" by which to write.[18]

His earliest poems show a willingness to dispense with forms, a sweet lyricism, and a simpler diction than even many Georgians were employing, as in "Bacchanal," from 1912:

> If life would only come
> As I would have her come,
> With sweet breasts for my bed,
> And my food her fiery wine;
> If life would only come,
> For we live not till it comes,
> And it comes not till we feel
> Its fire through all our veins.
> (185)

When war broke out, he wrote a short lyric, "August 1914," which shows his quick development into something closer to an Imagist, with such visually acute images as "a burnt space through ripe fields" and "a fair mouth's broken tooth" (70). But there is also a haunting symbolism, reminiscent of Yeats, as in the poem's middle stanza:

Three lives hath one life—
Iron, honey, gold.
The gold, the honey gone—
Left is the hard and cold.

Rosenberg wrote under more difficult conditions than any of the officer trench poets, who had some privacy and freedom of movement, better kit, and greater opportunities for leave and rest tours back to England. His production under these hardships was remarkable—not only short lyrics, but extended works, such as the verse dramas *Moses* and *The Unicorn*, as well as drawings, which he also sent to Marsh. He had a whimsical side, on the one hand, as in the poem "The Immortals," which begins as a particularly gruesome killing fest (his hands are "red in their gore"). We are not told who "they" are who are being killed until the last line:

I used to think the Devil hid
In women's smiles and wine's carouse.
I called him Satan, Balzebub.
But now I call him dirty louse.

(78)

His poem "God," on the other hand, is bitterer than anything Sassoon ever wrote. God has created wealth, strength, and beauty, it seems, only to make life harder for us:

Your wealth
Is but his cunning to make death more hard.
Your iron sinews take more pain in breaking.
And he has made the market for your beauty
Too poor to buy, although you die to sell.

(63)

In a turn on an old aphorism, Rosenberg makes what seems to be a comment about the omnipresence of rats in the trenches—"And when the cats come out the rats are sly"—but in the next line switches identities with the rats. God is the feline in this cat-and-mouse game, and men are rats: "Here we are safe till he slinks in at dawn." The poem ends "Ah! this miasma of a rotting God!"

"Break of Day in the Trenches" has Rosenberg actually addressing a rat:

Droll rat, they would shoot you if they knew
Your cosmopolitan sympathies.
Now you have touched this English hand
You will do the same to a German.

(103)

Rosenberg was not well-schooled in literature, but he was fond of Donne. One can see here a retelling of "The Flea": where Donne imagines a kind of sexual intercourse with a reluctant partner through the intermingling of blood in the belly of a flea, Rosenberg imagines the rat's touch of English and German hands as a similar consummation, much too cosmopolitan for the narrowly defined patriotism of either side. The rat, like Donne's flea, can do what man cannot. This has the effect of reducing Rosenberg lower than a rat, and in the next lines that is made explicit. The rat, he imagines, must "inwardly grin" passing healthy young men in the trenches, for they have a lesser chance at life than it does. At the "shrieking iron and flame" Rosenberg puts a poppy in his ear and tells us that it—and he—are safe. But the roots of poppies "are in man's veins"; they "drop, and are ever dropping." Rosenberg was killed in 1918, the same year as Owen.

The complete poems of Wilfrid Owen make the slimmest of volumes, smaller even than those of Rupert Brooke and Edward Thomas, also killed too early, but with this limited work Owen has achieved a major reputation. Owen makes for a truer comparison to Keats than does Sorley. Though Owen and Keats both died very young, in their mid-twenties, they produced a body of work of a quality that Sorley, like Thomas Chatterton, another boy genius of poetry, only hinted at. Owen and Keats both produced the best of their work in a single year: for Keats, the *annus mirabulis* was 1819; for Owen, from August 1917 in Craiglockhart War Hospital convalescing, where he met Sassoon and then Graves, until his return to the front in August 1918. The comparison is fairer for another reason as well, in that Owen loved Keats and studied him carefully. In this he was helped rather than hindered by not finding a place in a prestigious public school, as Keats was rather old-fashioned for study there but held a prominent place in the curriculum of the government schools. From Keats, Owen learned the technique of slant rhyme, in which only the final consonants match, which he later developed into pararhyme and made his own. Pararhyme is consonantal rhyme, with only the vowels varying, as in "Arms and the Boy," which rhymes "blade" with "blood" and "flash" with "flesh." The same poem employs slant rhyme with pairs such as "teeth" and "death" or "apple" and "supple" (*Owen*, 131).

It was meeting Sassoon at Craiglockhart that sped his development. Just as Robert Frost's acceptance of Edward Thomas as a poet helped break Thomas's silence, Sassoon's acceptance and the example of his courageous outspokenness liberated Owen. Sassoon disliked the sonnets Owen showed him but praised the lyricism of "Song of Songs." The next few weeks were a period of rich experimentation for Owen, for he seems then to have first tried out pararhyme in a sustained way (in "Has Your Soul Sipped"), and he also produced a poem in Sassoon's manner, "Inspection." The latter imagines a fresh new lieutenant inspecting his men and being offended by a spot on one soldier's uniform:

> Some days "confined to camp" he got,
> For being "dirty on parade."
> He told me, afterwards, the damned spot
> Was blood, his own. "Well, blood is dirt," I said.
> (*Owen*, 72)

The colloquialness of the language and the potentially bitter irony in the situation are pure Sassoon. The soldier's answer is pure Owen:

> "The world is washing out its stains," he said.
> "It doesn't like our cheeks so red."

The lines have a simple lyricism that goes beyond Sassoon's fire-breathing. They also use Owen's education in a more allusive way, not as simple parody: The washing out of stains recalls the guilt of Lady Macbeth and a hymn favored by his extremely religious mother, "Are You Washed in the Blood of the Lamb." A. E. Housman's dying, red-cheeked youths also lie behind these lines.

Owen was soon combining a Sassoon-like realism with his Keatsian lyricism. "Anthem for Doomed Youth" (for which Sassoon, Owen said, supplied the title) is an early example of Owen's new style:

> What passing bells for these who die as cattle?
> —Only the monstrous anger of the guns.

> Only the stuttering rifles' rapid rattle
> Can patter out their hasty orisons.
>
> (*Owen*, 76)

Owen's first line is a response to a war anthology he had been reading, whose preface claimed that the poetry within mingled "the bugle-call of Endeavour, and the passing-bells of Death" (76). The poem goes on to answer its opening question. There are no bells for those who die as cattle. Nothing mourns them, save "the choirs,— / The shrill, demented choirs of wailing shells." The words are from Keats ("in a wailful choir the small gnats mourn," line 27 of "To Autumn"), but those words are put to a Sassoon-like use in the way Owen replaces a natural image of fall in England with the mechanical wail of the shells falling toward the trenches.

Owen drafted or revised several dozen more poems in the next few months, and on New Year's Eve of 1917 wrote in a letter home "I go out of this year a Poet, my dear Mother, as which I did not enter it. I am held peer by the Georgians; I am a poet's poet" (*Owen*, xxii). Only five poems were published in his lifetime (two in *The Hydra*, three in *The Nation*). Sassoon brought out the first edition of Owen's work, consisting of 23 poems, in 1920 (adding a twenty-fourth a year later), and it was these two dozen poems alone that established his reputation in that decade, when he became a major influence on par with Eliot, Hardy, Yeats, and Hopkins (whose poetry had also been only recently revealed by Robert Bridges's edition of 1918).

The Irish and the War

Irish attitudes toward the war were conflicted. Some Irishmen, of course, fought for England, but many were either indifferent to or bitter toward the war. Its advent had stalled Irish hopes for Home Rule, fanning anti-British sentiments and leading some to pro-German sympathies. Irish patriotism focused on the struggle for Irish freedom, not on the battle of the British Empire against the Hun. Yeats was ambivalent. He wrote very little about the Great War; his great elegy "Easter 1916" is for the dead of that rebellion against British rule. His edition of *The Oxford Book of Modern Verse* (1936) includes no poems by Owen, Graves, Rosenburg, Gurney, Sorley, Coulson, or Aldington; only one each for Brooke and Thomas, though not connected with the war; four by Sassoon and four by Hardy, but none, again, about the war. Even Robert Nichols gets in, with nine lyrics and sonnets, but none of them are the war poems that made his reputation in England as one of the Three Musketeers (the other two being Graves and Sassoon). The exclusion of Owen in particular did not sit well with English readers. Yeats's private assessment, on aesthetic grounds, was that Owen was "all blood, dirt & sucked sugar stick" (Crawford, 107). One might suspect that politics played the larger part; in 1915 he had written Edith Wharton, on being asked for a war poem, the lines "I think it better that at times like these / We poets keep our mouths shut" (Crawford, 107).

Irish troops did fight for Britain, however, and Yeats did honor them in an important poem, "An Irish Airman Foresees His Death," which he included in the Oxford anthology. The poem's title pointedly declares the airman's loyalty to Irishness, not to England's cause, and its third and fourth lines make the political situation explicit: "Those that I fight I do not hate, / Those that I guard I do not love" (Yeats, 87). The airman in question was Major Robert Gregory, son of Yeats's patron, Lady Gregory. The poem examines not his bravery or his accomplishments, but rather his reasons for fighting: Not out of hope it would improve Ireland's lot; not from law; not duty; not cheering crowds; but because

> The years to come seemed waste of breath,
> A waste of breath the years behind
> In balance with this life, this death.

These reasons may or may not have been Gregory's own; they resonate deeply, however, with Irish feelings of hopelessness, expressed also in James Joyce's short story "The Dead," also from this period.

Imagists and the War

Like the Georgians, the Imagists did not form a well-defined movement. Ezra Pound himself struggled with trying to reconcile Imagism and Vorticism, both words of his invention, and at the same time distance himself from Amy Lowell's takeover of Imagism (Pound called it "Amygism"). If Imagism valued the image, Vorticism valued energy. It attracted painters especially, who gathered around the painter and writer Wyndham Lewis (1882–1957) to create the Rebel Art Centre in London in March 1914. In 1914 the prepublication notices of Amy Lowell's new book, *Sword Blades and Poppy Seed*, touted her as the foremost of the Imagists, and included in that group William Butler Yeats. It is true that Yeats and Pound were spending a great deal of time together talking about Japanese Noh plays and reading Robert Browning's *Sordello* out loud. Only the simplest definition of Imagist, however, such as anyone who is associated with Pound, could keep Yeats in that camp. In the same simplistic way, a Georgian at this time was anyone who wrote nature poems.

Unlike the Georgians, the Imagists were not a homegrown group. Pound, of course, was American, and championed the young American T. S. Eliot (1888–1965), as well as a young Irishman living in Trieste, James Joyce (1882–1941). His circle was always international and inclusive of all the arts, not just poetry. His friends in 1914 included the Japanese actor and dancer Michio Ito, the Japanese painter Tami Koume, and the French sculptor Henri Gaudier-Brzeska. This meant that the Imagists as a group did not possess that unflinching patriotism of the Georgians that moved them to enlist and slowed their turning against the war. For the Georgians, love of *the* country translated into love of country, effortlessly it seems. When war broke out, Pound was a bit cavalier about it. He later offered his services to the British government, he said, but was refused. For Pound and Eliot, the first two years of the war offered inconveniences—sometimes the locals, tumbling to the fact that they were foreigners, would want them to prove they were not Germans.

Those who had followed Pound from Imagism to Vorticism and who were English, however, did feel the tug of duty and eventually enlisted: Wyndham Lewis, Thomas Ernest Hulme (1883–1917), Ford Madox Ford (1873–1939), Richard Aldington (1892–1962), Herbert Read (1893–1968). Initially, however, even these English writers saw the war in France as a sideshow to the great war they were conducting over artistic principles. All through the winter of 1914 to 1915 Lewis and Pound worked on the second (and final) issue of *Blast*, their experimental publication meant to introduce the great whirl of Vorticism to the public. Neither seemed to realize that as Britain was being blasted from across the Channel by zeppelin air bombardments, British citizens felt little need to blast old ways of writing poetry. Exactly the opposite was true, of course, which is why conventionally patriotic versifiers such as Jessie Pope and dead Georgian soldier-poets such as Rupert Brooke were so popular. The issue appeared, in fact, just after Brooke's death and, unfortunately, contained a parody of his poetry written by Pound, which attracted public displeasure.

Hulme, before he was killed in 1917, wrote little poetry, and Ford, though he published eight volumes of poetry culminating in *Collected Poems* in 1913, was known mainly for prose. His masterwork of 1915, *The Good Soldier,* is not directly about the war, but is about a different war, the one that results from the desire that flows between men and women. Its title suggested a patriotic novel to the British public, but to Ford it referred ironically to the novel's hero, a man like him who soldiered on despite adversity. Ford enlisted later that year, at the age of 41. His war poems, collected mainly in *Poems Written on Active Service* (1918), were accepted by Pound as appropriately avant-grade, but their content oddly recalls the Georgians. "Footsloggers," a poem in 10 parts dedicated to the wartime minister of propaganda, C. F. G. Masterman, recalls Edward Thomas's stated reason for volunteering:

> What is the love of one's land? ...
>   I don't know very well.
> Is it something that sleeps
> For a year—for a day—
> For a month—something that keeps
> Very hidden and quiet and still
> And then takes
> The quiet heart like a wave,
> The quiet brain like a spell,
> The quiet will
> Like a tornado; and that shakes
> The whole of the soul.[19]

Ford, as we know him today, refused to change his German surname, Hueffer, until after the war, in 1919, even though during the war it made him a target of police suspicion. His patriotic war poetry sometimes seems a defense against his German ancestry.

Herbert Read, later knighted for his influence on British letters as teacher, editor, and critic, was born, inauspiciously for a poet, on a farm in Yorkshire, and went to university in the industrial town of Leeds. He was in the Officer's Training Corps there, so that when war broke out he was given an early commission, in January 1915. While at Leeds, he was most taken with Yeats and with the Imagists; in France, he attempted to write Imagist poems. His best trench poems, such as "Villages Demolis," show how different Imagist techniques were from Georgian self-reflection in presenting the war experience:

> The villages are strewn
> In red and yellow heaps of rubble:
>
> Here and there
> Interior walls
> Lie upturned and interrogate the skies amazedly.
>
> Walls that once held
> Within their cubic confines
> A soul that now lies strewn
> In red and yellow
> Heaps of rubble.[20]

In the 1930s, Read wrote a long philosophic poem, "The End of a War," still in the Imagist style, something not attempted by the Georgian and Imagist lyricists. It is broken into three parts: the first is the meditation of a dying German officer, beginning "Ich sterbe" (Yeats, 345); the second is a very Yeatsian dialogue between the body and soul of a dying girl; the third is another meditation, this time by a waking English officer. It was the only war poem included by Yeats in his 1936 anthology.

Richard Aldington was, along with Hilda Doolittle, the original Imagist, proclaimed by Pound in a teashop in 1912. Aldington attempted to enlist immediately in August 1914 (he was rejected as unfit for service); though he was patriotic, his poetry was not. Typical is "Sunsets" (from his 1915 volume *Images*), ending "And the wind / Blowing over London from Flanders / Has a bitter taste" (Aldington, *Collected*, 55). In 1916, worried that volunteers alone would not fill the army, Parliament passed a conscription act, lowering physical standards, and Aldington enlisted. From his first days in France in the trenches he began to jot down poems in a small notebook "for no other reason than the consolation of writing something," he said in his autobiography.[21] The short lyric "Insouciance" restates this purpose for poetry:

> In and out of the dreary trenches
> Trudging cheerily under the stars
> I make for myself little poems
> Delicate as a flock of doves.
>
> They fly away like white-winged doves.
> (Aldington, *Collected*, 71)

The image of little poems as doves is striking. Several conventional associations are at work here, from doves as signs of purity, peace, meekness, and holiness to the mundane detail that paper is white. The arresting image, however, as in the best of Imagist poems, holds the meaning so tightly, so instantaneously, that linear prose explications seem particularly inept. The poem seems to say that the best part of Aldington is captured in his poems, just as the noblest parts of human nature are signified by doves, and though they both hover around the trenches, both are set free to fly above it and away to a more appropriate place, which cannot even be imagined in the poem. The carefree attitude that the title ascribes to the poem is certainly presented, but its opposite is as well, in the very intensity of the image.

Imagist techniques in the hands of Hulme were used to create shocking images—men making paths in the dark "Through scattered dead horses, / Over a dead Belgian's belly" (Crawford, 83). Aldington also used Imagism to create this kind of objective realism, communicating emotions without stating them. In "A Ruined House," for example, we do not see those who once lived in the house, but rather

> Their marriage bed, rusty and bent,
> Thrown down aside as useless;
> And a broken toy left by their child....
> (Aldington, *Collected*, 85)

In "Three Little Girls," another poem written during the war, he again juxtaposes violence and children: He remembers that he used to see them, Marianne, Madeline, Alys, three little girls "who sold us sweets / Too near the shells" (84), but where are they now? This is the technique used later by Sergei Eisenstein in the famous "Odessa Steps" sequence from *The Battleship Potemkin* (1925); Eisenstein's

montage cuts between a baby carriage and soldiers' rifles to communicate the feeling of horror at one's vulnerability to violence. The
short lyric "Battlefield" describes landscape in the same terms *The
Waste Land* would later use, a "fruitless land, / Thorny with wire /
And foul with rotting clothes and sacks" (84).

Hulme's dry, hard classical verse style in Aldington's hands could
be used for more than just realistic or horrifying descriptions; Aldington used it to demonstrate the strange dislocation between this
war and any experience he had known before, as in "On the March":

> Bright berries on the roadside,
> Clear among your dusty leaves,
> Red mottled berries,
> You are beautiful
> As the points of a girl's breasts.
> (*Collected*, 70)

The situation is simple: Aldington, marching, notices red berries by
the roadside and is immediately off in a reverie. He moves from
imagining the nipples of a girl's breasts to memories of warm sun-
shine, freedom, and civilian life, until he is ready to

> throw away rifle and leather belt,
> Straps, khaki and heavy nailed boots,
> And run naked across the dewy grass
> Among the firm red berries!
> I will be free
> And sing of beauty and the women of Hellas,
> Of rent seas and the peace of olive gardens.

He continues in this ecstatic dream until he is suddenly interrupted
by the command "Party—HALT!" The poem is ended, as the flight
of imagination is ended, by the sobering military command. In
miniature, the command subsumes the poem: The gala party of day-
dream is halted. When the poetic imagination and the reality of the
army are in conflict, the last word goes to the army.

Aldington also mixed his realism with an element of lyricism that
is reminiscent of Owen. "Machine-Guns," for example, depicts the
feeling of being overwhelmed by an assault of bullets but in an
image that is mesmerizingly beautiful, like a fireworks display:

"Brother Lead and Sister Steel"

Gold flashes in the dark,
And on the road
Each side, behind, in front of us,
Gold sparks
Where the fierce bullets strike the stones.

(83)

The soldiers "cower shrinkingly against the ground," except for two—Aldington and an officer, who "stand upright" in the road, amid the gold sparks:

All differences of life and character smoothed out
And nothing left
Save that one foolish tie of caste
That will not let us shrink.

The tie of caste, or class, is usually marked in the army by rank—an enlisted man, no matter how high in responsibility he rises (say, to sergeant-major) is still just one of the men; an officer, no matter how lowly or how green (say, a subaltern just come from a university without having even been in a Training Corps) is still an officer and a gentleman, who would be owed a salute by that sergeant-major. Aldington, however, is a private; the tie of caste here is evidenced in a kind of public-school nonchalance that must not let the men see one afraid. That is, the tie of caste between Aldington and the officer comes from their educations and social, not military, ranks.

Aldington was quite aware of this class distinction in the army, playing with it in a poem called "Two Epitaphs." It is not a very good poem, proceeding mostly by abstractions and rhetorical repetitions. It breaks into two sections. The first is a panegyric dedicated to "H. S. R. Killed April, 1917." The fallen soldier is an officer whom Aldington loved "from the ranks" for his kindness, courtesy, and bravery. To him, Aldington's final words are "Brother, / Hail and farewell." The second section is dedicated to a fellow enlisted man who died a month later: "E. T. Killed May, 1917." E. T. is the shadow of the virtuous H. S. R., coarse, ignorant, carping, "cruel and evil-tongued." Aldington, however, mourns this man's death equally with the first:

Yet you died without a moan or a whimper.

Oh, not I, not I should dare to judge you!

But rather leave with tears your grave
Where the sweet grass will cover all your faults
And all your courage too.

Brother, hail and farewell.

(*Collected*, 94)

Unlike Sassoon's only partial embracing of the "common" ones, Aldington fully accepts his brotherhood with the coarse and ignorant dead man. Caste is here made unimportant. The ability to appreciate what is "high" is not the real distinction to be made among men. Even courage is not the most revered quality, though this soldier was courageous in the correct way of not whimpering. What connects Aldington and the dead man is, paradoxically, his death; before that, Aldington clearly disliked him. The sweet grass forgivingly covers his faults. And then Aldington realizes in the next line that the grass also covers his courage. If faults and courage are equally eradicated, what is the man to be remembered for, mourned for? What is left? Neither faults nor courage, but the tears on the grave, which are the feelings of the living, and the sweet grass, which is what passes for continuation and eternity in the war.

Aldington repeated the dual structure of "Two Epitaphs" in a pair of poems called "Soliloquy—I" and "Soliloquy—II." The first one declares "No, I'm not afraid of death" (86) and the speaker brags that he can "munch" his sandwich and make a joke as the stretchers are wheeled by. Except for one thing:

But—the way they wobble!—
God! that makes one sick.
Dead men should be so still, austere,
And beautiful,
Not wobbling carrion roped upon a cart ...

The second soliloquy answers the first. Beginning "I was wrong, quite wrong; / The dead men are not always carrion," Aldington describes advancing through trenches the Germans have evacuated and finding a dead English soldier lying upon a step, "his closed left hand touching the earth":

More beautiful than one can tell,
More subtly coloured than a perfect Goya,

And more austere and lovely in repose
Than Angelo's hand could ever carve in stone.

These last lines on the beauty of the dead are part of a long tradition of the homoerotic in war. The nude bathing scenes and beautiful youths of Rosenberg and Owen are in this tradition as well, as in "Louse Hunting" and "Arms and the Boy." Rosenberg's poem begins with an abrupt single word—"Nudes"—and follows it with a vivid description:

Nudes—stark and glistening,
Yelling in lurid glee.
Grinning faces
And raging limbs
Whirl over the floor one fire.
(79)

The soldiers, their "merry limbs in hot Highland fling," are stripping off their shirts to kill lice. Some are burning their shirts, and in the shadows thrown by the single candle "gargantuan hooked fingers / Pluck in supreme flesh / To smutch supreme littleness." In Owen's poem, the phallic bayonet blades are "famishing for flesh," while "blunt bullet-heads," which the curly-haired youth strokes, "long to nuzzle in the hearts of lads" (*Owen*, 131).

As Paul Fussell notes in his seminal *The Great War and Modern Memory*, there has always been an intercourse between love and war. Part of that is literal. Rape is a long-standing consequence—or instrument—of battle, from the rape of the Sabine women to the war in Bosnia in the 1990s. The language of war is also the language of rape—"assault," "attack," "penetration." Secondly, prostitution has been common among the camp followers of armies. In the Great War, there were official brothels—Blue Lights for officers and Red Lights for other ranks. On the psychological level, prolonged sexual deprivation of the kind experienced at the front can magnify feelings of sexuality and love. W. H. Auden claimed that "in times of war even the crudest kind of positive affection between persons seems extraordinarily beautiful, a noble symbol of the peace and forgiveness of which the whole world stands so desperately in need."[22] Additionally, fear brought on by the presence of violence often expends itself in hedonistic release and an attitude of *carpe diem* that overthrows peacetime inhibitions. In a Jungian view, the public and institutional hatred that war calls forth is balanced in the personal sphere by love among individuals: Mars returns to his tent to become the lover of Venus. The classical educations of soldiers such as Aldington gave them the supreme example of warriors in love—the love of Achilles for Patroclus in the *Iliad*.

In *Articulate Flesh: Male Homo-Eroticism and Modern Poetry*, Gregory Woods argues that three battles in particular have passed from whatever historical significance they once possessed into powerful mythic stories of the connections between homoerotic love and war. The first, the battle of Chaeronea in 338 B.C., was fought by Philip II of Macedon against the Theban Band, an army of 300 lovers. Philip wept at the sight of the slain Thebans, seeing "not only dead warriors who had warred and lost, but also sleeping lovers who had loved and won."[23] The second incident took place at Ichinotani in 1184, when the warrior Kumagai Naozane ripped off the helmet of his enemy to gaze upon a beautiful boy, whom he then beheaded, leaving himself with a complicated emotional cocktail of duty, sorrow, love, regret, and respect. This particular motif appears often in Japanese literature and film. The third battle is Cascina in 1364, when the Florentines accidentally came upon their Pisan enemies bathing and slew them as they struggled to dress and arm themselves. Woods sees the meaning of this episode, as portrayed in subsequent art (for example, Michelangelo's cartoon for the Palazzo Vecchio in 1504), as having little to do with war and everything to do with honoring "the vulnerability and beauty of male flesh" (60). The dead English soldier of Aldington's poem partakes of all three motifs.

Homosexuality, however, was repressed, socially and personally, during the Great War. It had only been 20 years since Oscar Wilde's trial, conviction, and imprisonment in 1895 for sodomy. Sassoon was open about his feelings, but Owen seemed unable to face his. Graves, too, was uncomfortable with the love affairs he had experienced at Charterhouse, his public school, and in later editions of his autobiography excised the line that it took him until age 21 (which would be 1916, the third year of the war) to "recover" from homosexuality (Fussell, 274). In another 20 years, the interlude of the Jazz Age would help to create greater public awareness of and tolerance for homosexuality; the Auden generation would be more open about homoerotic love than the generation that fought the war. They would also largely avoid active service, based in part on the disillusionment of the artists who fought the Great War.

Posthumously, Wilfrid Owen achieved a great reputation in the following decades. At the same time, he was obviously precluded from writing any more poetry or developing in new directions. The best poets to survive the war were two Georgians, one who fought and one who did not—Robert Graves and D. H. Lawrence. They had time to develop into important Modernists. Others of equal talent did not—Owen, Edward Thomas, Isaac Rosenberg, and perhaps Charles Sorley and Rupert Brooke. The majority of this generation of English Georgians was lost to poetry, leaving the field clear for Americans—Pound, Eliot, Stevens, Williams. Just as America suddenly emerged from the Great War as a leading world economic power, so American literature emerged from the shadows of British culture, no longer just a colonial subset of British literature. American writers became a dominant presence in Britain and France in the 1920s, and from the newest and most modern of countries, one that prided itself on not being bound to the past, came Modernism.

For the English survivors, even those open to the great tide of Modernism about to wash over the arts in the 1920s, the link to the prewar Georgian past proved strong. Just one example is the painter Paul Nash (1889–1946). Nash enlisted immediately in September 1914 in the Artist's Rifles; in 1917, as an officer in an infantry regiment, he was wounded at Ypres and invalided to London, where he mounted an exhibition of his watercolors. The "Ypres Salient" Exhibition was so popular that he was seconded for the rest of the war to the Ministry of Information as a War Artist and sent back to France, where he began for the first time to paint in oils. Along with Stanley Spencer (1891–1959), also an official War Artist by 1918, Nash painted some of the most memorable images of the war. Nash and Spencer again served as official War Artists during the Second World War, Spencer painting a series of large canvases on shipbuilding and Nash producing perhaps the most famous painting of that war, *Totes Meer* (1940–1941), depicting shot-down German planes, wings undulating like a dead sea.

Nash's *We Are Making a New World* (1918), used as the frontispiece for this volume, is an example of the balance he struck between the influences of Modernism and his attachment to the countryside. Before the war, Nash had experimented with abstraction, but his own vision was essentially romantic. He made watercolors of visionary landscapes in the tradition of William Blake. *We Are Making a New World* is also a landscape, but a blasted one. A blood-red sun rises over blackened and lumpish ground, ploughed into mounds and depressions by shells. The landscape is peopled only by the stiff remains of charred tree trunks still standing, all branches and foliage blown off. The painting's title is reminiscent of the programs of Pound and Lewis, to "make it new" and to "blast" old notions of the arts. "Yes," Nash's painting seems to be saying, "we are blasting away the old to make our new world." The strong graphic elements of the painting bespeak Modernism, as does the irony of the title. But it is an irony that drips with a longing for the recent past. English writers in the following decades would likewise make their compromises with Modernism.

· FOUR ·

"My Killed Friends Are With Me Where I Go": Survivors, Casualties, and Prisoners of War, 1919–1929

The 1920s saw the gradual rise to dominance of Modernism. The Anglo-American T. S. Eliot led the way, first in poetry (*Prufrock* in 1917 and *The Waste Land* in 1922) and then in criticism, presiding over English letters in the next three decades as its most powerful voice. The sense of dislocation wrought by the war—social, economic, and spiritual—seemed best reflected by the techniques of Modernism, which broke with traditional verse. Those techniques grew directly out of Pound's Imagism—free verse, the direct speaking voice, acutely visual images, popular and urban subject matter, and an insistence on the objectivity of the thing itself. Eliot's method in *The Waste Land* was to gather up the shards of western civilization and juxtapose them—"a heap of broken images"—in the hope that, Frankenstein-like, a new life could be created from the fragments of the old order. Pound, of course, was Eliot's editor and teacher for *The Waste Land*, cutting away large swaths of the manuscript and giving the poem its famously evocative title (Eliot had called it "He Do the Police in Different Voices," a reference to an overheard pub conversation that was itself a reference to a popular British comedian). For these services, Eliot acknowledged Pound in the poem's dedication as *"il miglior fabbro"* ("the better craftsman").

The leading seller of volumes of poetry just after the war, however, was still Rupert Brooke, with 300,000 copies. Poets who had served in the war, who for the most part still identified themselves as Georgians, could metaphorically be described as prisoners of that war still. They spent the next decade or more working out their experiences. The end of the twenties, in fact, saw a flurry of prose works from combatants: in 1927, T. E. Lawrence's *Revolt in the Desert;* in 1928, Edmund Blunden's *Undertones of War* and Siegfried Sassoon's *Memoirs of a Fox-Hunting Man;* in 1929, Robert Graves's *Good-Bye to All That,* Richard Aldington's *Death of a Hero,* Ernest Hemingway's *A Farewell to Arms,* Erich Maria Remarque's *All Quiet on the Western Front;* in 1930, Sassoon's *Memoirs of an Infantry Officer,* Frederic Manning's *Her Privates We,* the war correspondent H. M. Tomlinson's *All Our Yesterdays,* and Henry Williamson's *The Patriot's Progress.*

The war generation clearly produced much work in the 1920s, but the inheritors of postwar Britain seemed to be the noncombatants and others whose voices were not taken so seriously during the war—especially women. The Americans and the Irish, who had not been so directly involved, seemed to possess greater vigor. The English survivors were largely exhausted, shell-shocked, and numbed. A similar lack of confidence emerged in their poetic practice. King George V still sat on the throne, and Edward Marsh produced two more Georgian anthologies, but Georgianism itself was weak and dying. The finest poets of the movement—Edward Thomas and Wilfrid Owen—were dead. Robert Graves busied himself with marriage and making a living. The Georgian mantle passed to weaker poets who indulged in a taste for prewar nostalgia, which has since tainted the word "Georgian" with the smell of irrelevance. Modernism, with its infusion of energy from outside England, was the only movement bold enough to think it might, Humpty-Dumpty-like, put the pieces back together again, where all the king's men had failed.

This is the view if one is looking for the new and the emerging. In the popular mind, however, little had changed. Eliot was hardly a household name in the 1920s or even in the 1930s. Robert Bridges was poet laureate until his death in 1930, at which point another Edwardian stalwart succeeded him, John Masefield. The only British or American writer to be recognized with a Nobel Prize in literature was Rudyard Kipling, in 1907. In the 1920s two Irish writers were honored, William Butler Yeats in 1923 and George Bernard Shaw in 1925. But Yeats was born in 1865, Shaw in 1856, and both had done prominent work by the century's turn. The intellectual ferment that Eliot and Pound were a part of in the twenties would not be generally recognized until much later: Eliot won the Nobel in 1948, Bertrand Russell in 1950, and Ernest Hemingway in 1954. Eliot did not even win a Pulitzer Prize for *The Waste Land;* the best book in his homeland that year was judged to be a series of lovely but traditional sonnet sequences by Edna St. Vincent Millay. Public taste, even educated public taste, did not take to Modernism.

Even Eliot's future acolytes did not take to him at once. W. H. Auden, at Oxford from 1925 to 1928, did not read *The Waste Land* until December 1926 (at which point, Christopher Isherwood says, he threw over Thomas Hardy and Edward Thomas as models and began to speak an Eliot-jargon of "sigmoids" and "ligatures" and opine that all poetry must henceforth be "austere").[1] Eliot was still so little known among the general public in the 1930s that the American poet Howard Nemerov, though he grew up in New York City and attended Eliot's alma mater, Harvard, from 1937 to 1941, only "discovered" Eliot, as he said in conversation, as a sophomore in college.

One change in Modernism's favor, however, was taking place in the public consciousness, and that was the recognition of the urban lives of most people in Britain and America. In 1923 Houghton Mifflin published the first anthology of "city poetry," aimed at a popular audience. Titled *The Soul of the City: An Urban Anthology*, it laid out a short tradition for the genre: a few lines by Pope, Milton, and Goldsmith; Wordsworth's sonnet "Westminster Bridge" and a bit of *The Prelude;* Walt Whitman's Brooklyn and Manhattan poems; and much (forgettable) British and American contemporary poetry. What is striking is how quickly the city became as conventionally treated by poets as the country had been by the late Georgians. In fact, much of the new "city" poetry was simply the obverse of Georgian "country" poetry: conventional sentiments dressed out in traditional forms and language, as in this short lyric by Charles Hanson Towne, to whom the anthology is dedicated:

> Here surge the ceaseless caravans,
>   Here throbs the city's heart,
> And down the street each takes his way
>   To play his little part.
>
> The tides of life flow on, flow on,
>   And Laughter meets Despair;
> A heart might break along Broadway ...
>   I wonder who would care?[2]

Here are the themes of alienation, loss of individual identity, and despair that also inhabit the early poetry of Eliot. The anonymous multitudes are hardly human. They are waves, surges, tides that drown out the individual, with the resulting lack of any real community: Laughter can run into Despair on the street, but neither has time to stop, to encounter the other—all is a ceaseless flow. The desire for traditional forms and romantic sentiments, whether about the city or the country, is perhaps predictable as a reaction to the ending of the stress of the war.

The Armistice

When the Great War ended in an Armistice on the eleventh hour of the eleventh day of the eleventh month of 1918, the whole world, one expected, would break out singing. Despite the dreary weather in London that morning, the social activist Beatrice Webb (1858–1943) noted in her diary "a pandemonium of noise and revelry," mostly from soldiers and flappers.[3] That night Osbert Sitwell (1892–1969), having survived the trenches, found himself stuck in a taxicab in Trafalgar Square in the rain, surrounded by dancing crowds. He began a poem that he published a week later in *The Nation*, "How Shall We Rise to Greet the Dawn," which imagines dancing feet crushing the "Old Gods" who brought the war and then dancing a new dance that will "create and fashion a new God."[4] Even Ezra Pound was celebrating. Forty years later in *Canto 105* he described himself circumspectly as "in one November / a man who had willed no wrong," but his companion that night, Ford Madox Ford's mistress, Stella Bowen, recalls him "with his hair on end, smacking the bus-front with his stick and shouting" on their way into central London to celebrate.[5]

Siegfried Sassoon described his feelings on that day in a poem written six months later, "Everyone Sang":

> Everyone suddenly burst out singing;
> And I was filled with such delight
> As prisoned birds must find in freedom.
> *(War*, 144)

The poem ends as brashly optimistic as many of his war poems are bitterly satirical—"the singing will never be done." Just a year and a half before, in Craiglockhart War Hospital, he had written another version of the war's end, "Fight to a Finish":

"My Killed Friends Are With Me Where I Go"

> The boys came back. Bands played and flags were flying,
> And Yellow-Pressmen thronged the sunlit street
> To cheer the soldiers who'd refrained from dying.
>
> (96)

In this earlier poem, Sassoon imagines the soldiers suddenly "snapping their bayonets on to charge the mob," with him at their head; after killing the press and the civilian war supporters, they go "to clear those Junkers out of Parliament." This, the poem's last line, equates Parliament with the German warlords; it was published, uncensored, in October 1917 in *Cambridge Magazine*. No one but Sassoon had so openly flirted with treason during the war.

One survivor and one prisoner of war, however, were not singing. Robert Graves spent Armistice night "walking alone along the dyke above the marshes of Rhuddlan (an ancient Battlefield, the Flodden of Wales), cursing and sobbing and thinking of the dead" (*Good-Bye*, 278). Graves had just learned of the deaths of Wilfrid Owen and another friend, Frank Jones-Bateman. His choice of walking place is appropriately symbolic. He was in Wales with his regiment, the Royal Welch Fusiliers, which he had joined in part from his childhood connection to Wales. His family had built a holiday retreat on a high hill near Harlech, where Robert and his siblings had engaged in inventing their own mythologies for the place, much like the Brontë children had done in Haworth. The house faced Ireland (and was given the Welsh name "Erinfa," meaning "towards Ireland," in honor of the Graves's Irish heritage).[6] Partly Celtic by birth and Welsh by choice, he walks near the site of slain warriors, both historic and mythic. The slain are heroic but have died uselessly in a great disaster, as the Scots died uselessly at Flodden, and as Owen and the others died in France. They lie in the marshes below, with Graves now slightly higher, out of the swamp of the trenches. He walks along a dyke, which may or may not hold the flood of grief he feels. For the rest of his long life Graves suffered nightmares (as well as what he called "daymares") filled with trench imagery. He is both a survivor and a casualty.

There had been literal prisoners of war, such as the poet F. W. Harvey (1888–1957), a boyhood friend of Ivor Gurney, who was captured by the Germans in 1916 and spent the rest of the war in various prison camps. He figures prominently in Osborn's anthology of 1917; his memoir, *Comrades in Captivity*, was published in 1920. Basil

Bunting (1900–1985) was imprisoned in England as a conscientious objector in the last year of the war, when he turned 18. Better-connected pacifists, such as the Bloomsbury painter Duncan Grant and novelist David Garnett (1892–1981), spent the war on the farm of their patron, Lady Ottoline Morrell (1873–1938), churning butter and mowing hay for the war effort. England's most famous prisoner of war, however, was D. H. Lawrence (1885–1930), another struggling young artist in Morrell's circle. Lawrence spent the war years in a self-imposed internal exile in England, in various country cottages away from London. He was frequently harassed by the police and the conscription authorities. His wife, Frieda, was a cousin of the German flying ace Baron von Richthofen; she had just returned from a family visit in Germany at the outbreak of the war. Lawrence was not a conscientious objector, objecting only to this war, and many in England objected to him. His ill health kept him out of the service, but his protests against the fighting and vilifying of Germany, as well as the reputation he was receiving for obscenity (his novel *The Rainbow* was confiscated and banned in 1915), made him a social recluse.

On the evening of the Armistice, Lawrence and Frieda attended a party in London where David Garnett, having not seen him in three years, greeted him warmly. Lawrence began to lecture him:

I suppose you think the war is over and that we shall go back to the kind of world you lived in before it. But the war isn't over. The hate and evil is greater now than ever. Very soon war will break out again and overwhelm you. It makes me sick to see you rejoicing like a butterfly in the last rays of sun before the winter.[7]

That night the Lawrences left the party, London, and, soon, England, for a wandering exile in Italy, Australia, Mexico, New Mexico, and the South of France.

A third poet who did not celebrate that night was Thomas Hardy. Hardy by then was 78 years old and not particularly noted for his partying spirit; his life was now lived almost entirely in his upstairs study at Max Gate, Dorchester, with infrequent visits to London. He was busying himself with his autobiography and could hardly bring himself to think about the war; he dealt with it, characteristically, by comparing it to events in the past, observing the dates of Napoleonic battles rather than the current ones in France. Two years after this night he published a commemorative poem called " 'And There Was a Great Calm' (On the Signing of the Armistice, 11 Nov. 1918)." The poem provides curiously few particular details beyond its title, not even identifying who was fighting, or why, or who won or lost. It uses large abstractions and the passive voice, beginning "There had been years of Passion ... / And much Despair, and Anger" until "one morrow" (no particular morrow, it seems, just one morrow, arbitrarily picked) "there sounded 'War is done!' " (*Hardy,* 589). The poem is cautious rather than celebratory. When a subject or actor is referred to, it is still generalized, identified by function rather than name: "all was hushed. The about-to-fire fired not, / The aimed-at moved away."

In the first decade of the century, Hardy had written a verse drama of the Napoleonic Wars, *The Dynasts,* attempting in poetry what Tolstoy had done in prose. To represent the vast sweep of events, Hardy told the story from alternating perspectives—sometimes domestic close-ups, sometimes cosmic panoramas. For the cosmic point of view, he invented a spirit world, including such figures as the Spirit of the Years, the Sinister Spirit, and the Spirit of Pity. He again brought out those characters to comment on this war:

> Calm fell. From Heaven distilled a clemency;
> There was peace on earth, and silence in the sky;
> Some could, some could not, shake off misery:
> The Sinister Spirit sneered: "It had to be!"
> And again the Spirit of Pity whispered, "Why?"
>
> (*Hardy,* 590)

Human beings are not the actors here. Calm simply falls. Clemency distills from Heaven like rain and falls as well. There is a strangely neutral balance to "some could, some could not shake off misery," suggesting that recovery from misery is likewise not particularly within human control but instead distributed randomly among the survivors. The choice of verb—"shake off"—suggests a palsied sickness as much as a vigorous act. The Spirit of Pity, who speaks for humankind, asks the question the survivors in 1918 were soon asking: Why? What had it been for?

The sorrow of Graves, the anger of Lawrence, and the questioning of Hardy more accurately reflect the range of responses in Britain to the war's end than the brief day of celebration recorded by Sassoon. The famous statement attributed to Sir Edward Grey, British foreign secretary, in 1914—"The lamps are going out all over Europe. We shall not see them lit again in our time" (Hynes 1991, 3)—seemed as hauntingly true in 1918 as it had five years before, perhaps more so. The war had solved no problems, and it had created some new ones; it delayed dealing with Irish Home Rule, worker agitation and strikes, and the suffragette question; it reduced Britain from being the world's banker to being its debtor; its 37,000,000 European casualties gave a sobering literalism to the popular phrase "lost generation"; it replaced ancient monarchies by fractious new nation-states, and those new inheritors of the Habsburgs, Hohenzollerns, and Romanovs soon gave way to Horthy, Hitler, and Stalin. And another world war.

The sense that another phase of world combat must inevitably come was so strong that as quickly as 1919 the Great War was given a numerical prefix—it became the First World War. How far this is from the initial conception of the war. The newspapers had most commonly referred to it as "The Great War," "The European War," and "The War for Civilization." H. G. Wells had called it "The War That Will End War" (Hynes 1991, 260). Woodrow Wilson had sold it in America as a war to "Make the World Safe for Democracy." When Colonel Charles Repington, military correspondent for the *Morning Post,* called his memoirs *The First World War,* some reviewers protested at the cynicism of his title, but the name stuck (Hynes 1991, 261). "First" implied that there would be a "Second."

This is partly what lies behind Yeats's famous poem of 1919, "The Second Coming." Yeats, of course, is using a private myth more fully worked out in *A Vision* (1925), but to his readership, the lines "anarchy is loosed upon the world, / The blood-dimmed tide is loosed" seemed a literal prediction of the near future as well as an accurate description of the recent bloodbath. The poetry of the 1920s was aware of the opportunity for—and the necessity of—a fresh start, because the war had irrevocably changed everything and there was no going back. At the same time, the sense of incompletion that hovered over world affairs inevitably undermined some of the confidence of the new start. Another apocalypse, everyone felt, was somewhere on the horizon.

The search for something new was already underway before the war. That is what the Georgian and Imagist anthologies were all about, as well as the Postimpressionist exhibitions mounted by Roger Fry. The war disrupted the creative blossoming then taking place in London, however. The prewar avant-garde movements of Futurism, Imagism, and Vorticism did not survive as movements. Most of the budding Modernists were dispersed. Some enlisted immediately—Rupert Brooke, Paul Nash, David Jones, Stanley Spencer, Ivor Gurney, Siegfried Sassoon, Robert Graves, T. E. Hulme, and Henri Gaudier-Brzeska. Wyndham Lewis's *Blast* died with its second issue in 1915. Samuel Hynes argues that a notice in *Blast* no. 2 explains the difficulty of keeping the poetry wars going. It is the announcement of the death of Gaudier-Brzeska at Neuville St. Vaast on June 5, 1915. It is the only writing in the issue that is "not Vorticist, or metaphorical, and that has no note of belligerent excitement in it" (Hynes 1991, 66). Yet nothing in the journal, argues Hynes, has its simple force: "war-as-fact had overtaken war-as-metaphor." More artists joined the fight in successive years, interrupting their careers—Ford Madox Ford, Herbert Read, Richard Aldington, Wilfrid Owen, Edward Thomas, Isaac Rosenberg, Wyndham Lewis. As a pacifist, E. M. Forster (1879–1970) spent most of the war in Egypt, while two other members of the literary group known as Bloomsbury, Duncan Grant and David Garnett, engaged in alternative service at home.

The Sitwells

The poetry scene in London did not cease altogether, however. Two years before Eliot published *Prufrock*, a remarkable young woman, Edith Sitwell (1887–1964), self-published an unremarkable volume of poems, *The Mother* (1915). She had just escaped her mother (and her eccentric father, Sir George Sitwell) with the help of her governess, Helen Rootham, with whom she shared an apartment in a poorer part of London. The next year she began a poetry magazine with her friend, Nancy Cunard (1896–1965), called *Wheels* (after one of Cunard's poems), which championed literary Modernism against the Georgians. *Wheels* went through six issues (called "cycles") between 1916 and 1921.

Sitwell was the eldest of three siblings, who from an unhappy home life banded together while still children into an alliance that lasted throughout their lives. Born to wealth and privilege, Edith, Osbert, and Sacheverall were still the poor relations of the extended family. Her mother reminded Edith that she, as the daughter of an earl, was better born than Edith, the daughter only of a baronet. The childhoods of the three Sitwell children were lived in the opulence of the Edwardian autumn, especially when they stayed with the grander relations each year at Christmas, with "geriatric aunts," scores of cousins, troops of governesses, "hordes of tall, loud, tweed-clad male relatives joyfully slaughtering hundreds of furred and feathered creatures daily," amateur theatricals, Hungarian bands, and endless lavish meals.[8] The Sitwell children referred to them as "The Golden Horde" and "the fun brigade." It was this group that they saw as the Philistines who must be held at bay by Modernist art.

Edith's contribution to that art was *Wheels*. She began to recruit poets to join her circle and appear in the magazine—first, Robert Nichols (1893–1944), who declined, then Aldous Huxley (1894–1963). She organized a reading with T. S. Eliot, Nichols, and her siblings. She and her brothers were not taken very seriously at first. Huxley described them memorably, if condescendingly, to his brother Julian, after he agreed to appear in *Wheels:* "The folk who run it are a family called Sitwell, alias Shufflebottom, one sister and two brothers, Edith, Osbert and Sacheverell—isn't that superb—each of them larger and whiter than the other.... Their great object is to REBEL, which sounds quite charming; only one finds that the steps which they are prepared to take, the lengths they will go are so small as to be hardly perceptible to the naked eye."[9]

Nevertheless, Huxley soon became a regular at the Sitwells' table, as did Tom and Vivienne Eliot, who had in 1918 few friends in London. Likewise, *Wheels*, though never highly praised, was soon seriously treated by the reviewers, who usually compared it with the current Georgian anthology. T. S. Eliot's review of the second cycle called it a more serious book than the latest *Georgian Poetry*, but his praise was faint: "Instead of rainbows, cuckoos, daffodils and timid hares, they give us garden-gods, guitars, and mandolins."[10] By the end of 1918, the Sitwells were at the social center of the London arts scene. They planned a party for November 11, 1918, to which even Bloomsbury came; it happened to fall on Armistice night; it was the party at which D. H. Lawrence lectured David Garnett on the war Lawrence believed was soon to come.

Edith's greatest coup at *Wheels* was to publish seven poems of Wilfrid Owen in the fourth cycle (November 1919). Osbert, as an officer and a poet (though stationed mostly with the sons of the aristocracy in the Grenadiers' posh Chelsea barracks in West London), had been a friend of Siegfried Sassoon, who asked Osbert to look after Owen during a stay in London in the summer of 1918. Osbert, through Sassoon, got the manuscripts to Edith, who wrote to Owen's mother for permission to publish. The next year, 1920, a volume of Owen's poetry was brought out; it was Edith Sitwell who did the editing, but Siegfried Sassoon who usurped her editorship. The place of authority and authenticity still belonged to the male trench poets.

Osbert, with some claim to having been in the trenches, was the best-known poet of the three siblings at first. He was in harmony with Sassoon before they ever met, though Osbert's antiwar spirit owed more to his anger at his father than to his experience of war. "Rhapsode" (from October 1917) is addressed directly to the generation of the fathers:

> We know you now—and what you wish to be told;
> That the larks are singing in the trenches,
> That the fruit trees will again blossom in the spring,
> That Youth is always happy.
>
> (*Satires*, 14)

When Sassoon assumed the literary editorship in 1919 of the voice of the Labour Party, the *Daily Herald*, Osbert was one of his first contributors, with a bitter poem satirizing the homecoming parades as "Corpse-Day." Again, the fathers are the chief target:

> Old, fat men leant out to cheer
> From bone-built palaces.
> Gold flowed like blood
> Through the streets;
> Crowds became drunk
> On liquor distilled from corpses.
> (*Satires*, 32–33)

A week later Osbert contributed three more poems that savaged Winston Churchill. The *Herald* published them as editorial leaders, rather than as poems. Churchill was for all the Sitwells the incarnation of the worst of their childhood. He was a member of "The Golden Horde," those patriotic, card-playing, sporting, quail-shooting, country house–conservative old fathers who had presided over so much blood. Churchill, responsible for the slaughter at Gallipoli, now wanted to intervene against the Russian Bolsheviks. Osbert gives Churchill this monologue:

As I said in a great speech
After the last great war,
I begin to fear
That the nation's heroic mood
Is over.
Only three years ago
I was allowed to waste
A million lives in Gallipoli,
But now
They object
To my gambling
With a few thousand men
In Russia!
It does seem a shame.
I shall burn my *Daily Herald*.[11]

The poems were hurriedly reprinted by the local Bolsheviks at The Bomb Shop at 66 Charing Cross Road under the title *The Winstonburg Line;* it was Osbert's first book.

Osbert began to formulate a poetic manifesto; for him, the lark symbolized the lie that the old fathers, abetted by the Georgians, tried to sell the young. He argued that poets should turn from nature to their true role as "magicians," writing poems that are "like a crystal globe, with Truth imprisoned in it, like a fly in amber" (Pearson, 152). Edith's writing changed radically. She began to use favorite nursery-rhyme characters from her childhood in surreal situations suggested by the French symbolists, introduced to her by Helen Rootham. She often wrote now in ballad stanzas and rhymed couplets, and paid more attention to sound than to sense: "Jane, Jane, / Tall as a crane"; "Three poor witches / . . . Black and lean, / Are Moll and Meg, / And Myrrhaline"; "Queen Circe, the farmer's wife at the Fair / Met three sailor-men stumping there"; "Prince Absalom and Sir Rotherham Redde / Rode on a rocking-horse home to bed"; "Gargotte the goose-girl, bright as hail, / Has faded into a fairy-tale"; "The miller's daughter / Combs her hair, / Like flocks of doves / As soft as vair."[12]

Sacheverell, meanwhile, had gone up to Oxford to study; he lasted only a short while, but he did meet there a 16-year-old music student whom he thought a genius, the composer William Walton (later Sir William Walton, president of the Society for Twentieth Century Music). Walton came to live with the Sitwells as his patrons, becoming almost the fourth sibling. Soon he and Edith were collaborating on a piece of performance art called *Facade*. Its first performance was on January 24, 1922, in the upstairs drawing room at Osbert's house at Carlyle Square. The sculptor Frank Dobson had painted a curtain behind which the Sitwells took turns declaiming Edith's poems through a papier-mâché megaphone while Walton conducted his own music played by six instrumentalists—flute, clarinet, saxophone, trumpet, cello, and percussion. The event became the talk of London, perhaps validating F. R. Leavis's claim that the Sitwells should be remembered for publicity more than for poetry.

Without Walton's music and Edith's powerful personality and striking presence, the poems of *Facade* cannot be fairly judged. They seem on the page to validate the gossip that Virginia Woolf passed on to her sister Vanessa, that the Sitwells had been reciting "sheer nonsense through megaphones" (Glendinning, 77). But Edith always claimed to care more about rhythm and sound than sense. One poem from *Facade* begins "The octogenarian / Leaned from his window, / To the valerian / Growing below" (E. *Sitwell*, 133). When Sacheverell Sitwell (1897–1989) was himself 80 years old, he wrote a poem with the same title as this one, "The Octogenarian." It is a tribute to Edith's importance to him and also a description of her poetic practice. He recalls the summer of 1921 when every time he came to her flat, up four double-flights of stone stairs, she had a new poem for him:

> Poems in a rich vein of fantasy
>   invented for yourself,
> And all your own,
>   like nothing before or since.
>   (*Glendinning*, 72)

Though Edith thought Sacheverell the most talented of them all, his poetry looks oddly out of place with hers, like a belated Georgian among the Modernists.

Robert Graves and Laura Riding criticized her severely in their *Survey of Modernist Poetry* (1927) for obscurity that distances itself from an audience. This was a serious charge, for Graves and Riding were not opposed to difficult poetry. They praised E. E. Cummings (1894–1962) in the same volume for his compressed language that repaid readers willing to work to fill in the gaps. When Yeats, however, was choosing his Oxford anthology in 1936, he devoted 18 pages to her poetry (more than for Eliot and Hardy combined). In his preface, he provides a way to read her: She is "not to be read but spoken," and her "exaggerated metaphors" should be read as myth; that is, if in one poem a storm suggests to her "the bellowing of elephants," then one will understand the phrase in a later poem, "The elephant trunks of the sea" (Yeats, xix). Yeats praised her early poems of experimental wordplay for creating a world of "elegant, artificial childhood" and the later poems for a "nightmare vision."

The Sitwells' Jazz Age popularity declined almost immediately with the onset of the Depression and the Threadbare Thirties; Edith wrote little poetry herself during that decade, but she played a crucial role in encouraging younger poets, most notably Dylan Thomas. With the outbreak of the Second World War she became an important War Poet in her own right, breaking the pattern that gave soldier-authored poetry the only authority to speak of war. Part of the reason for Sitwell's being taken seriously as a War Poet in the 1940s was that the nature of war had changed. There was no longer the sharp demarcation between front lines and home front. As total war came to Europe, civilians, women, children, the aged, all were vulnerable to death and destruction raining down suddenly and unpredictably from the skies. A woman reading poems in a public hall in London with bombs falling outside (which Sitwell actually did) could claim to be present at the place of danger as truly as any soldier.

Unsoldierly Voices

Immediately after the First World War, however, the voices of women and other noncombatants were not particularly honored, as the story of Sassoon's dislodging of Sitwell from the editorship of Owen's poems shows. Their voices soon rose into more prominence, however, just as trench poetry began to move from primacy to a respected but background position. In part, no one wanted to be reminded of the soldiers' bitterness, of their sacrifice and their anger. (Osbert Sitwell had predicted this in a poem called "The Next War":

"My Killed Friends Are With Me Where I Go"

"Deaf men became difficult to talk to, / Heroes became bores" [*Satires*, 34].) In part, in the memorializing of the war dead, the grief and losses of the civilian world, and especially of women, could be more deeply acknowledged.

One route for noncombatants to have their poetry taken seriously was found by Ezra Pound, in his translations of the Chinese war poems of Li Po (701–762), which he published as *Cathay* in 1915. The great ideological divide that grew up in the Great War had split the world into two camps—those at the front (male) who had an authentic experience that they could only tell truthfully through a sharp irony, and those at home (female) who could not know the truth and so told and believed grandiose or sentimental illusions. By translating Li Po, Pound could use the correct male soldierly language without having to make false claims about his own experience, as in "Song of the Bowman of Shu" and "Lament of the Frontier Guard" (poems that Gaudier-Brzeska at the front picked as especially moving to his fellow soldiers there).[13]

He also translated poems in a female voice (which he did not send to the trenches), such as "The River-Merchant's Wife: A Letter." The speaker of the letter is in Pound's feminized situation: the one left behind. The wife describes how, in her arranged marriage, she has gradually come to desire "my dust to be mingled with yours / Forever and forever and forever."[14] Now her lord has been gone five months, and her longing for him, though stated discreetly, is palpable:

> The leaves fall early this autumn, in wind.
> The paired butterflies are already yellow with August
> Over the grass in the West garden;
> They hurt me.

The letter ends with the wife inquiring which route her lord will take home, for she wishes to go out to meet him. The sorrow of the wife, the obvious bonds of love and eroticism, affirm a connection between man and woman that the trench poets were only allowing between comrades in arms. These two are also meant to be in each other's arms. The focus on the wife's feelings, rather than upon descriptions of the world of combat, allows this poem to authenticate and validate women's experiences.

Eleanor Farjeon (1881–1965), a close friend of Edward Thomas, wrote a moving elegy for him in this vein, called "Easter Monday (*In Memoriam* E. T.)." The poem begins:

> In the last letter that I had from France
> You thanked me for the silver Easter egg
> Which I had hidden in the box of apples
> You liked to munch beyond all other fruit.
> You found the egg the Monday before Easter
> And said, "I will praise Easter Monday now—
> It was such a lovely morning." Then you spoke
> Of the coming battle and said "This is the eve.
> Good-bye. And may I have a letter soon."[15]

Thomas was married, but not happily so, and Farjeon played the role of intellectual companion in his life, a role that his wife, Helen Thomas, could not. He played in Farjeon's life the role of absent husband. The intimate attachment between the two, though unconsummated, is shown by the small and loving domestic details of the poem—the mention of his favorite fruit, the playful hiding of candy in the box. Because their relationship takes place in words more than in physical action or presence, Farjeon religiously preserves Thomas's words from his last letter.

The 14-line poem has the look of a sonnet, but a fractured, unrhyming one. The octet (though it is 9 lines) sets out the situation. The sestet (of 5 lines) consummates the grief:

> That Easter Monday was a day for praise,
> It was such a lovely morning. In our garden
> We sowed our earliest seeds, and in the orchard
> The apple-bud was ripe. It was the eve.
> There are three letters that you will not get.

Farjeon memorializes Thomas's words and the religious season of his death (ironically, Easter), but the actual date of his death, April 9, 1917, is not mentioned. What is important is the "eve." This word is mentioned twice, in rhyming position in a sonnet that otherwise has no rhymes. The first time it refers to when Thomas's letter was written, the eve before the battle. The second time is more mysterious, its subject ambiguous in its referent: "It was the eve." The eve of what? Easter Monday, back in England? The day he died? The date she learned of his death? One reading is that the eve is a repetition of the only eve that matters, the eve of the letter-writing. There is a dark undertone here: Is she the Eve who gave the apple that has led to her Adam's death? In that story, their fall into sin and death leads to a sexual consummation and a life together with children.

The stoical poignancy of the last line, "There are three letters that you will not get," is strongly controlled yet laced with the same intensity, and perhaps eroticism, as the letter of the River Merchant's wife. There is a deeply buried possibility that those three letters could be s-e-x. Nothing so bold occurs anywhere in the correspondence between Thomas and Farjeon, or in the poem, but the letter-writing is surely charged for the both of them, as evidenced by "may I have a letter soon" and her thrice-performed compliance. Farjeon demonstrates her faithfulness to Thomas, in the currency of their relationship, by the letters that travel to France. Continuity with him is emphasized, in the apple-bud in the garden, in the preserving of his words, and in the three letters.

There is also a fourth letter, in the sense that the poem itself, constructed of words, goes out to him, but with no hope of actually touching him (corresponding to the physical remoteness of their relationship). It echoes, in a more personal way, one of Thomas's most beautiful poems, from two years earlier, "In Memoriam (Easter, 1915)":

> The flowers left thick at nightfall in the wood
> This Eastertide call into mind the men,
> Now far from home, who, with their sweethearts, should
> Have gathered them and will never do again.
>
> (*Works*, 45)

Thomas and Farjeon in their elegies emphasize the love between men and women (as does Hardy in "In Time of 'The Breaking of Nations'" and Pound in his translations of Li Po). Men and women, when seen as lovers, can become, in this tradition, equals, both feeling absence, longing, and grief. More commonly, as with these poems, it is woman who feels grief, which is the experience of war she has as the one abandoned, while man feels fear and injury and anger, as the one who must fight.

This broken sonnet by Farjeon is from a collection she published as *First and Second Love* (1947), a sequence of 44 sonnets. Many of them seem also addressed to Thomas, and are, again, poems about absence. One of the most haunting of them addresses the children she never had:

"My Killed Friends Are With Me Where I Go"

> Farewell, you children that I might have borne.
> Now must I put you from me year by year.
> Sometimes I felt your lips and hands so close
> I almost could have plucked you from the dark.
>
> (37)

The ghostliness of their nearness in the dark is like that of Thomas, and the verb "plucked" recalls the ripeness and fruitfulness of the garden imagery in her elegy for him: "We sowed our earliest seeds, and in the orchard / The apple-bud was ripe." The poem's final couplet could be addressed to both the absent children and the absent husband: "I shall not see you laugh or hear you weep, / Kiss you awake, or cover up your sleep."

Charlotte Mew (1869–1928) was also husbandless and childless, but unlike Farjeon did not center her poetry on those states. One of her chief poetic preoccupations was madness, from a family history that saw two of her four siblings confined for life. Because of this history, both Mew and her sister pledged never to marry and never to conceive. After publishing a few poems in periodicals, she was discovered by Alida Monro, who brought out a slim volume of her poems from the Poetry Bookshop called *The Farmer's Bride* (1916), from the first poem in the volume. After reading it, Thomas Hardy proclaimed her the best woman poet then writing. This praise did not help her gain an audience and may have hurt; Virginia Woolf referred to her, mockingly, as Thomas Hardy's favorite "poetess," picking up on the unintended condescension in his praise. Later critics dismissed her as an example of Hardy's poor judgment. Her reputation is receiving a long overdue reevaluation.

Nothing in *The Farmer's Bride* indicates that Mew is interested in writing about the war, but when it was reissued in 1921 with 11 new poems added, one of them directly dealt with a contemporary issue, the construction of a public monument to memorialize the dead, called the "Cenotaph." In her poem by that name, Mew takes an ambivalent stance toward the memorial: "Not yet will those measureless fields be green again / Where only yesterday the wild, sweet, blood of wonderful youth was shed; / There is a grave whose earth must hold too long, too deep a stain."[16] In her extraordinarily long lines, Mew indicates the "measureless" quality of the loss, and the long time required for healing. The entire war is only "yesterday" on the time scale required for restoration. Mew seems here to have an environmentalist's sense of the fragility of nature and a pessimism about the difficulty of repairing destruction.

She describes those left behind as "watchers by lonely hearths." They were left behind first by the soldiers going off to war, and now by the death of those men. But they have felt violence, too, "from the thrust of an inward sword." With this imagery, Mew has linked the war story with her Catholicism, representing the situation of mothers and other supposed noncombatants everywhere by alluding to Mary, whose heart will be pierced by a sword at her son's death. From this inner violence, to the emotions, those left behind have "more slowly bled." And yet the government wants to build a glorious monument: "We shall build the Cenotaph: Victory, winged, with Peace, winged too, at the column's head. / And over the stairway, at the foot—oh!" In the midst of describing the grand architectural project, she breaks off at the thought of what lies at the foot. "Here, leave," she says, the monument uncluttered so that "desolate hands" may spread "violets, roses, and laurel" from "the little gardens of little places where son or sweetheart was born and bred." The Cenotaph becomes, then, not a place to celebrate victory or peace but rather to express loss.

And that, too, is a problem. To strew such beautiful flowers—purple violets, green laurel, red roses—is to commemorate loss too prettily: "It is all young life: it must break some women's hearts to see / Such a brave, gay coverlet to such a bed!" The government's version of memorializing has its own public agenda, and private grief cannot even be properly represented. What is left? God, "who is not mocked and neither are the dead":

> For this will stand in our Market-place—
>   Who'll sell, who'll buy
>   (Will you or I
> Lie to each other with the better grace)?
> While looking into every busy whore's and huckster's face
> As they drive their bargains, is the Face
> Of God: and some young, piteous, murdered face.
>
> (36)

The "Face of God" has an Old Testament suggestion of wrath to it; the buyers and sellers in the market had best beware of the profaning of these murdered dead.

"My Killed Friends Are With Me Where I Go"

In 1929, after Mew's suicide, Alida Monro posthumously published *The Rambling Sailor* with her memoir of Mew, remarking that very little poetry had survived house-movings, periods of depression, and her fastidious self-criticism, perhaps only a tenth of her total output. What remains is remarkable. Two companion pieces, "May, 1915" and "June, 1915" (42, 43), link Mew's environmentalism with her spirituality. Her treatment of nature deserves a new name, for which "environmentalist" may be best because of the ways it differs from the late Romanticism of Frost, Thomas, and the Georgians. "May, 1915" opens with a conventional romantic motif: "Let us remember Spring will come again / To the scorched, blackened woods, where the wounded trees / Wait, with their old wise patience for the heavenly rain." The first line of Mew's poem recalls the last line of Shelley's "Ode to the West Wind." She is able to start her poem with a confidence that he needed to build to. For Shelley, the coming of spring hints at the presence of a transcendence; this hint is hard won, asserted in his poem's grandly rhetorical last line. For Mew, belief is the beginning place, accepted and known; her poem does not feel the need to inquire about God. It turns instead to the trees, "sure of the sky: sure of the sea to send its healing breeze, / Sure of the sun."

The war enters the poem in its title and the "scorched woods," but the poem focuses not on soldiers' suffering in the war but on the trees' injuries. The "wounded trees" are not symbols of promise but real trees, which are blackened by fire and shelling. As real trees, they need water, air, and sun to heal. This is what is sure in the poem. Because Mew is also sure of God, she is not forced into Romanticism's passionate search for belief. She is free to leave God and nature as partners, rather than construct a proof of God by an examination of nature as the Romantics so often do. Nature, capitalized, does not have to stand in for God, but can remain in lowercase, as the thing itself.

Nature perseveres continuously but not predictably. Spring comes "like a divine surprise / To those who sit today with their great Dead, hands in their hands, eyes in their eyes, / At one with Love, at one with Grief: blind to the scattered things and changing skies." Mew's universe allows for both surety and surprise. We humans, our eyes looking into the eyes of our "great Dead," are temporarily blinded to our own emotional processes, but those processes do proceed. The progress of grieving, Mew seems to be saying, is slow and surprising and sure.

"June, 1915" also acknowledges the war's seriousness and the difficulty, maybe even the inappropriateness, of the Romantics and Georgians' faith in Nature: "Who thinks of June's first rose to-day?" The answer is "Only some child, perhaps," who "with shining eyes" in some "sunny green lane" will stop to smell it. In the conventional poetry of the day, we know where this poem would take us: The opposition between the child who smells the roses and we adults who are blind would be resolved in favor of the child, from whom we would learn. Mew ends the poem, however, with the two experiences, adult and child, juxtaposed, uncommented upon. Each has its validity, and we are allowed to remain open to both:

> What's little June to a great broken world with eyes gone dim
> From too much looking on the face of grief, the face of dread?
> Or what's the broken world to June and him
> Of the small eager hand, the shining eyes, the rough bright head?
>
> (43)

Two of Mew's best poems, "The Trees Are Down" and "Madeleine in Church," are longer, more ambitious works. The first begins with an epigraph from Revelation 7:3: "Hurt not the earth, neither the sea, nor the trees." The poem's opening lines then describe the cutting down of trees near her house in London: "They are coming down the great plane-trees at the end of the gardens" (48). Their crash is accompanied by "the 'Whoops' and the 'Whoas,' the loud common talk, the loud common laughs of the men, above it all." She finds a dead rat, which "unmakes" the spring for her for a moment. The loss of the trees unmakes more than a moment; it is half her life, and half the spring. "Madeleine in Church" is a dramatic monologue. Its girl speaker prefers the dark and the human to the bright and the godlike:

> Here, in the darkness, where this plaster saint
>   Stands nearer than God stands to our distress,
> And one small candle shines, but not so faint
>   As the far light of everlastingness
> I'd rather kneel than over there, in open day
>   Where Christ is hanging, rather pray
> To something more like my own clay,
>   Not too divine.
>
> (22)

This powerful and complex poem expresses her more ambivalent attitudes toward religion in a way that also applies to war, especially as related to the concepts of suffering, sacrifice, and victory.

After her death, Osbert Sitwell composed a six-part poem for "Miss Mew" that, throughout, used the image of her as a feather, "blown out of a pastel past, / Upon some shattering gale / Of which no one was ever told the nature" (*Satires*, 172). Her small output of poetry and the small facts known about her life have led to a sense of our having missed a great poet. Osbert Sitwell's lines on her express our wonder and our regret:

> How few
> The things we knew
> About Miss Mew!

Robert Graves and Laura Riding

In early 1918, while on leave, Robert Graves (1895–1985) married 18-year-old Nancy Nicholson, daughter of the artist William Nicholson. The Nicholsons had rented a house near Graves's parents' holiday cottage in Wales and become friends of the family during the war. Nancy was herself a promising young artist (she had designed a cover for *Vogue* at age 14) whose strong feminist attitudes appealed to Graves. When they met in 1916, he was writing the poems of *Fairies and Fusiliers*, trying to balance the claims of the imagination with the realities of the war in his odd title. When she showed him her illustrations to Robert Louis Stevenson's *A Child's Garden of Verses*, he felt that he had found a kindred spirit, someone else who saw a purity and perfection that lay behind childhood myths and stories, truths more powerful than the unpleasant reality he found around him. He had stated it succinctly in the poem "Babylon" in his new volume: "The child alone a poet is: / Spring and Fairyland are his."[17]

The marriage experienced many difficulties, however. They quickly had four children. One of their schemes for earning a living was to open a grocery shop, but they soon lost money. They survived one whole year on the charity of the publicity-shy T. E. Lawrence, who gave Graves an autographed copy of *Revolt in the Desert* to sell (it brought 330 pounds). Graves continued to publish in the immediate postwar years—*The Treasure Box* (1919), *Country Sentiment* (1920), *The Pier Glass* (1921), *Whipperginny* (1923), *Mock Beggar Hall* (1924)—but these volumes were dominated by ballads, songs, nursery rhymes, and playlets, which seemed an unsoldierly escape from reality.

A poem from *Whipperginny,* later dropped from the canon, deals specifically with money troubles and questions of poetic direction. The poem opens as a monologue in which Graves seems to be answering his publisher:

> "There's less and less cohesion
> In each collection
> Of my published poetries?"
> You are taking me to task?
> And "What were my last royalties?
> Reckoned in pounds, were they, or shillings,
> Or even perhaps in pence?"[18]

Graves immediately stops the money talk with a despairing admission—"I'm lost, in buyings and sellings." He does, however, ask to be permitted, just once more, the "irreconcilabilities" of his book. He offers a justification for the seeming lack of cohesion:

> For these are all the same stuff really,
> The obverse and reverse, if you look closely.

Whether he grows strong enough to "wrestle," as Jacob did, with a fiend or angel, or whether he grows childish and darts "to Mother-skirts of love and peace / To play with toys until those horrors leave"—"whichever way"—he finds "release":

> By fight or flight
> By being harsh or tame,
> The SPIRIT'S the same, the Pen-and-Ink's the same.

Graves rather aggressively, in the capitalized voice of the poem's last line, equates the lighter-seeming nursery rhyme poems he is writing with the grimmer war poetry of Owen and Sassoon then being celebrated. He makes two claims. First, the pen-and-ink process of writing is the same for either kind of poet. Graves is assuming that the purpose of poetry is therapeutic, and, in that case, it does not matter if one fights or flees, is harsh or tame, wrestles with demons or runs away from them back to childhood; the purpose and result is to deal with a powerful emotion, fear, and both formulas do it equally well. Second, the spirit behind the poetic enterprise is also the same, and this spirit has a name—the Muse. The seemingly irreconcilable content of his poetry is reconciled by assertion; the war poems in 1916's *Over the Brazier* and 1917's *Fairies and Fusiliers,* as well as those sometimes scattered in the later volumes, are not different from the ballads and songs and nursery rhymes. His need to write and the Muse make it so.

The entrance of American poet Laura Riding (1901–1991) into Graves's life in early 1926 was undoubtedly crucial, for she seemed to him to embody the Muse; but it is also true that Graves was fully conscious of a relationship to a Muse long before her arrival. In a poem from *Mock Beggar Hill,* "Antinomies," he observes a grasshopper and makes "her" the Muse:

> "What can I sing, Muse?" And she told me plainly,
> "Always the first thing floating in your mind.
> A formless, lumpish, nothing-in-particular.
> You take, toss, catch it, turn it inside out,
> Do new things with it."[19]

Riding proved to be a much better embodiment of the Muse than a grasshopper. Graves later said that during the years he knew her a kind of light shone from her. The poet Alastair Reid (b. 1926), who became Graves's friend and disciple, claimed that even in later years, whenever Riding's name was mentioned, Graves (as well as every other person Reid met who knew her) would get a "dazed faraway look" in his eyes.[20] Riding's ideas radically changed the direction of Graves's poetry. He renounced his Georgian past and laid out, in the book they wrote together, his own particular brand of Modernism.

The ideas of Riding and Graves about what makes one a Modern were brilliantly demonstrated in *A Survey of Modernist Poetry* (1927), which focused on specific poems of "moderns"such as E. E. Cummings, Edith Sitwell, and William Shakespeare. Riding and Graves invented "close reading," or if not invented, at least gave the earliest and fullest demonstration of its power in their explications. Both of them had been in communication with American poet John Crowe Ransom (1888–1974) and with Ransom heavily influenced the New Criticism that came to dominate English departments in the 1940s through the 1960s. The New Criticism (the name comes from Ransom's 1941 book of essays with that title) was written mostly by poets. It emphasized strict adherence to a text, which was seen as an artifact to explicate. Certain elements of Graves's early verse were congenial with the tenets of New Criticism—his humor and wit, his use of traditional forms, and his skill with tightly logical or powerfully intellectualized language. Those elements stayed with him all his life; they were put to the service of both expressing but also controlling and distancing experience and emotion.

Graves's poetry is inseparably wound up with his criticism, which is inseparably wound up with his life. The most famous event in the life of Riding and Graves is her suicidal leap from a fourth-floor window and his leap from the third floor on the way down to her. In her biography of Riding, Deborah Baker argues that it was not the emotions leading up to the suicide attempt, nor the attempt itself, which profoundly changed Graves, but visiting her in hospital afterwards, where she screamed and threw tantrums "for fun" or "just to have something to do."[21] She called the doctor whose surgical skill saved her from paralysis the "Insect." What Graves suddenly saw in Riding's contempt for appropriate behavior, even as she lay vulnerable and broken in a public ward at Charing Cross Hospital, was, Baker argues, his own "silenced rage" over the war. With her example, he, too, could feel beholden to no one. He dashed off his autobiography, *Good-Bye to All That* (1929), with its dismissive and slangily American title, in the next few months. It hit the right note with the public and quickly earned enough for the two of them to leave the scandal and the country behind. They settled in Majorca that year, on the advice of their friend Gertrude Stein, who told them, "It's paradise if you can stand it."[22] The peripatetic Riding could stand it for seven years, after which she made her way back to America. Graves made the island his home until his death at age 90, leaving only in wartime. Such wide-ranging minds as Graves's are not often content to remain in such an isolated and unsophisticated place as Majorca was then. Graves's real life was so lived in the poems that the literal insularity of an island was no drawback. For him, it was a paradise. The fairies—or the world of poetic truth they represented—won out over the Royal Welch Fusiliers.

During his long life, Graves repudiated much of his earlier poetry and almost every poet he knew or read. In 1927 he issued a collection of his poetry, *Poems 1914–1926*, from which he excised much of his earliest work. He continued to revise poems and his canon in new *Collected Poems* issued in 1938, 1948, 1955, 1959, 1961, 1965, and 1975. There was in his lifetime no authorized "Complete Poems," and each collection has some poems unique to it. One poet he did not repudiate was Thomas Hardy, perhaps because of the tradition Graves chose to construct for himself that by-passed the modernisms of Eliot, the Sitwells, Yeats, and Lawrence. Or perhaps it was the personal relationship that the not very sociable Hardy often was able to establish with younger persons, poets or not, which was sometimes closer than the relationship they had with the generation of their actual fathers. A lieutenant stationed at Blandford, Dorset, Elliott Felkin, described Hardy's capacity "of treating young people not as if you were pretending to make yourself young out of politeness, nor as if you were instructing or guiding by the wisdom of experience, but as if you really felt that age and youth had something to give each other."[23] Graves seemed to feel that from his brief personal relationship with Hardy a poetic mantle had passed on to him. He eschewed awards, prizes, and fame for a long time, steadily working on his island with a perseverance that matched Hardy's total dedication to a life of poetry. Like Hardy, he saw his prose works as a way to make money to support his poetry.

In his critical study of Graves's poetry, D. N. G. Carter begins by quoting a Hardy poem and a Graves poem side by side. In both poems, the poet is looking into a mirror at his own face. What Hardy sees is his "wasting skin," while at the same time he is aware that his heart is as unchanged and youthful as ever. Even though his "frame" is in the "eve" of life, he is still passionately shaken "with throbbings of noontide."[24] This attitude is quintessentially Victorian, but modern, too. Browning in a late monologue, "Cleon," presents the same dilemma of age:

> every day my sense of joy
> Grows more acute, my soul (intensified
> By power and insight) more enlarged, more keen;
> While every day my hairs fall more and more,
> My hand shakes, and he heavy years increase.[25]

The intensely alive mind is "fastened," as Yeats says in "Sailing to Byzantium," "to a dying animal."

Graves's poem is a much more exact, and exacting, description of his face:

> Grey haunted eyes, absent-mindedly glaring
> From wide, uneven orbits; one brow drooping

Somewhat over the eye
Because of a missile fragment still inhering,
Skin deep, as a foolish record of old-world fighting.

Crookedly broken nose—low tackling caused it;
Cheeks, furrowed; coarse grey hair, flying frenetic;
Forehead, wrinkled and high;
Jowls, prominent; ears, large; jaw, pugilistic;
Teeth, few; lips, full and ruddy; mouth, ascetic.[26]

Here we see Graves's biography worn into his face—the school boxing champion with his pugilistic jaw, the rugby player with a broken nose to show for it, the soldier with a drooping brow from shrapnel, the poet with frenetically flying hair, the self-deprecating humorist who claims to have "Teeth, few" in the catalogic phrasing of army-issued gear. His lifelong sexual conflicts are worn specifically on his mouth, full-lipped but ascetic.

In the third and final stanza, we see that this moment of self-reflection has come during his morning shaving ritual:

I pause with razor poised, scowling derision
At the mirrored man whose beard needs my attention,
And once more ask him why
He still stands ready, with a boy's presumption,
To court the queen in her high pavilion.

The final line is surprising in its upliftedness. Graves, like Hardy, Browning, and Yeats, is contrasting external aging with internal youthfulness but without the pain that that contrast normally brings. For him, age is irrelevant, for the best is yet to come. The queen, his Muse, is awaiting him. With his ritualistic action he will shave off the realities of manhood and enter once again the realm of boys, the realm of childhood, which alone dares to approach the throne. As Carter notes, Graves—"nobody's servant but his own"—is in the presence of the only being he "will bow before—the Muse" (Carter, 2). His personal history, which takes up the bulk of the poem, has ultimately no importance; all that matters is that surprising last line, the queen of poetry awaiting him in "her high silk pavilion."

In 1927 Graves began to write a more heavily intellectualized poetry that conformed more closely to the critical stance he and Riding were taking. One of the best of these poems, "The Cool Web," deals with the perennial issue for him of fight or flight—facing his war memories or escaping them. In the preface to *Whipperginny* (1923), he had refined the "fight or flight" formulation to a new pair of antimonies: whether to "demand unceasing emotional stress in poetry at whatever cost to the poet" or to write with "greater detachment" about a "series of problems in religion, psychology and philosophy" (v). His choice, with "no apology," was the latter.

"The Cool Web" (a permanent part of the canon, in every *Collected Poems*) is structured as a problem in logic, with the first two stanzas thesis and antithesis:

> Children are dumb to say how hot the day is,
> How hot the scent is of the summer rose,
> How dreadful the black wastes of evening sky,
> How dreadful the tall soldiers drumming by.
>
> But we have speech, to chill the angry day,
> And speech, to dull the rose's cruel scent.
> We spell away the overhanging night,
> We spell away the soldiers and the fright.
> (*Complete*, 1:323)

Children, before they are protected by language, are forced to face the emotional intensity of love and war—the scent of the rose, the soldiers drumming by. Adults, luckily, have the gift of speech to control rose and soldiers, angry day or smothering night. The naming of things is a spell that has power to control—to chill the hot day, to dull the rose's scent. Because spells often work by illusion, however, some uncertainty is thrown up here; perhaps language only gives the appearance of control. We must wait and see.

The third stanza slowly undermines whatever confidence the adults could take in language's power to charm:

> There's a cool web of language winds us in,
> Retreat from too much joy or too much fear:
> We grow sea-green at last and coldly die
> In brininess and volubility.
> (1:323)

The "cool web" of the title comes into play. "Cool" suggests a Jazz Age hipness, a detached savoir-faire, a slick and satisfying—maybe self-satisfied—way of using language. But the next word is faintly disturbing, not cool, not hip, not in control. "Web" brings the image of the spider into the poem, and an instinctive uneasiness. The verb "winds" confirms our worst fears, as it evokes the "winding sheet" of the dead, while the image of being wound in a web brings involuntary shudders at feelings of entrapment, engulfment, and death. Language is the spider's lair, into which we think we are voluntarily retreating, only to be wound into a cocoonlike pod, still alive but paralyzed, as the spider's meal is. In the image of the next two lines, we are pickled, drowning in brine. Again, we are food—something organic, living or once-living, but now to be gobbled up, just as our volubility gobbles up our life and ends it. The way "volubility" fills the mouth but does not visually fill out the line shows the mumbling murderousness of words. They are both too much and too little.

Is there a way out? Graves tries a new hypothesis, signaled by "if":

> But if we let our tongues lose self-possession,
> Throwing off language and its watery clasp
> Before our death, instead of when death comes,
> Facing the wide glare of the children's day,
> Facing the rose, the dark sky and the drums,
>
> (1:324)

The rhetorical repetitions are here heroic, the poem building in energy as it revisits its earlier images, building to a conclusion in its final line: "We shall go mad no doubt and die that way." How the wind is knocked out of us! There is no way out. To control, to diminish, to dull our experience of life is the way to death; to embrace life without some control is to go mad. Philosophy is dead; visions are mad. The offhand phrase "no doubt" in the last line, however, actually raises some doubt. Is there a middle road, perhaps? Or, perhaps, is there no real dilemma, just a trick of rhetoric? Is Graves choosing one of the two alternatives he provides us? The "no doubt" invites us to question the poem, and the poem remains more clever than we. To modify what Churchill once said of Russia, the poem is a riddle inside an enigma inside a box.

In the second half of his life, Graves was valued by the generation of poets coming of age in the 1950s, much as Graves had valued Hardy. He was admired for his independence from movements (Georgian, Imagist, Modernist) and for his longevity and persistence. Just as the last poem in Hardy's last volume, *Winter Words*

(1928), is "He Resolves to Say No More," Graves placed at the end of his works a poem that is aware of both death and posterity, "Leaving the Rest Unsaid." He uses the image of a book with *Finis* on its last page, wondering if he must also repeat that word in his book, the one the reader is holding. The Gravesian humor is here, arguing that to announce the end of the book is superfluous, because it is ended by the poet's death, "And to die once is death enough, / Be sure, for any life-time."[27] His bristly courage and argumentativeness are also here:

> Must the book end, as you would end it,
> With testamentary appendices
> And graveyard indices?

No, says the poet, punning on his name, he will not allow such appendices and graveyard mournings,

> So now, my solemn ones, leaving the rest unsaid,
> Rising in air as on a gander's wing
> At a careless comma,

The comma lifts into the sky like a droopy, careless wing and the poem drifts away, already ended before we were ready. We are left catching our breath, quite literally, at this moving and brilliant enactment of the suddenness and surprise of death. And there are also appendices and indices in the back of the volume—an extra-textual Gravesian irony. He leaves us watching his flight to join the Muse, and when he is already out of sight we get the joke. We are left with the irony of Troilus's cosmic laugh at the silliness of earthly worries, once one is safely elevated. Unfortunately, we are not elevated but still holding the book—and still trying to end the poem. And then we are elevated too. By our imaginative reading of the poem, we enter the realm of the Muse, which is the point that Graves has been making all his life—that one can live in heaven while on earth, through a life of poetry.

D. H. Lawrence and Anna Wickham

The *Last Poems* (1932) of D. H. Lawrence (1885–1930) also rose to the occasion—or, more appropriately for Lawrence's metaphorical universe, his last poems descended. That is, Lawrence played with some of our most fundamental metaphors, such as directionality. Where heaven, light, cheer, and health are normally "up," Lawrence in his novels and poems often directs his hero to take a downward journey into darkness to find enlightenment. The most famous of the *Last Poems*, "Bavarian Gentians" and "The Ship of Death," are some of the few Lawrence poems always anthologized, along with "Snake" and some of the other poems from *Birds, Beasts, and Flowers* (1923), usually ones from the "Tortoises" sequence. These are very fine individual poems, and it is upon them that his reputation as a poet commonly rests, even for educated readers, who know him chiefly as one of the most important Modernist novelists of the twentieth century.

Lawrence, however, like Graves and Hardy, saw himself chiefly as a poet, not a novelist. He wrote poetry throughout his life and published enough to rival Hardy or Yeats or Wordsworth in bulk. That is a lot of bulk, and much of it has been dismissed, especially the poems in *Pansies* (1929), as "rantings," by even so perceptive a critic as David Perkins. But it was Lawrence's chief occupation and must be treated seriously if we wish to treat him seriously. Given his devotion to poetry, it is not surprising that the prose style he brought to novel-writing has a lyrical and rhythmical quality that was new in prose works for the time.

Lawrence was first published in both the Georgian and the Imagist anthologies. That both groups claimed him, and that he had no trouble appearing in either anthology, is an indication that Modernism and Georgianism were not as vehemently opposed to each other before the Great War as after, when more hardened positions had set in. His first volume of poetry was *Look! We Have Come Through!* (1917), a sequence of free-verse lyrics showing his debt to Walt Whitman. Lawrence's short preface is worth quoting: "These poems should not be considered separately, as so many single pieces. They are intended as an essential story, or history, or confession, unfolding one from the other in organic development, the whole revealing the intrinsic experience of a man during the crisis of manhood, when he marries and comes into himself."[28] The confidence and joy of the title (and perhaps a note of surprise) refer to the success of his unlikely elopement with the married Frieda von Richthofen Weekley. It is a strange title for 1917, when the nation was war-weary and despondent and not at all sure it was going to come through. It is one more mark of Lawrence's dissociation from the war, or his reducing of it to second or third place behind the more personal wars he was fighting, with himself and society, for an openness in sexual and artistic freedom.

The preface is important for how it instructs us to read the poetry, not taking any single poem as the final word. When the poetry is read this way, the effect is close to Whitman's. Poems that answer each other or contradict each other, become obsessive on some points and flippant on others, show a Lawrence who contains multitudes. This approach has been argued most strongly by champions of Lawrence's 1923 collection *Birds, Beasts, and Flowers*. Lawrence thought this his best collection, and most critics agree. Patricia Hagen, in her sensitive reading of the "Fruits" section, demonstrates how to read Lawrence sequentially. The first poem in the volume, "Pomegranate," she argues, functions "as a sort of 'seed' poem, introducing the 'nucleus' of *Birds, Beasts, and Flowers*, the metaphors and imagery that will divide and subdivide as the volume continues."[29]

The metaphors start with the title of the volume. The title probably comes from a hymn of Sabine Baring-Gould (1834–1924), the novelist-hymnist who composed "Onward Christian Soldiers." The second stanza of Baring-Gould's "Evening Hymn" supplies the image:

> Now the darkness gathers,
>   Stars begin to peep,
> Birds and beasts and flowers
>   Soon will be asleep.
>   (995)

Baring-Gould's hymn gives Lawrence his catalog of creatures and his setting of darkness. The subsections or sequences of *Birds, Beasts, and Flowers* seem a disorderly lot: "Fruits," "Trees," "Flowers," "The Evangelistic Beasts," "Creatures," "Reptiles," "Birds," "Animals," and "Ghosts." While not the classification of a biologist, the groupings make more sense than first appears. "Creatures," for example, contains the poems "Mosquito," "Fish," and "Bat"—three different phyla. But the epigraph to the sequence describes "those things that love darkness," for whom "the light of day is cruel" yet who have no fear of the light of "lamps and candles"; this is the thematic link for the three disparate creatures, who are joined this way because it allows Lawrence to talk of our similar life as "things flying / Between the day and the night" (340). Each plant and animal in the collection becomes a metaphor for Lawrence's thoughts about humankind, yet each is also treated as the thing itself, quite remote from human understandings and feelings.

Lawrence's next volume, *Pansies* (1929), has seldom been admired. David Perkins speaks for many when he calls the shorter poems in the volume "splenetic" epigrams and the longer ones "tooth-gnashing invectives" (Perkins, 444). A few critics, such as Neil Roberts, make a case for them: To praise *Birds, Beasts, and Flowers* for a few "perfected" poems and to dismiss *Pansies* for lacking such poems misses the point for both volumes, he says. Both are, rather, "open and informal" sequences, which should be read "whole, and more rapidly than one normally reads a volume of poetry."[30] Thus even the physical speed of reading must be changed for the new kind of poetry Lawrence is trying to write. This is a fundamental challenge to the way poetry is perceived and studied in an academic setting.

The debate over Lawrence's status as a poet focuses on both theme and craft. Thematically, Lawrence rails against capitalism, socialism, over-intellectualization, women, the bourgeoisie, Oxford accents, revolutionaries, Boots Pharmacy, movies, Thomas Earp, Nottingham University, and many other seemingly random topics. The unifying theme of the poetry is his attitude toward these disparate topics. For Lawrence, all of them partake in the mechanization of life and love. This is a powerful theme, one that reflects the times. It finds expression in everything Lawrence wrote. Just one example is the condition of Clifford Chatterly, the mine owner who is cuckolded in *Lady Chatterly's Lover* (1928): He is paralyzed from the waist down. This is Lawrence's critique of Western civilization, over-rational, afraid of the body, pretending that people consist only of the parts from the waist up.

This idea was not Lawrence's fevered invention. It was latent in the times. Prewar clerks who read Georgian poetry on nature walks were aware of the numbing repetitiveness and emptiness of their jobs—hence the escape into nature. Rural immigrants to the city felt keenly the disappearance of communal village life, as well as the changed nature of work. In the factory, one responded to the rhythm of the clock rather than to the sun and the seasons. The resulting depersonalization and loss of social networks issued in violence and drunkenness as escape. The middle classes, too, recognized the explosion in growth, the overcrowding, the huge change in scale that urban life had undergone in just the past century—hence the creation of suburbs, which, alas, replicated more of the city than of the village. Postwar citizens were aware of the destruction that had been wrought. Blame was placed on women, the public schools, chivalry, sport, the generation of the fathers, and also on the machine. Soldiers in the war had cited not just lice, mud, and death as their enemies but also mechanization as the force that had changed everything: "A consumptive machine-gunner, too scared in an attack to bolt, can sit in a lucky hole in the ground and scupper a company of the best as they advance. Courage isn't what it used to be. The machine runs us over and we can't stop it" (Crawford, 21). That consummate Edwardian, Gilbert Keith Chesterton (1874–1936), wrote anti–Henry Ford poems such as "The Peace of Petrol" and this little ditty:

> The people they left the land, the land,
> But they went on working hard;
> And the village green that had got mislaid
> Turned up in the squire's back-yard:
> But twenty men of us all got work
> On a bit of his motor car;
> And we all became, with the world's acclaim,
> The marvellous mugs we are.[31]

Banished from the village green (which now the capitalist cum aristocrat owns), men become assemblyline workers, each one doing a "bit" of the car.

It is this vein that Lawrence mines. The argument about the impact of machines on human life which is in Chesterton's poem went on for most of the nineteenth century. Mary Shelley's *Frankenstein* (1818) is our dominant myth about the interaction of science and technology with the human and moral spheres. Thomas Carlyle, in an influential essay from 1829, "Signs of the Times," somewhat ambivalently calls the new age he is living in not what literary historians later name it, the Victorian period, but the Age of Machinery. In *Sartor Resartus* (1836), furthermore, Carlyle praises the gun as an invention that ends the tyranny of strength that heretofore a larger man could impress upon a smaller one. For Carlyle, the gun symbolized the power of mind and spirit over brute force. But Lawrence, standing a century removed from Carlyle and after the slaughter of the Great War, cannot allow machinery even a metaphorical beneficence.

For Lawrence, the machine is the creation of the rational mind, which has overbalanced every other way of knowing and being in Western culture. Poetry, as an artifact of that same Western culture, cannot be immune to charges of that same imbalance. This puts Lawrence in a ticklish situation, because he clearly admires the poetry of the past—Shakespeare, Shelley, Keats, Hardy. His solution, in a short but important preface called "Poetry of the Present" (1918), is to honor the poetry of the past but to argue for a new poetry of the present. Lawrence begins by making an analogy to songbirds, quite appropriate for a Georgian. He notes that birds sing "on the horizons ... out of the blue, beyond us ... at dawn and sunset"; poets likewise "sit by the gateways ... as we arrive and as we go out" (181). Birds and poets thus speak to the boundaries of things, the past and the future, the beginning and the end. This poetry must have a "finality," a "perfection," for it is from the realm of the perfect: "Perfected bygone moments, perfected moments in the glimmering futurity, these are the treasured gem-like lyrics of Shelley and Keats" (182).

But there is another kind of poetry, Lawrence argues, the "poetry of that which is at hand," and this ordinary poetry we do not as often listen to, just as we do not really listen to the "poor, shrill, tame canaries whistle while we talk." Lawrence's intention is to try for this "unrestful, ungraspable poetry," even if it means he may not be listened to, or thought shrill, or thought a poor poet.

Despite this clear declaration of intention, Lawrence is still frequently dismissed for his unmusical or unfocused lines. He can be blamed for defective intent, if one wishes, but hardly for defective craftsmanship: He refuses to write a poem that is a complete, whole object ready for analysis. His poems cannot be gem-encrusted music boxes awaiting a New Critical miner to make them glister and sing. They are coal, not gems; a "wind-like transit," not a crystallized moment; a breath, not an artifact. To write in such a way, Lawrence acknowledges, may be nearly impossible. But Whitman succeeds sometimes, so Lawrence intends to try: "We can break down those artificial conduits and canals through which we do so love to force our utterance. We can break the stiff neck of habit" (184).

Lawrence's defects might disappear faster if one reads quickly, but his utterances are best read slowly, as aphorisms are, or prophecies, or prayers. His utterances are usually highly metaphorical, and often switch metaphors, so that a new universe of connotations and entailments needs time to unfold. Lawrence speaks with a prophetic voice; if one hears his voice as shrill, high-pitched, and whinging, the poetry seems thin or ranting; if one hears the deep conviction and the profound desire to speak to the world, the poetry mesmerizes and inspires. Like Whitman, Lawrence draws heavily upon the rhythms and repetitions of the prose of the King James Bible. Ironically, he breaks the neck of habit in poetry by absorbing traditional prose.

There are many beautiful poems in *Pansies* (Lawrence saw puns in his title: *pensées* in French is both "thoughts" and "pansies"; *panser* means "to soothe a wound"). A brief sequence, "The Scientific Doctor" followed by "Healing" (620), shows Lawrence at his most flippant and most profound, side by side, with each poem adding to the other:

When I went to the scientific doctor
I realised what a lust there was in him to wreak his so-called science on me
and reduce me to the level of a thing.
So I said: Good morning! and left him.

The indignation of this door-slamming exit is followed by a deeper anger, which becomes more philosophical than angry:

I am not a mechanism, an assembly of various sections.
And it is not because the mechanism is working wrongly, that I am ill.
I am ill because of wounds to the soul, to the deep emotional self
and wounds to the soul take a long, long time, only time can help.

The biblical use of repetitions here begins to have the effect of biblical injunctions:

and patience, and a certain difficult repentance
long difficult repentance.

But the injunctions are more forgiving, more New Testament than Old:

realisation of life's mistake, and the freeing of oneself
from the endless repetition of the mistake.

Until the poem's last line, which allows in again the Old Testament and the note of condemnation: "which mankind at large has chosen to sanctify."

The poems of *Pansies* belong with the better-known *Last Poems* that mark Lawrence's unflinching spiritual journey downward into death. If there had been extraordinary measures available in 1930 to keep him alive, life-support systems and breathing machines, those, too, he undoubtedly would have rejected as he does the "scientific doctor." Lawrence, though he had many faults in life, could not be accused of hypocrisy on this issue. Whatever his emotional dependencies, he was extraordinarily self-sufficient in the ordinary, physical realm of life. It was he who did all the cooking and cleaning in his marriage to Frieda, often under the most primitive conditions, even while frequently ill, and of course without servants and "labor-saving" appliances. He did not look to science and rationality to save him. His last poem, written in a failing hand, optimistically balances darkness and light as he faces death. The poem, called "Prayer," asks for his feet to be placed on the crescent of the moon: "O let my ankles be bathed in moonlight, that I may go / sure and moon-shod, cool and bright-footed / towards my goal" (684). The poem ends with a familiar Lawrence symbol, the sun as a representative of pure light, reason, science, the male, and Western rationality: "For the sun is hostile, now / his face is like the red lion." Lawrence's early death at the age of 45 in 1930 marks the end of the decade, with the same sense of the passing of a prophet that Yeats's death in 1939, on the eve of the Second World War, gives to the end of that decade.

Lawrence is most commonly thought of in relation to sex. This is no doubt due to the notoriety surrounding, initially, *The Rainbow*, confiscated for obscenity in 1915, and then *Lady Chatterly's Lover* (1928), banned in England until the 1960 obscenity trial that allowed its unexpurgated publication by Penguin. Further, Lawrence's poetry and novels are thematically focused on the relationship between the sexes, in line with his goal as a writer to "do my work for women, better than the suffrage."[32] During his life, Lawrence was close to many women—he seemed to have a genius for intense friendships with women—and especially to the writers H. D., Katherine Mansfield (1888–1923), and Anna Wickham (1884–1947). Wickham, an important but now neglected poet, wrote an extraordinary analysis of Lawrence's work called "The Spirit of the Lawrence Women," not published until 1966. It is part memoir—"I remember

Lawrence. My nerves remember him, and, perhaps as he would have liked it, also my blood"—and part criticism.[33] She explains Lawrence's class background in a way not usually appreciated by upper middle-class writers such as Auden, who see Lawrence as working class, a miner's son. Wickham points out that she and Lawrence came from the Board Schools and that he was a teacher. They were the "rising" working class, which separated them from their families while not really allowing them into the middle class. She especially criticized Lawrence for his lack of understanding of the role of children in a woman's life. Aside from its first-hand help in understanding Lawrence, the essay reveals Wickham's fine mind and poetic concerns, telling us in addition much about the role of women in the first decades of the twentieth century.

Wickham was born Edith Alice Mary Harper; when she was 6, her parents moved from London to Australia, where at the age of 10, while residing at Wickham Terrace, Brisbane, she apparently promised her father that she would be a poet (hence her pen name). Back in England at the age of 21 she married a solicitor, Patrick Hepburn, and had four sons. Unhappy with marriage and domestic life, she began to write poetry that is more feminist and erotic than anything produced by her contemporaries Charlotte Mew (1869–1928), Eleanor Farjeon (1881–1965), Mina Loy (1882–1966), H. D. (1886–1961), Edith Sitwell (1887–1964), and Ruth Pitter (1897–1992). Her themes of sexual repression and domestic confinement put her closer to the work of the feminist novelists of the time—May Sinclair (1863–1946), Dorothy Richardson (1873–1957), Virginia Woolf (1882–1941), and Rebecca West (1892–1983). She said that these lines must preface all of her books:

> Here is no sacrificial I,
> Here are more I's than yet were in one human,
> Here I reveal our common mystery:
> I give you *woman*.
>
> (*Wickham*, 1)

This, her "womanifesto," makes explicit her exhuberance, her variety, and her feminism.

The best-known of Wickham's poems, if any are known, are the four reprinted by Sandra M. Gilbert and Susan Gubar in *The Norton Anthology of Literature by Women* (1996), "The Affinity," "Divorce,"

"Meditation at Kew," and "Dedication of the Cook." The last of these answers head-on the most frequent male criticism of women's suitability for the arts, especially poetry:

> If any ask why there's no great She-Poet,
> Let him come live with me, and he will know it.
> If I'd indite an ode or mend a sonnet,
> I must go choose a dish or tie a bonnet.[34]

The reason, of course, that the she-poet must cook or clothe before writing is children. And the reason for children is marriage: "for she who serves in forced virginity / Since I am wedded will not have me free." If a woman is heterosexual and expresses love physically, she will not be free of children. Marie Stopes's *Married Love,* giving advice on contraception, was only published in 1918; by then Wickham was 34 years old. It was 1921 before Stopes opened the first birth control clinic in London, and dependable methods were still far in the future. Wickham's poem ends uneasily. She is not willing to give up children ("Yet had I chosen Dian's barrenness / I'm not full woman, and can't be less"), and she is not of a class to have servants; she herself is both servant and mistress. Therefore, like a kind mistress, she imagines nurturing her servant self, giving that self a few hours off to write ("I will make the servant's cause my own / That she in pity leave me hours alone"). Yet the final image of the poem is more apocalyptic than this modest compromise prepares us for: Imagined as flowers which her garden "is so rich in," her poems "will blossom"—so far, a conventional image of controlled growth— "from the ashes of my kitchen." The phoenix rising from the ashes is appropriate as an energetic vision of the creation of poetry, but the more mundane connotation of a kitchen in ashes suggests a destructive fire aimed at the heart of maternal home life.

Wickham's poetry feels the extremes of the everyday and the sublime. She responds to two kinds of creation, birth and writing. Though the one is usually imaged as mundane and the other as liberating, both are valued. She never forgets the tug of children during the rush of writing. The funniest poems take a dim view of contemporary married life, as in "Meditation at Kew": "Alas! for all the pretty women who marry dull men / Go into the suburbs and never come out again" (Gilbert and Gubar 1996, 1380). Others are emotionally overwhelming, as in "Divorce" (1381). This poem begins with a traditional image of the woman as preserver of culture, keeping the home fires burning while the man is away on the world's business:

> A voice from the dark is calling me.
> In the close house I nurse a fire.
> Out in the dark, cold winds rush free,
> To the rock heights of my desire.

The fourth line reveals that the fire that the woman nurses is an internal one, akin to the phoenix and ashes of her kitchen from "Dedication of the Cook." The next couplet takes on the rhythms and language of Tennyson's "Charge of the Light Brigade": "I smother in the house in the valley below, / Let me out to the night, let me go, let me go!" (1382). In Tennyson's geography, the valley below is the Valley of Death. Like the Israelites in bondage in Egypt, it is good to be let go from such a place. On the other hand, going "out to the night" and the "dark, cold winds" is not particularly cheering, especially given the 600 cavalrymen charging down upon the house. The desperation of the speaker builds:

> High on the hills are beating drums,
> Clear from a line of marching men
> To the rock's edge the hero comes.
> He calls me, and he calls again.

She is called out, not to freedom but to battle: "On the hill there is fighting, victory, or quick death." But even death in this battle is better than staying where she is: "In the house is the fire, which I fan with sick breath / I smother in the house in the valley below, / Let me out in the dark, let me go, let me go!"

For every poem like "Divorce" that longs to escape bonds, there is one equally valuing the importance of what those bonds teach, such as "Sehnsucht" ("Because of hunger is our work well done") and "Self-Analysis" ("I am like a man who fears to take a wife, / And frets his soul with wantons all his life"). Sometimes there is such a perfect blend of escape and attachment that it is difficult to see which predominates, as in her poem for D. H. Lawrence, "Multiplication":

> Had I married you, dear,
> When I was nineteen,

I had been little since
But a printing machine;
For, before my fortieth year had run,
I well had produced you
A twenty-first son.

Your ingenious love
Had expressed through me
Automatic, unreasoned, fecundity.
I had scattered the earth
With the seed of your loins,
And stamped you on boys
Like a king's head on coins.

(*Wickham*, 318)

One of the ambivalences implied by this seemingly light poem is that if Wickham had been satisfied in marriage to a kindred spirit (which she considered Lawrence to be), then she would have had no life as an artist. She can print poetry or sons.

Louis Untermeyer championed her poems, "struggling between dreams and domesticity," citing her "genius for the firm epithet and quick-thrusting phrase—and an unforgettable power of emotion" (Untermeyer, 277). After her suicide in 1947, her poetry plunged into instant obscurity, a neglect that Stanley Kunitz called "one of the great mysteries of contemporary literature."[35] She wrote more than 1,400 poems, of uneven quality, but much was destroyed in 1943 when her house in Hampstead was bombed.

In the 1930s, an Oxford professor who had fought in the Great War, J. R. R. Tolkien (1892–1973), wrote down the bedtime stories he was telling his son as a small novel, *The Hobbit* (1937), whose world was later expanded into a trilogy, *The Lord of the Rings* (1954–1955). This work, which became immensely popular in the 1960s, avoided all mention of sex and gendered relationships, but it continued the debate about the machine. Tolkien took the nostalgic, conservative, "English" side of the debate. Tolkien's hobbits are small, plump creatures who like to eat good meals and smoke their pipes afterward, much like Oxford dons. They live in a small shire, far away from the belching smoke, noise, and commotion of the great world beyond. That world, however, eventually impinges upon the shire and almost destroys it. The forces arrayed against the shire are vast and tyrannical, the land of "Mordor" ruled by a "Dark Lord" who has enslaved neighboring kings. If the shire stands for little England—conservative, Christian, and antimodern—Mordor stands for the Soviet Union, Stalin, communism, industrialization, and Modernism.

The same year in which Tolkien became Oxford's Professor of Anglo-Saxon, 1925, a student arrived who would later, in the 1930s, for a time embrace everything Tolkien hated. W. H. Auden and the circle of young poets he led abandoned Anglicanism for communism, employed in their poetry images of the factory and the urban landscape, loved the modern spareness of the early T. S. Eliot, modern art, modern jazz, decadent Berlin, and brash America. The pendulum continued to swing toward the modern and the new—though before long it would reverse direction again, and Auden would become one of Tolkien's most enthusiastic supporters, writing imitations of Anglo-Saxon verse in the forties and in the fifties championing *The Lord of the Rings*. Ironically, or perhaps predictably, it is when Auden lives in England that he speaks urgently for reform and change. When he leaves England, he becomes converted to the older traditions that the new poets of the thirties were trying to reform. Perhaps this is simply the nostalgia for an idealized English past which the Georgians also felt. The power of that image of the rural English village, church, and shire, however, is an unmistakable constant in English poetry, one to which Auden and even Eliot return.

The twenties as a decade was summed up by the editor of Lawrence's poetry, Vivian de Sola Pinto, in his autobiography, *The City That Shone*. For Pinto, the "city that shone" was Oxford. He was an upper middle-class youth dragged from college to serve in the Great War as a subaltern, where he had the luck to have a poet for his company commander, Captain Siegfried Sassoon; after the war, he returned to continue his undergraduate studies and eventually become a well-known scholar. Pinto knew Lawrence, but he knew best his own social class, so that when he writes about poetry or intellectual life, it is the life of his class, taking place at Oxford. Despite this blindness, what Pinto says has a general ring of truth for the poets of the twenties, thirties, and forties: "In the 1930s, I understand, most intelligent Oxford undergraduates were politically minded and in the forties they were nearly all religious, but for us in the years immediately following World War I it seemed that salvation could only come from the arts."[36]

· FIVE ·

"Nothing Yet Was Ever Done / Till It Was Done Again": The Thirties and the Coming War, 1930–1939

Unlike the First World War, which seemed to take everyone by surprise, not necessarily by its coming, but by its ferocity and duration, the approach of the Second World War surprised no one. It was heralded in the thirties by the rise of fascism, the polarization into left and right, the breakout of the Spanish Civil War in 1936, and then a growing exodus from Europe. The poetic response was sure and certain, with Yeats's "rough beast ... slouching toward Bethlehem" preparing for the coming catastrophe with the same broad symbolic power that Eliot's *Waste Land* theme achieved in describing the aftermath of the first war.

The 1930s are sometimes known as the decade of the Auden Generation, after the title of an influential book by Samuel Hynes.[1] The decade saw the emergence of poets who were in school during the Great War, including W. H. Auden (1907–1973), Louis MacNeice (1907–1963), Stephen Spender (1909–1995), William Empson (1906–1984), Cecil Day Lewis (1904–1972), and John Betjeman (1906–1984); these last two became poet laureates, in 1968 and 1972. In mid-decade a Romantic revival led by Dylan Thomas (1914–1953) reacted against the Audenian School, or Pylon Poets, as they were sometimes called because of their celebration of industrial imagery.

Of course, the older generations that had come of age as late Victorians, Edwardians, Georgians, or Modernists were still writing. Rudyard Kipling, W. B. Yeats, Arthur Symons, G. K. Chesterton, and A. E. Housman, all of whom had volumes in the 1890s, were still publishing 40 years later. John Masefield and Walter de la Mare between them brought out 16 volumes of verse in the thirties. The Georgians, except for those killed in the war, were still active:

"Nothing Yet Was Ever Done / Till It Was Done Again"

Siegfried Sassoon, W. H. Davies, Wilfrid Gibson, John Drinkwater, Laurence Binyon, Edmund Blunden. Their traditional style continued to be the most popular with the general public and was enthusiastically adopted by those in the next generation who did not take much account of Modernism—poets such as Peter Quennell (1905–1993), published in the last of Marsh's Georgian anthologies; Anne Ridler (b. 1912), a Christian poet influenced by that side of Auden and Eliot; and Roy Campbell (1902–1957), known mainly for satires. Campbell, who grew up in South Africa and came to England at the age of 16, satirized Afrikaner ways in *The Wayzgoose* (1928), then attacked Bloomsbury and the remaining Georgians in *The Georgiad* (1931), and ended the thirties praising Franco as the upholder of Christian values in *Flowering Rifle* (1939). Writing and publishing as Modernists were Basil Bunting, David Jones, Edith Sitwell, and T. S. Eliot (and, of course, Ezra Pound, though he had abandoned London in 1920 for four years in Paris, and then gone to Italy, where he was working on *The Cantos*). Robert Graves, on Majorca until the Spanish Civil War drove him back to England, was still a decade away from writing *The White Goddess* (1948). Thomas Hardy and D. H. Lawrence had only just recently died, and their posthumously published last volumes, in 1928 and 1932, were also stiff competition for the younger generation of poets grouped around Auden. Nevertheless, the new generation quickly rose to prominence.

They had been raised on Hardy, Hopkins, Yeats, Eliot, and Lawrence. An Oxford-educated group, they brought to poetry a modern vocabulary of politics and social science. Auden especially added a deeper understanding of Freud and Marx, who gave him an awareness of the enemies within. Marx taught him about the class wars in England, and Freud revealed the wars in the psyche. The consciousness of war behind and ahead made them acutely aware of politics and world affairs. It was difficult to avoid taking a stance, left or right, on events of the day. From the very beginning Betjeman was backward-looking, to Thomas Hardy and traditions of the past; the others chose liberal or leftist positions but expressed them in muted tones of traditional form and understatement. As they aged, however, these poets, too, became more conservative, Day Lewis especially, who became a devotee of Hardy and instructed that he be buried in Stinsford churchyard near the master.

The thirties also saw a flurry of new anthologies and magazines (many with the word "new" prominently trumpeted in their titles):

"Nothing Yet Was Ever Done / Till It Was Done Again"

New Signatures (1932), *New Verse* (1933), *New Country* (1933), *New Writing* (1936), *Twentieth Century Verse* (1937), *Poetry London* (1939), *Poets of Tomorrow* (1939), *Poems for Spain* (1939), *The New Apocalypse* (1939). These publications had learned from Edward Marsh's Georgian anthologies, Ezra Pound's editorship of *The Little Review*, Richard Aldington's Imagist anthologies, Wyndham Lewis's *Blast*, and Edith Sitwell's *Wheels* how effective it could be to introduce new poets or new movements by way of anthologies and periodicals, even when cheaply produced. The technique became a staple of the 1930s and after.

New Signatures was founded by Michael Roberts (1902–1948), who first presented Auden, Day Lewis, and Empson as members of a coherent movement. The next year Geoffrey Grigson (1905–1985) began *New Verse*, leading off with poems by MacNeice and Auden. Grigson was a scathing reviewer but a good editor; he preferred what was authentic in language and emotion, showing great preference for the conversational style of Auden and MacNeice. During the magazine's run, from 1933 to 1939, he published many writers who would later win larger reputations: Norman Cameron (1905–1953), who published little during his life but whose *Collected Poems* were brought out in 1957 by his friend Robert Graves and enlarged in 1985 and 1990; Bernard Spencer (1909–1963), a British Council officer living most of his life abroad and writing about exile; Kenneth Allott (1912–1973), a poet of skillful rhetoric influenced by Auden; Roy Fuller (1912–1991), a poet of the Second World War, later a solicitor, board member of the BBC, and Oxford Professor of Poetry from 1968 to 1973; Gavin Ewart (b. 1916), whose *Pleasures of the Flesh* caused a stir in 1966 with its explicit sexual references (especially poems about such animals as the Dildo and the Masturbon); and, of course, Auden, MacNeice, Spender, Day Lewis, and Dylan Thomas. Grigson did not bring out a volume of his own verse until 1939.

New Country, New Writing, Poets of Tomorrow, and *Poems for Spain* were published by the poet John Lehmann (1907–1987); the first, an anthology, helped define the new left-wing literary movement represented by Auden, Isherwood, and Spender; the second, a periodical, persisted into World War II and became *Penguin New Writing* (after its collapse Lehmann started *The London Magazine* in 1954). *Twentieth Century Verse* was started by Julian Symons (1912–1994); Symons published many of the same poets as Grigson, and when the war began both magazines folded, replaced by James Tambimuttu's

Poetry London, which during the 1940s published Kathleen Raine (b. 1908), Lawrence Durrell (1912–1990), David Gascoyne (b. 1916), Keith Douglas (1920–1944), and Michael Hamburger (b. 1924).

In 1934 Dylan Thomas burst upon the scene at the age of 20 with his first book, *18 Poems*, championed by Edith Sitwell. The suddenness of his rise had much to do with his pyrotechnics of language, sounds not heard in the early thirties dominated by Auden's spareness, understatement, and controlled tones. Auden, it should be noted, was still only 27 but already an established force to be in reaction against. Richard Ellmann notes that in his American readings Thomas used to say that his poems had to be read "very soft or very loud" (Ellmann and O'Clair, 917), not in the middle range of Auden or Hardy. He was claimed as the leader of "The New Apocalypse" in the 1939 anthology with that name, but he did not sign the manifesto worked up the year before by the anthology's editors, Henry Treece (1912–1966) and J. P. Hendry (1912–1986). Treece and Hendry claimed their principles were formed "two or three years before Munich," in reaction to the Auden Generation's belief in the possibility of politics to create a better world (Perkins, 195). Thomas did not appear in the second anthology of the movement, *The White Horseman* (1941), though his close friend Vernon Watkins (1909–1967) did. Claimed as an apocalyptic writer and a surrealist, Thomas in retrospect appears more fittingly as the leader of a general revival of romantic tendencies in English poetry, poetry of the heart and not of the head. George Barker (1913–1991) emerged as a prodigy at about the same time as Thomas but remained in Thomas's shadow as the poor man's dissolute Romantic.

In 1936 two events importantly influenced poetry: the outbreak of the Spanish Civil War and the International Surrealist Exhibition in London. The first, a battle that all Europe saw as a prelude to the coming showdown between fascism and communism, absorbed the attention of Auden and his group, as well as that of a younger generation that included Christopher Caudwell (1907–1937), Julian Bell (1908–1937), and John Cornford (1915–1936), all of whom were killed in Spain. The second event more widely introduced the ideas of French surrealism to England, which were already appearing in the poetry of the precocious David Gascoyne, who had published *Man's Life Is This Meat* two years before, at the age of 18, and *A Short Survey of Surrealism* the following year. Surrealism explored the irrational, often by the startling juxtaposition of unrelated images to give a sense of a fantastic reality outside of the ordinary. One of the Surrealist's favorite texts was a line of the French poet Lautréamont (1846–1870): "Beautiful as the chance encounter of a sewing machine and an umbrella on an operating table."[2] Gascoyne translated that principle into lines of poetry that surprised readers with such metaphors as "the face of the precipice is black with lovers; / The sun above them is a bag of nails" (Larkin, 489). These lines begin a poem titled "Salvador Dali," for the Spanish painter whose images of melting watches and burning giraffes were moving the ideas of Surrealism into the public mind. The end of the 1930s saw a brief flowering of Surrealist poetry, by Gascoyne, Charles Madge (b. 1912), Kenneth Allott, and Lawrence Durrell. The new taste in poetry that elevated these poets in the late 1930s occurred against the backdrop of an apocalyptic changing of European alliances in 1939, with the revelation of a Soviet-German Non-Aggression Pact. Communism had gotten into bed with fascism, to the dismay and disillusionment of the leftist poets. The poetry that reacted to Auden was appropriately supercharged in thought and language. Almost any lines by Dylan Thomas could serve as an example:

> This was the crucifixion on the mountain,
> Time's nerve in vinegar, the gallow grave
> As tarred with blood as the bright thorns I wept;
> The world's my wound.[3]

Another significance of the reaction to Auden in the mid-thirties was the entrance of voices from outside the traditional centers of power in British life. Where the Auden Generation was Oxford-educated and spoke in its accents, Thomas and Watkins were Welsh. The Scots Edwin Muir (1887–1959) and Hugh MacDiarmid (1892–1978), who had long been writing, came into prominence. Raine, though born in London, made much of her childhood in the wilds of Northumberland. From the fringes, these poets spoke with a new, wild, off-center voice. Thomas especially played the role to the hilt, the bardic prophet from a strange and ancient country. With the coming war, prophetic utterance seemed appropriate. The modern social science of Auden had failed and now one had to reach back to older, darker traditions, ancient pagan or Christian, to deal with what was about to happen.

Women's Voices

At the same time, another grouping of poets, also outsiders, earned notice. These were women, and their relationship to tradition was ambivalent. In *No Man's Land: The Place of the Woman Writer in the Twentieth Century* (1988), Sandra M. Gilbert and Susan Gubar argue that the intellectual ferment and linguistic experimentations of Modernism were, for both men and women, a product of the ongoing battle of the sexes begun by the late nineteenth-century rise of feminism. Partly as a result of the work of Gilbert and Gubar, attention to women writers of this period has mostly been focused on Modernist women writers, because it is they who are on the front lines of the battle and, presumably, most seriously grappling with the issues being contested there: H. D., Edith Sitwell, Katherine Mansfield, Virginia Woolf, Nancy Cunard, Mina Loy, Jean Rhys, May Sinclair, Rebecca West, Rose Macaulay, Dorothy Richardson, Antonia White, Radclyffe Hall, Doris Lessing, to name a few. Women whose work is not experimental in form or overtly feminist in subject matter have been less interesting for scholars, despite a high level of merit recognized by other poets in their day. This may in part be due to their popularity with the general reader, evidence that they did not ruffle many feathers in acquiescing to received taste. This phenomenon was common in America, with such popular writers as Kathleen Norris (1880–1966) and Edna Ferber (1887–1968) being derisively dismissed by Dorothy Parker (1893–1978) and Elinor Wylie (1885–1928), mostly, it seems, for having too cheerful an outlook on life. "Ferber," Parker said, "whistles at her typewriter."[4]

A deeper reason for their neglect is offered by Celeste Schenck, that women writers are always subjected to two competing stereotypes: They are both "beneath" culture and "upholders of" culture.[5] Thus any woman who writes as a Modernist is damned for a lack of seriousness and a lack of craft, because she is too "mired in nature" to master the proper tradition, and any woman who writes traditionally is damned as a conservative enemy of experimentation, upholding genteel Georgian values. To follow Schenck's argument to its logical conclusion, it does not matter how a woman writes; because the stereotypes are there for all women, any woman writer at any time can be damned by either charge, as an unserious lady poetess. We must listen more carefully to the "rear-guard," says

Schenck, as well as to the "avant-garde." It is no accident that "rear-guard" is English and "avant-garde"is French. After World War II, British poets such as Donald Davie and Philip Larkin were at pains to establish a "native" English tradition that by-passed the "foreign" influences of Modernism. For Larkin, the three greatest evils to befall the arts were Pound, Picasso, and Parker, two Americans and a Spaniard who all lived in France and ruined poetry, painting, and jazz.

Some writers, like Stevie (Florence Margaret) Smith (1902–1971), are difficult to classify as either rear-guard or avant-garde. Smith seems the consummate poetic outsider, living with an aunt in the London suburb Palmers Green most of her life and working as a secretary until she was 51 years old. She accompanied her poems with drawings, "something like doodling," she said (Ellmann and O'Clair, 653), which gave her often naive-seeming and comic verse a further look of unseriousness. But there was always a depth beneath her light touch, as in "Valuable," whose epigraph tells us that the poem is a response to "reading two paragraphs in a newspaper."6 The poem begins rather prosaically, in the voice of a middle-aged lady disgusted with the younger generation, such as might appear in a letter to the editor:

> All these illegitimate babies ...
> Oh girls, girls,
> Silly little cheap things,
> Why do you not put some value on yourselves,
> Learn to say, No?
> Did nobody teach you?
> Nobody teaches anybody to say No nowadays,
> People should teach people to say No.

The second stanza, evidently responding to a different paragraph in the newspaper, begins just as simplistically as the first stanza: "Oh poor panther, / Oh you poor black animal, / At large for a few moments in a school for young children in Paris." The panther is now back in its cage again, but Smith imagines its eyes, "angry and innocent," saying something to us: "I am too valuable to be kept in a cage." This is still bordering on the conventional and the sentimental, but it no longer has the unlettered feel of the opening complaint. The final stanza joins the two disconnected pieces—"Girls, you are valuable, / And you, Panther, you are valuable"—and ends with a sweetness unimagined by the woman who begins the poem: "If everybody says he is valuable / It will be comforting for him." The poem's movement is from the simplistic to simplicity.

Sylvia Townsend Warner (1893–1978), too, was difficult to classify. Like Auden, she was homosexual, a communist in the 1930s, and profoundly moved by the events in Spain. But her poetry seems oddly Georgian in its employment of traditional forms and lyrical tones. In "Woman's Song," housewifery and God are treated with a delicate seriousness not congruent with conventional notions of homosexuality and communism. The poem is modeled on a litany: "Kind kettle on my hearth / Whisper to avert God's wrath, / Scoured table, pray for me."[7] The use of inversion to achieve rhyme—for example, "Wrung dishclout on the line / Sweeten to those nostrils fine, / Patched apron, pray for me"—mixes a very old poetic practice with an unusually modern colloquialism. Similarly, in "Hymn for Holy Deconsecration," Warner's down-to-earth housewifely knowledge contrasts strongly with her elevated subject. The deconsecration ritual, to make an Anglican church "unholy" again so that it can be used for commercial purposes, is likened to the church having its "own detergent" (Hall, 65). This detergent is named in the second stanza: "O mystical emulsion! / O supervenient Tide!" It can be used to wash and cleanse in a parody of baptism and communion: "Unchanged in outward seeming / But inwardly renewed" the church is "disblest," released "from every grace," and, humorously, "disempewed." Though few in number, the faithful gather to "disencumber / This edifice of God." The wry notion that the church is working to make the world unholy is reminiscent of Philip Larkin in such poems as "Church Going" and "High Windows," which treat ecclesiastical subjects with an irreverence that clearly shows a longing for religion to live up to its promise. Warner's uncertain status is shown by the history of her place in anthologies. During her lifetime, she was one of the few women included by Louis Untermeyer in his editions of *Modern British Poetry*. She was not included, however, in Gilbert and Gubar's influential *Norton Anthology of Literature by Women* in either 1985 or 1996, missing out on the resurrection so many neglected women received then. She has been reprinted in the 1990s in Bonnie Kime Scott's *The Gender of Modernism* and Linda Hall's *An Anthology of Poetry by Women: Tracing the Tradition*, both of which include women writers who are not particularly interested in linguistic experimentation.

Another group of women clearly fit Schenck's notion of a rearguard. Frances Cornford (1886–1960), Rupert Brooke's friend from Cambridge days, published eight volumes of poetry between 1910 and 1960. She was often eclipsed by others in her famous family: her father, Francis, Charles Darwin's third son and a Cambridge botanist; her husband, Francis, a classics professor at Cambridge who influenced Auden; and her son Rupert John Cornford (born the year Brooke died and named after him), another poet-prodigy who died too young in war after producing an initial body of interesting work, thus becoming, like his namesake, something of a legend for the time. Frances Cornford's poetry is traditional in form and theme, often dealing with small domestic moments, and with husbands, fathers, and sons. In "Family Likeness" she comments upon her famous family:

> That eager, honouring look
> Through microscope or a picture-book,
> That quick, responsive, curious delight—
> For half a century I have seen it now
> Under the shaggy or the baby brow,
> And always blessed the sight.
>
> (81)

She often celebrated the Cambridgeshire countryside, as in "Travelling Home":

> The train. A hot July. On either hand
> Our sober, fruitful, unemphatic land;
> This Cambridge country plain beneath the sky
> Where I was born, and grew, and hope to die.
>
> (77)

The adjectives describing her beloved home could stand for the qualities of her poetry as well—unemphatic, yes, and more sober than anything by Dylan Thomas, but in its plain way as fruitful as more exotic places such as Wales, the Lake District, or Cornwall.

Ruth Pitter (1897–1992), like Cornford, wrote poems in traditional prosody on conventional "women's" themes—mostly God and gardening. The two subjects might seem easily combined, but for Pitter they were separate. She called her volumes *The Rude Potato* (1941) and *Pitter on Cats* (1947) her "profane" poems. Her religious verse has the imaginativeness and toughness of Gerard Manley Hopkins, as in a poem published in 1936 with this mathematical title:

$$\frac{1}{\infty} = 0$$

$$\therefore 0 \times \infty = 1$$

The last lines explicate the formula: "I'll be the humble zero, accept division / As life itself, leave me the infinite / To multiply me into integrity."[8] Another popular writer of the day, Mary Webb (1881–1927), is known mostly as a regional novelist celebrating Shropshire, though her poetry has seen a revival in the *Selected Poems* edited by Gladys Mary Coles in 1981 following Coles's 1978 biography of Webb, *The Flower of Light*. Similarly, Vita Sackville-West (1892–1962) is more noted for her relationship with Virginia Woolf than for her poetry, which is considerable. Both Webb and Sackville-West, incidentally, were famous gardeners, and that source of imagery, as with Pitter, fructifies their poetry. Sackville-West published long poems on her garden at Sissinghurst Castle in Kent, *Sissinghurst* (1931) and *The Garden* (1946). Webb wrote poems describing gardens and flowers, but she also employed that imagery even when the subject was unrelated, as in two poems published in 1939 in the slim, posthumous volume *Fifty-One Poems*. "Autumn, 1914" describes the war's outbreak in terms of the bees and trees moaning for one who does not come: "He's gone, her man, so good with his hands / In the harvest field and the lambing shed."[9] The second poem is an epitaph, perhaps for Webb herself:

> Here lies a lover of roses. All her years
> She fashioned shrouds in a cellar underground.
> At last she owns a rose-tree; all around
> Where she reposes fragrant petals fall,
> Clear pink and shelly and ethereal,
> Raining upon the daisied grass like tears—
> Only she does not know and cannot see:
> Darker than any cellar lieth she.
>
> (46)

The reputations of this group of women writers hardly survived their deaths. Anna Wickham's poetry (see chapter 4) has been reprinted by Virago and Cornford's by Enitharmon Press, but Pitter, Warner, and Webb have been consigned to the libraries and a few anthologies, and Edward Thomas's friend Eleanor Farjeon (1881–1965) hardly ever exists even there, except for her children's books. Having been ignored by male arbiters of the canon, they were initially equally ignored in feminist canon reformation. They fall into a gap: traditional but not male, female but not modernist or overtly feminist. Their tradition extends from such nineteenth-century poets as Mary Elizabeth Coleridge (1861–1907) and Alice Meynell (1847–1922), women too conventional and religious to receive the kind of attention devoted initially to those who broke new ground following Virginia Woolf. Coleridge, Meynell, and Charlotte Mew are beginning to receive more attention from feminist critics, for although traditional in form and theme, their concerns subtly (and sometimes not so subtly) differ from those of their male contemporaries. For their high level of craftsmanship, Cornford, Pitter, Warner, and Webb merit more attention, but they are in danger of being assigned to the same grave as Kathleen Norris and Edna Ferber, with a headstone marked "matriarchal sentimentalist essentialism."[10]

The coming of the Second World War in 1939 closed the decade abruptly. Early that year Yeats died, at the age of 73, the wild, wicked, respected old man. Auden left England for America. The war was even grimmer—and its outcome less sure—than the First World War. It was also a less literary war than the first one, or so it seemed to the newspapers, which wondered why no new Rupert Brooke had stepped forward to inspire the nation. Cecil Day Lewis's "Where are the War Poets?" answered that often asked question with the disenchantment felt by anyone who was young, religious, socialist, or idealistic. Day Lewis was all of these, as well as a poet, and poetry had learned from the First World War never to be patriotic again:

> They who in folly or mere greed
> Enslaved religion, markets, laws,
> Borrow our language now and bid
> Us to speak up in freedom's cause.
>
> It is the logic of our times,
> No subject for immortal verse—
> That we who lived by honest dreams
> Defend the bad against the worse.
>   (Larkin, 353)

Nevertheless, a great deal of war poetry was written: some by exceptional young poets such as Henry Reed (1914–1986), Alun Lewis (1915–1944), Charles Causely (b. 1917), Keith Douglas (1920–1944), and Sidney Keyes (1922–1943); some by important writers of the older generation, such as Virginia Woolf, T. S. Eliot, Edith Sitwell, W. H. Auden, and Dylan Thomas.

Another answer to the question "Where are the War Poets?" is that those of the First World War were still there. Robert Graves, Herbert Read, Edmund Blunden, and Siegfried Sassoon addressed the war, if sometimes only obliquely, as in Graves's "The Persian Version" from 1945, which teaches that the victors get to write the history. Even more powerfully, the poets who had died in the first war were still alive in the minds of those facing the second. As Robert Hewison points out, when Keith Douglas attempted to portray Libya's wartime desert landscape, he admitted that "Rosenberg I only repeat what you were saying."[11] Brooke was in everyone's mind as the poet to avoid, and Owen the poet to admire. Owen's success, however, made it much more difficult to write freshly of the war. Roy Fuller suggests that it was difficult even to be sure of one's own response, so powerful was the weight of the past: "Our fathers felt these things before / In another half-forgotten war. / And our emotions are caught part / From them" (Hewison, 96). Auden, Spender, and MacNeice turned inward. In his February 1939 elegy for W. B. Yeats, who had died the month before, Auden already begins his turn from political activism to note that "poetry makes nothing happen."[12] What is its role? "It survives, / A way of happening, a mouth." Edith Sitwell's reemergence as a poet was the most surprising. She had published no poetry since 1929's *Gold Coast Customs*, but the war brought her back with a voice that was more direct, less fanciful than before. In what became her most famous poem, "Still Falls the Rain," she uses the Christian symbolism favored by her protégé, Dylan Thomas:

> Still falls the Rain—
> Dark as the world of man, black as our loss—
> Blind as the nineteen hundred and forty nails
> Upon the Cross.
>
> (*E. Sitwell*, 265)

The nineteen hundred and forty nails refer to the poem's subtitle, "The Raids, 1940. Night and Dawn." Old poems gained new currency, as had happened with A. E. Housman's *A Shropshire Lad* during the first war. A single line by Dylan Thomas from 1934 resonated anew: "I see the boys of summer in their ruin" (*D. Thomas*, 91).

Just as the First World War had put a quick halt to Modernist experimentations, when the Second World War broke out, poets and audiences also turned to a more traditional, romantic view of poetry. The poetry editors at two of the major publishing houses were two poets of the older generation, T. S. Eliot at Faber's and Herbert Read at Routledge's. They divided poetry sent them according to their differing tastes, Eliot favoring the toned-down Modernism of Auden and Read preferring the new Romantic poets. Thus when Sidney Keyes sent Eliot a collection of "romantic" poetry from students at Oxford, Eliot sent it on to Read, who published them as *Eight Oxford Poets* (1941). The anthology included Keyes, Keith Douglas, and Drummond Allison (1921–1943), all of whom were killed in the war. Keyes was not yet 21, Douglas only 24, Allison 22. The Welsh poet Alun Lewis died in Burma in 1944, at 29. The early deaths of these poets helped to establish their reputations as the successors of Owen, Sassoon, Sorley, and Rosenberg.

Alun Lewis, especially, was hailed as the poet the papers had been looking for. The son of two Welsh schoolteachers, Lewis's biography reads a little like D. H. Lawrence's, a little like Edward Thomas's. He was university-educated, though at Manchester, not Oxford. He was not quite of the right class but still his poetry received early attention, first from Robert Graves. Indecisive about military service like Thomas, he eventually became an officer in a Welsh regiment like Graves, the South Wales Borderers. His poem "All Day It Has Rained ..." was widely admired; Bernard Bergonzi claims it as the archetypal war poem of the Second World War, as it "contains no hint of heroics" and "takes the form of a Romantic meditative monologue, describing the surroundings and then moving into inner consciousness."[13] It begins with a repetition of its title, and indeed the word "rain" is soggily repeated throughout the poem: "All day it has rained, and we on the edge of the moors / Have sprawled in our bell-tents, moody and dull as boors, / Groundsheets and blankets spread on the muddy ground" (Larkin, 480). The bivouacking soldiers find "no refuge from the skirmishing fine rain" and sit idly in their tents all day "stretched out, unbuttoning our braces, / Smoking a Woodbine, darning dirty socks, / Reading the Sunday papers—I saw a fox." At this unexpected entry of the fox—or memory of its entry—a new note of excitement momentarily captures the poem, and a dash of color is added. But quickly that dies down in the droning, drenching boredom of the war, a boredom symbolized by the rain. The pervasiveness of both rain and ennui, and the feeling of their interminableness, no matter what one does, is evident in the lines after the memory of the fox, when bombs and girls are routinely intermixed in the soldiers' conversations: "I saw a fox / And mentioned it in the note I scribbled home;— / And we talked of girls, and dropping bombs on Rome." The poem ends with a reverie of childhood, Lewis walking to a hill near Steep, "where Edward Thomas brooded long / On death and beauty—till a bullet stopped his song." Thomas was Lewis's personal hero. Steep is Thomas's village, and "Rain" one of Thomas's best poems. The death of Lewis, like the loss of Thomas in the first war, deprived England of an extraordinarily gifted writer. But just as Thomas was overshadowed by Wilfrid Owen, so Lewis is not now remembered as the best poet of the war years. That honor goes to Keith Douglas. Because this study must end with 1939, no more poetry of the 1940s can be discussed here, except for a brief overview of what followed the war.

The poetry that emerged after the war was called "The Movement," from an anonymous article in the *Spectator*. Robert Conquest's anthology *New Lines* (1956) canonized the poets of the Movement. Three were his friends from Oxford in the 1940s—Philip Larkin, Kingsley Amis, and John Wain. The others were also Oxbridge-educated, John Holloway and Elizabeth Jennings at Oxford and Thom Gunn, Donald Davie, and D. J. Enright at Cambridge, where they studied under the eminent scholar F. R. Leavis (1895–1978). Movement poetry had a taste for the quiet, the moderate, the less ambitious—in reaction against Dylan Thomas's domination of the intervening years. In form it was traditional and in language colloquial—much like the Georgians'. The hegemony of Eliot began to seem like an aberration in British poetry, or an interlude. In truth, the Movement poets made good use of all that had come before them. In the poetry of the best of them, Philip Larkin (1922–1985), one can detect Hardy, Yeats, Lawrence, Eliot, and Auden, though not in equal measures. A small poem called "An April Sunday Brings the Snow," not published in Larkin's lifetime, demonstrates the qualities of Movement verse: simple, direct expression of modest themes; lyricism combined with emotional restraint; an acceptance of the limits of form yoked to a colloquialness of diction and syntactical enjambment that keep the form from declaring itself too loudly as POETRY. The poem, an elegy for Larkin's father, begins with the poet spending an hour or so observing a sudden April snow shower's effect on his plum trees:

> Strange that I spend that hour moving between
> Cupboard and cupboard, shifting the store
> Of jam you made of fruit from these same trees:
> Five loads—a hundred pounds or more—
> More than enough for all next summer's teas,
>
> Which now you will not sit and eat.
> Behind the glass, under the cellophane,
> Remains your final summer—sweet
> And meaningless, and not to come again.[14]

Larkin was the same age as Sidney Keyes, whom he knew slightly at Oxford during the war. He considered Keyes and the others published in *Eight Oxford Poets*, such as John Heath-Stubbs (b. 1918) and Keith Douglas, a little too flashy in their poetry. Keyes and Douglas admired W. B. Yeats and Rainer Maria Rilke. Larkin's man, from his teens, was D. H. Lawrence.

John Heath-Stubbs describes the pendulum-swings of poetic fashion from the thirties through the fifties in a comic poem, "The Poet of Bray," which may summarize this chapter's discussion to this point:

> Back in the dear old thirties' days
>   When politics was passion
> A harmless left-wing bard was I
>   And so I grew in fashion:
> Although I never really *joined*
>   The Party of the Masses
> I was most awfully chummy with
>   The Proletarian classes.[15]

At this point, the poem breaks into a chorus that at first seems to imply that the poet will forever swear allegiance to politically informed poetry: "This is the course I'll always steer / Until the stars grow dim, sir—." That is, he will steer the course of harmless left-wing versifying until the stars dim at the end of time. But the remainder of the chorus turns the meaning around, as we realize that "this is the course I'll always steer" refers to the lines that follow, not to those that have just preceded: "That howsoever taste may veer / I'll be in the swim, sir." That is, the poet will always steer the course of taste and fashion, in order to be "in the swim." The "stars" that grow dim now seem to be more on the order of media or movie stars, who when they dim are to be immediately abandoned for whatever is new. And the new will surely come:

> But as the tide of war swept on
>   I turned Apocalyptic:
> With symbol, myth and archetype
>   My verse grew crammed and cryptic.
> With New Romantic zeal I swore
>   That Auden was a fake, sir,
> And found the mind of Nicky Moore
>   More interesting than Blake, sir.
>
> White Horsemen down New Roads had run
>   But taste required improvement:
> I turned to greet the rising sun
>   And so I joined the Movement!
> Glittering and ambiguous
>   In villanelles I sported:
> With Dr. Leavis I concurred,
>   And when he sneezed I snorted.
>
>   (294–95)

Nicholas Moore (1918–1986), poet and nephew of the Edwardian poet T. Sturge Moore (1870–1944), published many of the New Apocalyptic writers; when that movement "had run" its course, F. R. Leavis and his disciples ("Leavisites") rose up to argue for the civilization-saving value of poetry. Another hiccup later, Heath-Stubbs claims to become a Beat and an Angry Young Man, railing against the Establishment, until he finds himself in the Establishment, and younger poets, presumably, can rail at him. It is unclear if with success and age he has opted out of these changing fashions, or if the next one has simply not come along yet. What is clear, in the comic tone of this history of verse, is that the seriousness with which Pound and Eliot began the movement to Modernism is long gone. Poetry is a minor art, akin to styles of dress. Such modest aim suggests that Heath-Stubbs is, here at least, not the opportunist he claims to be, but moving toward a Movement position, as it was popularly defined and received.

The Movement poet Donald Davie (1922–1995), in an influential book called *Thomas Hardy and British Poetry* (1972), argues that, for good or ill, the chief influence in British poetry has been the poetry of Hardy. For the next 25 years, this thesis was acknowledged by more and more poets and critics, until it became a commonplace, with the reputation of Hardy rising as Eliot's waned. Given the cyclical and reactive nature of British poetry throughout the century, one might have predicted that this opinion, too, would have been more quickly subjected to the pendulum's swing. One reason for its persistence, and even growing strength, is that it forms a counterweight to another trend that does not show any signs of reversal—the opening up of the canon. Just as more and more voices from outside the mainstream emerged from the thirties through the nineties—regionalist literatures, women writers, working-class writers, colonial and postcolonial voices—so new outsiders continue to claim their place in print. Opposed to this liberal openness is a conservative narrowness that places a high value on Hardy and "Englishness." The poetry wars once again reflect the larger cultural and social struggles of the nation. Hardy, and then Larkin, became identified with Thatcherism and the Conservative party in England, against immigration, the expansion of educational opportunity, and life on the dole. Regionalist voices, immigrants, the unemployed, and members of those classes who were for the first time finding places in the expanding polytechnics and red-brick universities (the new institutions, of which Larkin's University of Hull was one), felt differently.

Oxford Voices

W. H. Auden holds an important place in this literary-historical melting pot of British life. As Stan Smith points out, there are really two stories about Auden.[16] In one, he is the young leftist who finally gets some common sense and returns to Christianity, repudiating his earlier foolishness. In the other, he is the brilliant Marxist overtaken by bourgeois doubt, lapsing into a caricature of a poet. Smith's reading is that neither view, though both are popular in Britain, takes into account Auden's keen understanding of the instability of the ego and questioning of who or what we really are.

An important jumping-off point is Auden's revision of Jung's statement about Hitler being the unconscious of the German people.

In his commencement address at Smith College in 1940, Auden said that Hitler "comes uncomfortably near being the unconscious of most of us" (Smith, 13). This view comes from Auden's understanding of both Freud and Marx, that human beings as subjects operate out of self-interest and yet are not fully in control of their destinies. "We are lived by powers we pretend to understand," he says in his elegy for another writer, "In Memory of Ernst Toller," written the month of Toller's death, May 1939: "They arrange our loves; it is they who direct at the end / The enemy bullet, the sickness, or even our hand."[17] Toller had died by his own hand.

The enemy within revealed by Freud and Jung is born from the socialization that all of us have undergone. It resides potently within us, a kind of inner Hitler, fed from the energies of desires we have agreed to repress. Thus we are usually in conflict, usually wearing a mask to hide deeper feelings, and often surprised by them when they emerge. We are both bushwhacked and self-deceived. The agent of socialization is education, often imaged by Auden as fascist. He described school as "an absolute dictatorship where the assistant staff play, as it were, Goering Roehm Goebbels Himmler to a headmaster Hitler. There are the same intrigues for favour, the same gossip campaigns, and from time to time the same purges."[18] In his famous parody of totalitarian state control, "The Unknown Citizen," from March 1939, Auden lets the voice of the state declare with satisfaction that Citizen JS/07/M/378 "never interfered" with his children's education, and that the citizen was never "odd in his views." There is perhaps a buried pun in "odd in" ("Auden") that suggests Auden's own "oddnesses" in British society—politically, sexually, and vocationally.

Auden was sent away to boarding school at the age of 8, to St. Edmund's in Surrey, where he suffered the irrational rages of his tutors. He befriended there a fellow sufferer, Christopher Isherwood (1904–1986), who would later become Auden's lover and an important novelist. At 13, Auden went to Gresham in Norfolk, an up-and-coming public school that emphasized science, which appealed to his father, who was a medical doctor. St. Edmund's was scary, but Gresham was the fascist state. It was there that in his unhappiness he turned to poetry. He described the moment of epiphany in a poem from 1939, not printed in his *Collected Poems*, "Pascal": "Even the ablest can recall a day / Of diagnosis when the first stab of his talent / Ran through the beardless boy" (*English Auden*, 452). Auden recounts his personal "day of diagnosis" when he turned from engineering to poetry as a day in March 1922, when he was just 16. He was already excited by the unusual teaching of his tutor, Frank McEachran, who had his students stand on chairs to speak aloud passages of great poetry he had collected and which he called "Spells" (Davenport-Hines, 40). When a school chum asked Auden whether he wrote poetry, Auden felt that "like a lucky orphan he had been discovered / And instantly adopted by a Gift" (*English Auden*, 452). The dedication of his collection of essays *The Dyer's Hand* (1962) is to his Oxford tutor, Nevill Coghill (to whom he announced he was going to be not just a poet but a great poet), but also points to his father and earlier tutors: "Three grateful memories: a home full of books, a childhood spent in country provinces, a tutor in whom one could confide."

Auden was already extraordinarily well read when he came up to Oxford in 1925. His first poetry, from 1923, shows an identification with Wordsworth, in such juvenilia as "The Tarn" or "Rookhope." A year later he threw over Wordsworth for Hardy, as in the ironic "The Miner's Wife," the haunted "He Revisits the Spot," and the philosophical sonnet that begins "There was desolate silence on the world / For who shall say how many million years."[19] He then devoured the Georgians—Walter de la Mare, W. H. Davies, Wilfrid Gibson, Edward Thomas, Robert Frost, Edmund Blunden, Richard Jefferies, and D. H. Lawrence, and their influence shows, too, in these early poems from 1923 and 1924. At Oxford, where he met up again with Christopher Isherwood at the end of 1925, all were impressed with his intellect and the uses he had put it to, but even more by his vitality and dedication to poetry. Auden held court in his rooms, recruiting a literary following of friends that included Cecil Day Lewis, Louis MacNeice, and in Auden's last year at Oxford, 1928, the 19-year-old Stephen Spender. The poetry of this group would be quite directly aware of the times: first of the Depression; then of politics, issuing in the violence of the Spanish Civil War; then of world war, prison camps, and refugees.

Auden's favorite landscape for walks and contemplation was urban—usually the gasworks, the municipal rubbish dump, canals, or electrical towers (Auden was born in York but grew up, like Tolkien, on the outskirts of industrial Birmingham). These landscapes, as well as machines, make frequent appearances in his earliest poetry: "By the Gasworks, Solihull," "The Traction-engine," "The Pumping Engine,

Cashwell," "The Mail-train, Crewe," "The Canal, Froghall." It was Stephen Spender, however, who most often celebrated this imagery and gave the group early on its derisive name, the Pylon Poets, from a 1933 poem "The Pylons," which images those structures as "nude giant girls" that are "tall with prophecy" of the future.[20] Spender was the most overtly leftist of Auden's gang in his imagery, but even for Spender communism ultimately did not run very deep. There is a continual romantic strain singing through his poetry, and that tradition has a conservative influence on the poetry. Such celebrations of modern machinery as "The Landscape Near an Aerodrome" and "The Express" are not far removed from Wordsworth's and Whitman's poems about railway locomotives. Spender's description of a train ride during which scenes outside the window seem like motion pictures, "vivid but unreal," recalls Siegfried Sassoon's train poem (see chapter 3), which likewise replaces standard Georgian imagery with the antiromantic and the urban:

> Real were iron rails, and, smashing the grass,
> Real these wheels on which I rode, real our compelled time:
> Unreal those cows, those wave-winged storks, that lime
> Painted on enamel behind the moving glass.
> Those burned in a clear world from which we pass
> Like *rose* and *love* in a forgotten rhyme.
>
> (8)

Spender's linking of an older poetry using "love" and "rose" to an older, now unreal, landscape of cows suggests that the new landscape of iron demands a new style; but the poem itself certainly demonstrates that Spender has not forgotten the implications of the words "rose" or "love," or forgotten how to rhyme.

The poetry of Spender, Day Lewis, MacNeice, and Auden gains some of its similarities from the shared class background of the four, and that background is High Church–Anglican and upper middle class, despite the Irish births of Day Lewis and MacNeice, and Spender's attempt to portray himself as coming from a family too poor to send him to public school. This is the central contention of Adrian Caesar's *Dividing Lines: Poetry, Class, and Ideology in the 1930s*, which argues with the conception of an Auden Generation "representative of a decade" and with the "literary-historical myth" that sees the development of poetry as a cycle of actions and reactions.[21]

The actions and reactions of poets to each other are real, demonstrable, and observable. Art often engenders art. This is the basic point of Harold Bloom's *The Anxiety of Influence,* that writers must consume, translate, and transcend strong writers of the past, or else be consumed by them and be silenced.[22] (Gilbert and Gubar extend Bloom, showing that the situation for men is more complex, as the formerly willing female muse has in the twentieth century become self-willing and a competitor [1988, 161]). Caesar's first contention, however, is amply demonstrated, that the poetry of Auden and his followers represents only a slice of the richness of the thirties, that it is a very particular upper middle-class slice, and that, despite the trappings of leftist beliefs, it betrays a deep liberalism, which Caesar takes to be a nonrevolutionary and conservative critique of society. Thus Auden's "conversion" to Christianity in the early 1940s, Spender's knighthood, and Day Lewis's appointment to the laureateship are not surprising events but predictable outcomes for successful men of their class.

Auden contributed to the confusion over his "leftist" years and his "Christian" years by changing, suppressing, and mythologizing his poetry from the first period. In 1973 he described his well-known lyric from 40 years earlier, "Out on the lawn I lie in bed," as a "Vision of Agape," responsible for bringing him back to the Christian faith several years later.[23] The poem describes an idyllic summer evening out on the lawn conversing with sympathetic colleagues (his fellow teachers at the Downs School, Colwall, where Auden taught English, arithmetic, French, gymnastics, and biology in 1933). The poem has a vision, but it is of peace, contentment, and pleasantness, reminiscent of Rupert Brooke's feelings for Grantchester in both charm and nostalgia, right down to the appreciation of bathing. One searches the poem in vain for a vision of agape. What is plainly there is Auden's awareness, not of love, but of guilt, that his comfort is built upon the sufferings of others. The disturbing stanzas that most directly show this were cut by Auden when he published his *Collected Poems* in 1945:

> And, gentle, do not care to know,
> Where Poland draws her Eastern bow,
>   What violence is done;
> Nor ask what doubtful act allows
> Our freedom in this English house,
>   Our picnics in the sun.

> The creepered wall stands up to hide
> The gathering multitudes outside
>   Whose glances hunger worsens;
> Concealing from their wretchedness
> Our metaphorical distress,
>   Our kindness to ten persons.
>   (*English Auden*, 137)

The ivy walls are barriers of class. Within, one feels "metaphorical" distress, not the more basic kinds. Kindness to 10 persons in this context is not commendable but self-blaming. Kindness to those within the walls does nothing to salvage one's complicity in the doubtful acts that make privilege possible.

Auden similarly excised a stanza from another poem from these early years, "Here on the cropped grass of the narrow ridge I stand." In this poem, the outside world does intrude. The poem appears to be in the tradition of eighteenth-century landscape poetry, conducting the eye from scenic view to scenic view, much like portions of William Cowper's *The Task* (1785). Current world politics enter peripherally in the seventh stanza with the sighting of a hawk. The hawk suggests to the poet water and canals, which then further suggest central state control (which is how canals get built). In the next stanza, the situation in Germany may be implied, though the poem still appears to be a rural idyll: "And over the Cotswolds now the thunder mutters" (*English Auden*, 143). The final stanza recalls the final lines of Rupert Brooke's "Grantchester" ("The Priory clock chimes briefly") and alludes to Wilfrid Owen and war (" 'The poetry is in the pity,' Wilfrid said"). Despite these allusions to dangers beyond England, the poem measures, controls, and contains them. The first three of the excised lines, originally occurring between the seventh and eighth stanzas, moves the danger into England: "Guilty, I look towards the Nottinghamshire mines / Where one we quoted in the restaurants received / His first perceptions of the human flame" (423). With this memory of D. H. Lawrence, miners, Marxists, and class warfare invade the squire's tour of his property. Such lines are not inconsistent with Auden's later return to the church, but they show an active, troubled, and aware political consciousness as well.

What political consciousness meant in the early 1930s was, in large part, an awareness of Germany, where communism, fascism, and liberal democracy were battling for control. Where Eliot and the Modernists had looked to France for new ideas and found them, the writers of the 1930s began to take account of Germany. Auden and Isherwood had traveled to Berlin in 1928 and made good literary use of it. Isherwood stayed until 1933 and produced *Goodbye to Berlin* (1939), made into the musical *Cabaret* in 1968. Auden began to write poems in German, continuing even after his return to Britain in 1929. Despite less than a year in Germany and no formal training in the language, he achieved a level of accomplishment that amazed Isherwood and their Berlin circle. Just a portion of one poem deserves quoting for the offhand ease with which Auden employs colloquial language in the formal Shakespearean sonnet:

> Es regnet auf mir in den Schottische Laende
> Wo ich mit Dir noch nie gewesen bin
> Man redet hier von Kunst am Wochenende
> Bin jetzt zu Hause, nicht mehr in Berlin.[24]

Literally, the poem says "It's raining on me in the Scottish lands" (Auden's first teaching job back in Britain was at Larchfield Academy, Dumbartonshire, Scotland, where he taught English, French, and rugby); "where I with you have never been / people talk here about art on the weekends / I'm now at home, no more in Berlin." The last line has the brevity and conventionality of a postcard, but the language of tourism is reversed to dramatize Auden's situation. Rather than "I'm in Berlin. Having a wonderful time. Wish you were here," Auden is at home, in the rain, wishing his addressee were here, or that Auden were there. There is resignation in "Bin jetzt zu Hause" that comes from how the third line defines home: "I know I'm home," the poem says, "because people here treat art trivially, unlike Berlin where it is a part of daily life." Such a marriage of modern colloquial language and the sonnet is difficult enough in English; what Auden achieves with his imperfectly learned German is stunning.[25]

If frequency of anthologizing means anything, then Auden's best poems were written in the 1930s: "This Lunar Beauty," "As I Walked Out One Evening," "Out on the Lawn I Lie in Bed," "Stop All the Clocks," "The Unknown Citizen," "Spain 1937," "Musée des Beaux Arts," "Yes, We Are Going to Suffer, Now," "September 1, 1939," "In Memory of Sigmund Freud," "In Memory of W. B. Yeats." These last four, as powerful markers of the end of the decade, will be discussed in the concluding section.

Though far from an Oxford voice (though she was of the right class), the anomalous Stevie Smith also visited Germany, in 1929 and

1931. She was drawn "deutsch-wards" both geographically and culturally by her mixed feelings for a German friend, Karl Eckinger.[26] She turned her experience of Germany into a novel to rival Isherwood's. It was her first book, called *Novel on Yellow Paper* (1936) because it was typed without any title on the yellow copying paper of her employer, which led her publisher's readers to refer to it as "the novel on yellow paper." Its heroine-narrator is a witty, caustic observer of the darkness coming over Germany. The instant success of the novel led her publisher, Jonathan Cape, to take a chance on Smith's poetry, which had been found too quirky for a book before, and bring out *A Good Time Was Had By All*, with her James Thurber–like drawings, in 1937. The voice of the novel was even more clearly present in the poems, and it was for her poetry that she would eventually be known, her novels about Germany forgotten in favor of Isherwood's.

Like the early Edith Sitwell and Robert Graves, Smith turned to nursery rhymes to people her short narrative poems, but she was just as likely to use a person, a historical event, or a newspaper article as her jumping-off point. Thus we have such poems as "Admire Cranmer!," "Thoughts about the Person from Porlock," and "Valuable." Her best-known poem, "Not Waving But Drowning," ends with lines that could stand for her poetry: "I was much too far out all my life / And not waving but drowning" (303). Her poetry was often seen as light or comic, like a swimmer waving happily to those on shore; just as humor can be a defense for pain, the comic poet can really be a swimmer in trouble, flailing her arms in gestures that from a distance appear playful and benign. She was particularly drawn to religious issues and often took a contrarian stance, seeing the lions' side of things in the battle between the Christians and the lions ("Sunt Leones"), or questioning Jesus in "Was He Married?" This poem makes humans, and especially Stevie Smith, one feels, all the more admirable for dealing with problems that Jesus never faced, including feeling remorse for doing wrong, or feeling that his life was pointless ("He was not wrong"; "From his cradle he was purposeful"). Did Jesus ever feel the day brighten for a moment "because a mood had been conquered, or a sin? / I tell you, he did not sin" (389–91).

After a severe bout of illness that disturbed her ability to speak (later discovered to be a rapidly growing brain tumor), Smith began work on a companion poem to one she had written for her very first volume in 1937, "Come, Death." This early poem became "Come, Death (1)" and the one from January 1971 "Come, Death (2)." Together they show her struggle with Christianity, right to the end. The first has a seventeenth-century feel:

> How foolish are the words of the old monks,
> In Life remember Death.
> Who would forget
> Thou closer hangst on every finished breath?
> How vain the work of Christianity.
>
> (108)

The work of Christianity is both vain and in vain because its message is so obvious to anyone noticing the difficulty of living: "Foolish illusion, what has Life to give? / Why should man more fear Death than fear to live?" The second poem is as colloquial as the first is formal, beginning "I feel ill. What can the matter be?" Rather than turn to God in this illness, she turns to one who is more familiar to her and more dependable:

> Ah me, sweet Death, you are the only god
> Who comes as a servant when he is called, you know,
> Listen then to this sound I make, it is sharp,
> Come, Death. Do not be slow.
>
> (571)

In the sixties and seventies she was more popular with readers and audiences than Auden, but that very popularity, along with her conservative valuing of tradition, made her suspect to critics, as has happened with Philip Larkin, J. R. R. Tolkien, and C. S. Lewis.

One other Oxford voice deserves notice, though she is certainly not a part of the Auden Generation. Elizabeth Daryush (1887–1977), the daughter of Robert Bridges, grew up at Boar's Hill near Oxford. Because of her father, she knew Thomas Hardy, John Masefield, and Robert Graves, and a family tradition holds that Gerard Manley Hopkins looked in on her lying in her cradle. With her husband in his native Persia between 1923 and 1927, she made a study of the language and translated the Sufi mystic poet Rumi. She produced an outpouring of poetry in the 1930s, six volumes, all unashamedly traditional but employing metrical experiments like her father and Hopkins. She wrote in traditional meters, syllabics, and accentual syllabics (in effect, Hopkins's "sprung rhythm"). An example of syllabics is "War Poem," written with six syllables to the line:

> Plant no poppy (he said)
> no frail lily sublime,
> for in war's famine time
> thou'lt need but corn for bread.
>
> Hoard no jewel (he cried)
> no dazzling laboured gem:
> thou'lt be forced to sell them
> for steel, so now decide.
>
> Set no flower in thy word
> (he besought, but none heard)
> cut no flash to thy wit,
> if thou must disown it
> when see'st thou sorrow's sword.[27]

The poem's diction, dialogic structure, and theme of diminishment owe much to a Hardy poem from 1898, "Heiress and Architect." Daryush, in her faithfulness to Hardy and Hopkins, sometimes seems the last Victorian. Donald Davie introduced her *Collected Poems* (1976), arguing that she deserved a wider readership.

Scottish, Irish, and Welsh Voices

The triangle formed by Oxford, Cambridge, and London has long been the center of power in England. The dialect of Middle English spoken there in the fourteenth century became the basis for Modern English, partly as a result of a bit of literary luck. Chaucer, England's first great poet, wrote in the vernacular of this region, and Caxton, England's first printer, also a southerner, gave Chaucer's words a relatively fixed spelling, from which the language of poets writing in English derives. Even without this literary luck, however, the civil, governmental, and economic power of this triangle would probably have predominated linguistically. "English" and "England" have thus for a long time stood as the names of the language and the country, so that "England" is often used interchangeably with "Britain," "Great Britain," or the "United Kingdom." Such usage grates on Scots, Irish, and Welsh ears, for "England" more properly refers only to one country among four entities bound up in a "united" kingdom. "Great Britain" denotes the island that is divided among England, Scotland, and Wales. It also refers to the nation created in 1707 when the English and Scottish parliaments voted to unite. A fourth entity, first Ireland and then Northern Ireland, gives the nation its proper name today, the United Kingdom of Great Britain and Northern Ireland. Wales, though it has been incorporated into England since its thirteenth-century conquest by Edward I, still retains a nominal status as a "country" (evidenced mainly in this century by its right to select its own national team for the World Cup soccer matches, as do Scotland and England).

Northern Ireland cannot be described as a country on the level of Scotland and Wales, but a province still being battled over by internal forces preferring allegiance to either the United Kingdom or Eire (the Republic of Ireland). Political allegiances for Belfast-born poets are also divided. Though they are technically British citizens, those who identify with Irishness, such as the Nobel laureate Seamus Heaney (b. 1939), have preferred that they be discussed not in books about British literature but in those dealing with Irish literature. Louis MacNeice and Cecil Day Lewis, though born in Northern Ireland, were thoroughly Anglicized and are usually discussed as members of Auden's circle. But even they cannot be treated simply as Oxford voices. As MacNeice wrote, "I come from an island, Ireland, a nation / Built upon violence and morose vendettas."[28] Because of the complexity and of limited space, Anglo-Irish poets cannot be discussed here, leaving the focus to Scotland and Wales.

Scotland has a long history of opposition to and separation from England, with local institutions of self-government that led it in 1997 to win acceptance of a Scottish Parliament with power over most Home Rule issues. The Welsh sometimes evidence localized anti-English sentiment, as in the vandalizing of English-owned holiday cottages, but there is no similarly current Welsh tradition of self-government to agitate like the Scots for a parliament of their own. Welsh speakers have their own television station and dual English-Welsh signs, but theirs is not the majority language in their own country; ironically, their country's name, "Wales," is derived from the Anglo-Saxon word "weales," meaning "foreigner," "stranger," or "slave." Named by the English conquerors, the Welsh are strangers in their own land. Dylan Thomas's ramshackle home "The Boathouse" in

Swansea has become the main tourist attraction in Wales, and his legend provides one of the major stereotypes by which the Welsh are known today—hard-drinking, glib-tongued lads. But except for a smattering of words, Thomas could not speak Welsh, nor could most of the Welsh poets publishing in the thirties and forties—David Jones, Vernon Watkins, Alun Lewis. Those who lived longer, Glyn Jones (1905–1995) and R. S. Thomas (b. 1913), steeped themselves in the language.

Scotland has fewer Gaelic speakers than Wales has Welsh speakers, but the local dialects are strong, and through the efforts of Hugh MacDiarmid (1892–1978), those dialects have a written form in poetry that has reestablished Scottish traditions and identity in the twentieth century. MacDiarmid (born Christopher Murray Grieve) was a Scottish nationalist and a communist. His creation of a literary dialect (which he called "synthetic Scots") from several local dialects and sprinkled with archaic words he found in dictionaries was for him a political act as much as his role in founding the Scottish Nationalist Party. The poetry written in this dialect, called "Lallans," is usually not overtly political, perhaps because the act of writing in Lallans is itself a political statement. Typical is this poem from 1926 about Noah loading the ark, the "Parley of Beasts": "Auld Noah was at hame wi' them a', / The lion and the lamb," the poem begins, and then concludes, by contrast, that "noo-a-days e'en wi' ain's se / At hame it's hard to feel."[29] Though many things in the modern world militate against feeling at home even with oneself, an obvious obstacle for a Scot is the feeling that home is an occupied territory.

MacDiarmid also wrote poems in standard English, and these usually make a political point to an English audience, as in "British Leftish Poetry, 1930–1940": "Auden, MacNeice, Day Lewis, I have read them all, / Hoping against hope to hear the authentic call" (*MacDiarmid*, 418). To the Edwardians still active in English letters, such as the poet laureate John Masefield, and to the Modernists such as Pound and Eliot (and Yeats), whose politics were conservative bordering on fascist, the Auden club looked like a gang of leftists. To MacDiarmid, however, they were a "tragical disappointment," like a bad night at the theater. His "Another Epitaph on an Army of Mercenaries" from 1935 is an answer to A. E. Housman's lyric in *Last Poems* (1922) in praise of mercenaries for saving "what God abandoned" (Housman, 144). On the facing page of Housman's epitaph is another lyric pleading with a lad to stay home at the plough because "too full already is the grave / Of fellows that were good and brave" (Housman, 145). MacDiarmid, with his internationalist sentiments, reacts strongly to Housman: "It is a God-damned lie to say that these / Saved, or knew, anything worth any man's pride. / They were professional murderers and they took / Their blood money and impious risks and died" (*MacDiarmid*, 313). The anger in these lines abates only a little in the couplet that ends the poem: "In spite of all their kind some elements of worth / With difficulty persist here and there on earth." Though he vigorously protested against English hegemony over Scotland, MacDiarmid could find "some elements of worth" even in England; one of his mottos in life, he said, was taken from that most English of writers Thomas Hardy: "Literature is the written expression of revolt against accepted things."[30]

During the Spanish Civil War, MacDiarmid wrote poems so polemical that it is hard to call them poems, as in "Fascists, You Have Killed My Comrades." "And, Above All, My Poetry Is Marxist" ends with a quotation from the immortal words of the Central Committee of the Revolutionary Communist Party:

> This is the poetry I want—all
> I can regard now as poetry at all,
> As poetry of today, not of the past,
> A Communist poetry that bases itself
> On the Resolution of the C. C. of the R. C. P.
> In Spring 1925: "The Party must vigorously oppose
> Thoughtless and contemptuous treatment
> Of the old cultural heritage
> As well as of the literary specialists ...
> It must likewise combat the tendency
> Towards a purely hothouse proletarian literature.[31]

Even in his most exquisite ranting, MacDiarmid often allows a line or two of poetry to shine through. His poem questioning the erecting of war memorials, "At the Cenotaph," begins with a stunning challenge: "Are the living so much use / That we need to mourn the dead?" (*Socialist*, 57). In an attack on Siegfried Sassoon from the 1930s, "An English War-Poet," he notes Sassoon's recovery from wounds in hospital, "where members of the royal family stopped by his bed / To offer forty-five seconds of polite sympathy" (*Socialist*, 68). His commemoration of a princess's wedding ("Royal Wedding Gifts") notes that she is "daughter of a base and brainless breed," a line worthy of Milton's and Shelley's heavy alliterations in their antiroyalist sonnets (*Socialist*, 16). Both shocking and funny is his gratuitous insult to the wife of George V on her launching of the ocean liner named for her, the *Queen Mary*. His opening couplet borrows from Homer: "Was *this* the face that launched a thousand ships? / No! But it frightened one right smartly down the slips" (*Socialist*, 15). MacDiarmid was aware that he was often dismissed as a propagandist. His defense is best given in the concluding couplet of "Poetry and Propaganda": "In short, any utterance that is not pure / Propaganda is impure propaganda for sure!" (*Socialist*, 14).

Edwin Muir (1887–1959), though only five years older than Mac-Diarmid, was born in a Scotland hundreds of years older than Mac-Diarmid's. Muir grew up in the Orkney Islands, isolated from the Scottish mainland, the son of a tenant farmer in a place where subsistence agriculture and local custom had changed little since the Middle Ages. When he was 14, his family was forced to give up farming; they moved to Glasgow, then infamous for its industrial ugliness and degraded slums, and he gave up school for work. In his autobiography, he gives special emphasis to the impact of this change: "My father and mother and two of my brothers died in Glasgow within two years of one another. Four members of our family died there within two years. That is a measure of the violence of the change."[32] Muir's subsequent poetry returns again and again to this split experience of his childhood. Orkney figures as a lost Eden. His parents, he says in the same passage about the move to Glasgow, did not know about ambition, did not know what competition was. The farm folk lived an ordered life based on custom, with a cultural life made up of legend, folk song, and the poetry of the Bible. His favorite reading as a boy was William Morris and the Greek gods and goddesses, whom he pictured living as he did under a "low Northern sky" (*Autobiography*, 77). His poetry likewise is allegorical and mythical, as even the titles assert in such poems as "Ballad of Hector in Hades," "The Mythical Journey," "One Foot in Eden," and "The Myth," which begins "My childhood all a myth / Enacted in a distant isle; / Time with his hourglass and his scythe / Stood dreaming on the dial."[33]

The move from Orkney to Glasgow was for Muir the Fall from the Garden of Eden. It is a fall from a timeless, archetypal world into the world of modern progress. In one of his earliest poems, "Horses," from *First Poems* (1925), the primitive elements of weather, landscape, and animals are combined to present an image of power and meaning that lies outside the merely human:

> Those lumbering horses in the steady plough
> On the bare field—I wonder why, just now,
> They seemed terrible, so wild and strange,
> Like magic power on the stony grange.
>
> Perhaps some childish hour has come again,
> When I watched fearful, through the blackening rain
> Their hooves like pistons in an ancient mill
> Move up and down, yet seem as standing still.
>
> (19–20)

The image of horses, representing some lost prelapsarian existence full of magic and power, is used again in 1956 in a poem T. S. Eliot praised as the most terrifying work about the atomic age, "The Horses": "Barely a twelvemonth after / The seven days war that put the world to sleep, / Late in the evening the strange horses came" (246–47). The nuclear war that has destroyed the world in seven days mimics the seven-days creation story of Genesis. In the midst of the devastation, the strange horses bring back the agricultural past of early humankind in their willingness to serve, freely, as partners in our need to begin again: "Since then they have pulled our ploughs and borne our loads / But the free servitude still can pierce our hearts. / Our life is changed; their coming our beginning."

Muir could also write politically, but when he did he was at odds with the Scotland that MacDiarmid was trying to resurrect. Muir felt at the edges of Scottish life (the Orkneys were originally a Viking settlement) and in touch with an agricultural way of life that was itself more in touch with the timeless realities of which myth speaks. Thus in a poem such as "Scotland 1941," he attacks the more recent Scottish past that MacDiarmid is trying to celebrate in his revival. For Muir, "we were a tribe, a family, a people" (97). That unity was broken by the Calvinist reformers Knox, Melville, and Peden, who bequeathed to Scotland a mean materialism:

> Now smoke and dearth and money everywhere,
> Mean heirlooms of each fainter generation,
> And mummied housegods in their musty niches.
> Burns and Scott, sham bards of a sham nation,
> And spiritual defeat wrapped warm in riches.
>
> (97)

The cure for this state of things is found not in political action but in myth, which is the only resource that can truly recover what is lost, by rituals of reenactment. "Twice-Done, Once-Done" makes the paradox plain:

> Nothing yet was ever done
>   Till it was done again,
> And no man was ever one
>   Except through dead men.
>
>   (134)

That is, ritual and custom, which connect us to the past, are the real restoratives. Thus Scotland's two best-known twentieth-century poets present a divided front: MacDiarmid, creator of literary Scots and agitator for a revived, independent Scotland, and Muir, writing in English but claiming an older vision that makes kilt-wearing, Burns-loving nationalism a sorry sham.

A third Scottish poet, Andrew Young (1885–1971), is an anomaly for both Scotland and the thirties. Born and educated in Edinburgh, he published his first book of poems, *Songs of Night*, in 1910, when W. H. Auden was three years old. Later he disavowed all of his work published before 1933. Young became a Presbyterian clergyman and was appointed minister to a village in Midlothian in 1914. By 1920 he had moved south to a parish in Sussex. He wrote in English about local flora, making him appear a late Georgian. He read and reread Thomas Hardy, and, not surprisingly, his poetry has many similarities to that of Edward Thomas in its use of rural settings and themes. He was deeply aware of the layers of time and death inhering in the present. Just as Thomas's World War I lyric "Digging" meditates on his own clay pipe that he is burying in the earth, where it mixes with the forgotten pipe of an unknown eighteenth-century soldier, so Young examines a similar homely object in "The Flesh-Scraper," from his 1939 volume *Speak to the Earth:*

> If I had sight enough
> Might I not find a fingerprint
> Left on this flint
> By Neolithic man or Kelt?
> So knapped to scrape a wild beast's pelt,
> The thumb below, fingers above,
> See, my hand fits it like a glove.[34]

The last line vividly marks his own connection to the past and to death. In 1939 Young converted to the Church of England and was made vicar of a small country parish, Stonegate, Sussex. He became an expert on rare wildflowers, publishing three books on the subject, as well as writing poems; he became almost a type of the Victorian gentleman clergy, leaving his Scottish identity rather far behind.

There have been other regionalisms reflected in twentieth-century British poetry, less obvious than Scots nationalism. The county of Northumberland, still aware of its heritage as an Anglo-Saxon kingdom and as the border country ruled by the Percys against Scottish cattle raiders, felt itself almost as far as the Scots from the center of power in England. It was the home of Basil Bunting and, during the years of the Great War, of Kathleen Raine. Both poets made use of the early history of the area, Raine in her "Northumbrian Sequence," which opens with the story of the sparrow's flight (from the Venerable Bede's *History of the English Church and People*), and Bunting in *Briggflatts* (1966), which alludes to the same story. Bunting was also devoted to Northumbrian dialect; in a note published with the poem, he warned "Americans who may not know how much Northumberland differs from the Saxon south" that "Southrons would maul the music" of many of the lines (210). Raine and Bunting replicate, in a rough way, the differences of Muir and MacDiarmid. She is concerned with myth and he with politics.

Though he is heavily indebted to Pound and to Modernism, Bunting's sympathies are rural and socialist. In 1930, at the beginning of the Depression in England, he wrote about the already depressed agricultural laborers of the north, using local dialect words, in "Gin the Goodwife Stint" and "The Complaint of the Morpethshire Farmer." In both poems, the greed of the landlords drives rural folk out. In the first poem, "the ploughland has gone to bent / and the pasture to heather," so the "goodwife" and her "bairns" spend two pounds each on a "C. P. R. packet"—that is, the Canadian Pacific Railroad's packet ship for emigrants (92). The reason for the land's deterioration into gorse and heather is, from Bunting's perspective, shameful: It is to make good hunting land for the Duke's shooting parties. The Duke in question is not Bunting's abstraction, but the Duke of Northumberland, the largest landholder in the county. In the second poem, the farmer from Morpeth, just north of Newcastle, makes this point more directly:

> Canada's a bare land
> for the North wind and the snow.
> Northumberland's a bare land
> for men have made it so.
>
> Sheep and cattle are poor men's food,
> grouse is sport for the rich;
> heather grows where the sweet grass might grow
> for the cost of cleaning the ditch.
>
> A liner lying in the Clyde
> will take me to Quebec.
> My sons'll see the land I'm leaving
> as barren as her deck.
>
> (97)

Though this poem dates from the Depression and is identified by a specific place-name, it can stand for a generalized feeling in the north of Britain that from this time forward it has been left behind by the south. Northern cities such as Glasgow, Newcastle, Liverpool, Leeds, Sheffield, and Manchester were early entrants in the industrial revolution, soon becoming industrial powerhouses attracting an influx of labor to their rough and robust districts. With the waning of shipbuilding and heavy industry in the twentieth century, the north drifted into unemployment and impoverishment. It soon became identified with socialism and the Labour Party, the south with conservatism and the Tories. This division began to have an effect on the production and reception of poetry. In the north, especially in the sixties, more and more working-class and regional voices were heard, such as Tony Harrison (b. 1937) from Leeds and Roger McGough (b. 1937) from Liverpool. They looked to different traditions than Modernism and Georgianism had offered; they mined ballads, folk songs, popular culture, and colloquial speech more heavily than Auden ever could. In the class perspective of these new poets, both the Georgians and the Modernists looked conservative, but the Georgians and the traditional poets who followed them especially fell into disfavor. The thatched cottages, wildflowers, and quaint hedgerows so often celebrated by the Georgians are essentially a feature of the rural southern counties, and those counties are economically prosperous in part from a booming tourist industry that exploits the rural stereotypes of this poetry. It is the poetry of Bunting and MacDiarmid especially that breaks ground for the proliferation of regional voices later.

The Welsh poets David Jones, Dylan Thomas, and Vernon Watkins also contributed to this emphasis on regionalism, but their relationship to their Celtic roots was more complicated than for the Scots and the Northerners. Foremost is the issue of language. Donald Davie explains that "Welsh is far nearer to being an alternative national tongue than Gaelic is for the Irish or the Scots; yet on the other hand, the English spoken and written by Welshmen diverges from the metropolitan English, lexically and syntactically, much less than the English of Ireland and Scotland does."[35] What this means, says Davie, is that a Welsh writer who chooses to write in English "feels especially guilty." There is no third option, such as Hugh Mac-Diarmid's concocted Lallans for the Scots.

David Jones (1895–1974) felt this division keenly. A contemporary of Robert Graves and a private in Graves's regiment, the Royal Welch Fusiliers, during the Great War, Jones had an English mother and a Welsh father. He worked on an ambitious long poem after the war, *In Parenthesis,* which he finally published with difficulty in 1937. The work is Modernist, though not because Jones had much acquaintance with the works of either Eliot or Pound. He is a "natural" Modernist from surviving the war. His letters are a nightmare for editors, for he continually added afterthoughts in margins, on the backs of sheets, on the envelope, attached by various arrows and lines or not marked except by the new color of ink, looking something like James Joyce's manuscript of *Finnegan's Wake. In Parenthesis* weaves Welsh mythology, Sir Thomas Malory, Catholicism, and the daily experiences of ordinary soldiers into a narrative rich in allusion and cross-reference. Jones provided his own notes to the poem, but as T. S. Eliot says in his introduction to the edition brought out by Faber, "author's notes (as is illustrated by *The Waste Land*) are no prophylactic against interpretation and dissection: they merely provide the serious researcher with more material to interpret and dissect."[36] A brief example of Jones's style is this description of two trench soldiers talking:

> I am the Single Horn thrusting
> by night-stream margin
> in Helyon.

Cripes-a-mighty-strike-me-stone-cold—you don't say.
Where's that birth-mark, young 'un.
Wot the Melchizzydix!—and still fading—jump to it Rotherhithe.
  Never die never die
  Never die never die
  Old soljers never die.

(84)

Jones's notes identify as sources for these lines the Welsh Percival story (*Peredur ap Evrawc*), a story about Moses in the *Itinerarium Joannis de Hese*, a phrase from Hebrews 7:3, and the lyrics of a popular song. David Perkins calls *In Parenthesis* "certainly the greatest literary text that deals with the First World War" (Perkins, 302). It was also heavily praised by T. S. Eliot and W. H. Auden, but it is still not well-known to modern readers. No poem of its length and difficulty, however, has been successful with modern readers (and even competent readers of the great epics of the past have sometimes repeated what Samuel Johnson said of *Paradise Lost,* that they thought the work worthy but did not wish it one word longer than it was).

Vernon Watkins (1906–1967) was a friend of Jones and of Thomas; he saved their letters to him, though his own to them are mostly lost. This has less to do with Watkins's importance to them than with the poverty and distractedness of Jones and the self-absorption and profligacy of Thomas. The Welsh poet Glyn Jones (1905–1995), a devotee of Thomas, hypothesizes the reason Thomas trusted Watkins so thoroughly and leaned upon him so heavily was that "in the mounting disorder of Dylan's affairs the serene dedication and the Christian acceptance of Vernon must have seemed like a still centre, a point of unattainable sanity."[37] The three of them wrote in English, though their correspondence is sprinkled with Welsh words added for flavoring or more exact meaning. Watkins was the most accomplished in Welsh, which was the first language of both his mother and father. He read it with the aid of a dictionary, though he did not speak it.

Watkins wrote poetry from childhood on but did not publish until Thomas urged him to in the late 1930s. His poetry was at first romantic, as in "Griefs of the Sea," from the first number of *Wales* in 1937: "It is fitting to mourn dead sailors, / To crown the sea with a blind wreath of foam / Though the deaf wave hear nothing" (Norris, 23). But with his first volume, *Ballad of the Mari Lwyd* (1941), rougher rhythms and coarser life emerged, as in "The Mummy": "His eyes are closed. They are closed. His eyes are closed. / His hands are clenched. They are clenched. His hands are clenched. / The messenger comes. The letters are disciplined; they are disposed."[38] The title poem of the volume was especially stunning:

> The sands in the glass, the shrinking sands,
> And the picklock, picklock, picklock hands.
>
> Midnight. Midnight. Midnight. Midnight.
> Hark at the hands of the clock.
>
> (72)

In a note Watkins explained that the "Mari Lwyd" was the "Grey Mare," a New Year's Eve tradition that he had witnessed as a boy, when "singers, wits, and impromptu poets" would arrive on the doorstep with a horse's skull to engage in a rhyming contest. If they won, they would "bring their horse's head in, lay it on the table, and eat and drink with the losers of the contest" (89). The ballad (really a playlet with stage directions) is typical of Watkins's later work in its attempt to bring together in a timeless moment the sacred and the profane.

Watkins worked all his life as a cashier in a Lloyd's bank in Swansea, refusing promotions so that he could devote his energy to poetry. The Anglo-Welsh poet and Anglican priest R. S. Thomas (b. 1913) provided a poem, "The Bank Clerk," for a commemorative volume after Watkins's death. The poem plays on money metaphors, making the point that the "real coinage" in our lives is the coinage of poetic language, not the "dry cheques" offered by the bank's Customers. The poem ends with a challenge:

> Clerks, businessmen,
> Grousers about the cost
> Of a poet, he has balanced honourably
> His accounts, but—what about you?
> (Norris, 34)

The question of this last line is too confrontational for the gentle, uncritical Watkins, but the poem admirably blends the elements of Watkins's life: his sane and responsible family and work life, his devotion to his writing life, and his concern for the timeless spiritual.

"Nothing Yet Was Ever Done / Till It Was Done Again"

In his question to us, R. S. Thomas asks how we will balance the claims of the world and the claims of the spirit. This is a lofty, priest-like question, but it is also crucial in a quite practical way for any poet.

The greatest of the Anglo-Welsh writers in the first half of the century, the one who dazzled them all, solved the problem of employment by his gift for performance. Dylan Thomas (1914–1953), with his beautiful, dramatic, mesmerizing voice, found his greatest fame on the BBC and lecture tours of America. He often did not read his own poetry, playing rather the role of the poet, which people adored. The worse his behavior the better, it seemed, so that at readings the audience appreciated hints of his audacious boozing and philandering as much as the poetry. Thomas thought, oddly, that another quality of a true poet was to be fat, and this he also quickly attained in his mercurial rise. He embodied and enacted poetry for the modern audience, much as Elvis Presley and Marilyn Monroe would in the 1950s embody sexuality, glamor, fame, and fortune for the masses. Thomas was deeply offended when a book of criticism referred to him throughout as "Dylan" rather than the more customary and respectful "Mr. Thomas," but the familiar usage is another sign of his stardom. Like Elvis and Marilyn, he could, for a while, be known by one name. His fame was stolen shortly after his death by a young American folk singer, Robert Zimmerman, from Minnesota, who shrewdly seized Thomas's name to engineer his own rise to the top in the 1960s, becoming Bob Dylan.

Thomas, like Edith Sitwell, was found by many to be too obscure to understand, though after the poetry of the Surrealists his exuberant language did not seem such a big hurdle. The sounds he spoke, in his lilting accent, were rich and glorious. Most of his poems from the thirties are little read today; his reputation rests on a few more accessible works from later in his career, such as the radio play *Under Milk Wood* (1952) and three poems from 1945, "A Refusal to Mourn the Death, by Fire, of a Child in London," "Fern Hill," and "In My Craft or Sullen Art." His most frequently read and quoted poem, probably rivaled only by Robert Frost's poem for Edward Thomas, "The Road Not Taken," is the villanelle written as his father was dying in 1951, "Do Not Go Gentle into That Good Night." Despite the appearance of natural if untidy genius that he projected, Thomas was a careful craftsman. "Fern Hill" reputedly went through more than 300 drafts. Thomas worked sometimes in syllable counts, sometimes in traditional forms such as the villanelle, and sometimes in puzzles of form he gave himself to solve. "Vision and Prayer" from *The Poems of Dylan Thomas*, edited by his childhood friend and some-time collaborator Daniel Jones, is written in geometric shapes, such as diamonds and hourglasses. In "Prologue," written specially to lead off *Collected Poems* in 1952, Thomas wrote two verses of 51 lines each, with the second verse rhyming *"backward* with the first.... Why I acrosticked myself like this, don't ask me" (*D. Thomas*, 250).

What was most admired in Thomas by other poets was already there in the thirties, a wonderful compression of metaphor. Edith Sitwell cited the short phrase "altarwise by owl-light" for a compactness that yet could conjure up whole mythologies of meaning. One of the early poems that has made it into the anthologies, "The Force That through the Green Fuse Drives the Flower," likewise gets its special power from Thomas's startling metaphor. The force that Thomas is writing about is natural, sexual, and contradictory, both a creator and destroyer: "The force that through the green fuse drives the flower / Drives my green age; that blasts the roots of trees / Is my destroyer" (*D. Thomas*, 77). The "green fuse" serves as a visual image of the stem of a plant, through which a life force surges like electric power or burns like gunpowder on its way to an explosion of bloom. Behind this simple, two-word image lie deeper and deeper resonances, to the Green Man of the Woods who is Nature, to the Roman conception of one's genius as a driving force within, to dynamite and electricity and phalluses. His wife, Caitlan Thomas, said, in her anger and grief after his early death from drinking in 1953, "Dylan was a shit."[39] He was also a considerable poet. Like Byron, Shelley, Wilde, and Lawrence, however, he will probably be remembered as much for his life as for his poetry, which seems to be the fate of writers who are associated with sexual excess lived publicly on a grand scale. Especially if they die young.

The Eve of the Second World War

The year 1939 enjoyed a richness in publication that would not soon be seen again, if only for the practical matter of the paper shortage during the war. A deeper reason is the dispersal of the intellectual richness of the thirties, a richness that this chapter has only briefly described. Just as the ferment taking place in England in 1912 and

1913 was suddenly quashed by the outbreak of the First World War, so the Second World War caused citizens and writers to hunker down for the long haul, though for some, notably T. S. Eliot, the war years saw important work done.

The main works of 1939 were Christoper Isherwood's *Goodbye to Berlin;* W. H. Auden's elegies for Freud and Yeats, both of whom died that year; Auden and Isherwood's *Journey to a War,* about the Sino-Japanese War they had witnessed the year before; Dylan Thomas's *Map of Love;* Stephen Spender's *The Still Centre;* Roy Campbell's celebration of Franco, *Flowering Rifle;* and first books by Geoffrey Grigson, Anne Ridler, Roy Fuller, and Glyn Jones. William Empson was preparing a volume of poems with the ominous title *The Gathering Storm* (1940). The conventional wisdom about the thirties poets (excluding Dylan Thomas), that they were political up until the war, appears true if one examines these titles. During the war, especially under the influence of Eliot, Auden, Betjeman, Thomas, Vernon Watkins, Edith Sitwell, and Kathleen Raine, Christian themes made a comeback, and Marxism, indeed politics, seemed dead. George Orwell, in his prose satire *Animal Farm* (1945), was certainly writing about politics, but only to put a nail in its coffin. In 1939 it was apparent that politics of the left and the right, communism and fascism, had ended in totalitarianism. The liberal democracies appeared enfeebled. Politics at worst was the problem and at best was inadequate.

The year 1939 was, in Samuel Hynes's words, "a sort of war-year *before* the war, when the life of Europe had already become a wartime life, a period of waiting for the end" (Hynes 1972, 340). The Spanish Civil War had finally ended in March, just in time for Czechoslovakia to be occupied by German troops. German and Russian troops were massed on the western and eastern borders of Poland by August, right after the signing of a nonaggression pact between Hitler and Stalin, and on September first the long wait of anticipation was over. The thirties, that "low dishonest decade," in Auden's phrase from "September 1, 1939," were ended, and the Second World War had officially begun.

Auden's contribution to his book with Isherwood on the war in China was a sonnet sequence, titled "In Time of War." The middle sonnet of the sequence, number 14, opens with a line that speaks not of China but of Europe: "Yes, we are going to suffer, now" (*English Auden,* 256). The sonnet describes a nighttime air raid, but Auden

uses the images of the air raid as a metaphor to point to the evil
within our hearts that leads to war:

> Yes, we are going to suffer, now; the sky
> Throbs like a feverish forehead; pain is real;
> The groping searchlights suddenly reveal
> The little natures that will make us cry,
>
> Who never quite believed they could exist,
> Not where we were. They take us by surprise
> Like ugly long-forgotten memories,
> And like a conscience all the guns resist.

We are taken by surprise—by the planes, by ugly memories, and by
conscience—because we never thought we would have to pay a
price. But our "private massacres"—those whom we daily slaughter—have made us sick. Our heads throb with fever. Our private
hatreds—of "all Women, Jews, the Rich, the Human Race"—are
erupting now. It is for this that we are going to suffer.

Geoffrey Grigson wrote the most appreciative review of "In Time
of War," in what turned out to be the last issue of *New Verse*. The
review has an elegiac tone: "*New Verse* came into existence because
of Auden. It has published more poems by Auden than by anyone
else.... Auden is now clear, absolutely clear of foolish journalists,
Cambridge detractors ... and the new crop of loony and eccentric
small magazines in England and America. He is something good
and creative in European life in a time of the very greatest evil"
(Hynes 1972, 348–49). Grigson is bidding good-bye to Auden, to his
journal, and to what is "good and creative" in European life. What is
left is the very greatest evil. It would be difficult now to want to start
a new journal, a new movement, any new work.

The year before, in March 1938, Grigson had printed a display
page in *New Verse* headed "BE WARNED BY RUPERT BROOKE,"
which recounted Churchill's funeral oration over Brooke and ended
with the warning that Churchill was still young enough "for a
funeral oration about you."[40] This was not the majority view in the
popular press, however, which was searching for the new Rupert
Brooke. C. Day Lewis's "Where Are the War Poets?" (quoted at the
beginning of this chapter) gave the cynical answer. As an example of
how little war poetry there was at first, Roy Fuller cites his own first

wartime book, not published until 1942 but yet cited as the first clear look at the "life of the Forces" (Fuller, 130). Fuller cites as the reason "the ease of avoidance by poets of active service"; the answer is more complex than that, but it is true that England's best poets were dead, abroad, pacifist, openly gay, rejecting of military service, rejected for military service, seeking alternative service, too old, or too young.

Louis MacNeice's brilliant *Autumn Journal* (1938) records his thoughts on the approaching war almost like a rhymed diary. Jon Stallworthy regards it as the thirties' version of *The Prelude*, except that Wordsworth "looks back to the rapids of the French Revolution, whereas MacNeice can hear the premonitory thunder of the Falls ahead."[41] The poem is about Ireland as well as war: "The minority always guilty. / Why should I want to go back / To you, Ireland, my Ireland?" (MacNeice, *Collected*, 133). It is also about the unemployment of the thirties: "And the North, where I was a boy, / Is still the North, veneered with the grime of Glasgow, / Thousands of men whom nobody will employ" (133). A surprising theme is the twin attack on Rupert Brookeish emotions and the Georgian countryside, as if they still have power in English poetry in 1938. The soil, which inspired Brooke and for which Edward Thomas fought, is "tired and the profit little" (136). The rivers are "beer-brown" with pollution. Laborers and shepherds work under a "mackerel sky." Because of this post-Eliot landscape, MacNeice declares:

> Sing us no more idylls, no more pastorals,
>   No more epics of the English earth;
> The country is a dwindling annexe to the factory,
>   Squalid as an after-birth.
>   (136–137)

These endings intoned by Grigson, Auden, and MacNeice were not to be the final word, of course. Poetry will go on. There were new magazines. There were to be idylls and pastorals. And they were even to be written by the MacNeice who had forsworn idylls. As in the First World War, the destruction and despair attendant upon warfare would drive poets quickly back to old traditions for what comfort they could provide. In October 1940, MacNeice wrote "Cradle song for Eleanor," a lullaby that offers a way out of what is about to befall:

> Sleep, my darling, sleep;
> The pity of it all
> Is all we compass if
> We watch disaster fall.
> (190)

The "pity of it all" is reminiscent of Owen's penciled preface to his poems: "the poetry is in the pity." MacNeice seems to be saying that war, beheld, is solely about the pity which Owen said was the only proper way to behold it. But sleep, a creeping into "the robber's cave," into withdrawal or into childhood, offers a protection—but only for a while: "Life will tap the window / Only too soon again." The image is of Sleeping Beauty under glass. She will be awakened not by a kiss but by a tap that threatens to break the glass, which has functioned as a symbol of her sheltered virginity:

> When the winsome bubble
> Shivers, when the bough
> Breaks, will be the moment
> But not here or now.
> (190)

The poem ends with lines that are often quoted:

> Sleep and, asleep, forget
> The watchers on the wall
> Awake all night who know
> The pity of it all.
> (190)

The roles of sleeper and watcher called up here seem at first quite gender-specific: MacNeice takes on the role of father and guardian, the watcher on the wall, who protects the women and children within. But the image also recalls Adam and Eve in the Garden, protected by angels upon the walls of Paradise—all in vain, of course, as the Fall will come. In the context of the lullaby, MacNeice is a guardian angel; in the context of the war, he is a sentry, though a civilian one. In the context of poetry, he is the nurse who sings us to sleep. In all his roles, he is doomed to failure. The cradle falls. The enemy comes. And we awaken. But if our fall is certain, it can be, the poem hints, something of a fortunate fall; at the very least, we will be refreshed and better able to join the fight.

This very traditional attitude to poetry was evident, says Linda Shires, in the outpouring of poetry by hundreds of men and women in military or government service between 1939 and 1945: "[W]riting out of the extreme conditions of exile, fear, isolation and danger, they made their way into print via Forces magazines now long forgotten."[42] One of these Forces magazines, *Khaki and Blue,* addressed its amateurishness directly: "We cannot attain the high quality of a Sidney Keyes or an Alun Lewis ... [but] we can record and interpret—even in a modest anthology like our own—the issues confronting and shaping the future and fate of our bewildering time" (Shires, 68). How modest and restrained an aim this is, if one remembers the claims made by anthologists during the First World War. Then, the purpose of poetry was to celebrate the nation's soldiers as heros. Now, it is to allow those soldiers the chance themselves to make sense out of bewilderment. Without Owen's and Sassoon's protests this could not have happened, but without the responses to war and destruction by Eliot and Auden, Sitwell and Farjeon, who showed that civilians and women had to deal with what war had wrought, it also would not have occurred to ordinary people that poetry was a way to make sense from brutal experience.

Owen's editor, the poet Jon Stallworthy, during a much later war made a very traditional claim for the primacy of experience, in "A poem about Poems About Vietnam":

> . . . .
> Lord George Byron cared for Greece,
> Auden and Cornford cared for Spain,
> confronted bullets and disease
> to make their poems' meaning plain;
> but you—by what right did you wear
> suffering like a service medal,
> numbering the nerve that they laid bare,
> when you were at the Albert Hall?[43]

John Cornford's mother, who wrote the famous epitaph for Rupert Brooke, may or may not have cared about Spain, but what she cared about, she wrote about:

> This once protected flesh the War-god uses
> Like any gadget of a great machine;

"Nothing Yet Was Ever Done / Till It Was Done Again"

> This flesh once pitied where a gnat had been,
> And kissed with passion on invisible bruises.
>
> (88)

Frances Cornford, then, has the last word. British poetry from 1900 to 1939 saw many poets, many movements, many manifestos, many crises. But from the most mundane lines of Wilfrid Gibson to the most ecstatic lines of Dylan Thomas, poetry served a human purpose, kissing our invisible bruises.

· Notes ·

Chapter One

1. John Osborne, *Look Back In Anger* (New York: S. G. Phillips, 1959), 17.
2. Osbert Sitwell, *Great Morning* (London: Macmillan, 1948), 232.
3. Charles Masterman, *The Condition of England* (London: Methuen, 1909), 12.
4. Alfred Austin, *Lyrical Poems* (London: Macmillan, 1896), 116–17. Austin's poetry is difficult to find; though he was the laureate, not a single verse is reprinted by Yeats or Larkin in their Oxford anthologies, and modern anthologies ignore him as well.
5. Samuel Hynes, *Edwardian Occasions* (New York: Oxford University Press, 1972), 2.
6. William Dean Howells, "The Laureate of the Larger England," in *Kipling: The Critical Heritage,* ed. Roger Lancelyn Green (New York: Barnes & Noble, 1971), 192.
7. *The Works of Rudyard Kipling* (Ware: Wordsworth, 1994), 329. Hereafter cited in the text as *Kipling*.
8. George Orwell, "Rudyard Kipling," rpt. in *Kipling and the Critics,* ed. Elliot L. Gilbert (New York: New York University Press, 1965), 80.
9. Louise Bennett, "Colonisation in Reverse," in *The Penguin Book of Caribbean Verse in English,* ed. Paula Burnett (London: Penguin, 1986), 32–33.
10. Quoted in William Vaughan, *Romanticism and Art* (New York: Thames and Hudson, 1994), 263.
11. *The Complete Poems of Thomas Hardy,* ed. James Gibson (London: Macmillan, 1976), 150. Hereafter cited in the text as *Hardy.*
12. W. B. Yeats, ed., *The Oxford Book of Modern Verse* (New York: Oxford University Press, 1936), xi–xii. Hereafter cited in the text.
13. Quoted in Robert L. Herbert, *Impressionism: Art, Leisure, and Parisian Society* (New Haven: Yale University Press, 1988), 74. Herbert hereafter cited in the text.
14. *Arthur Symons: Poetry and Prose,* sel. and intro. by R. V. Holdsworth (Chatham: Fyfield/Carcanet Press, 1974), 34. Hereafter cited in the text as *Symons.*
15. Robert Graves, *Good-Bye to All That* (rev. & rpt. 1985; New York: Doubleday, 1929), 307. Hereafter cited in the text as *Good-Bye.*
16. Edward Marsh, ed., *Georgian Poetry, 1911–1912* (London: The Poetry Bookshop, 1912), unpaginated prefatory note.

Notes

17. *The Works of Rupert Brooke* (Ware: Wordsworth, 1994), 97. Hereafter cited in the text as *Brooke.*

18. Frances Cornford, *Collected Poems* (London: Cresset, 1954), 19. Further quotations are from this edition.

19. David Perkins, *A History of Modern Poetry: From the 1890s to the High Modernist Mode* (Cambridge, Mass.: Belknap Press of Harvard University Press, 1976), 329. Hereafter cited in the text.

20. Michael Reck, *Ezra Pound: A Close-Up* (New York: McGraw-Hill, 1967), 20.

21. J. J. Wilhelm, *Ezra Pound in London and Paris: 1908–1925* (University Park: Pennsylvannia State University Press, 1990), 92.

22. Quoted in Glenn Hughes, *Imagism & The Imagists: A Study in Modern Poetry* (New York: Biblo and Tannen, 1972), 17. Hughes hereafter cited in the text.

23. H. D., *Collected Poems: 1912–1944*, ed. Louis Martz (New York: New Directions, 1983), 25. Further quotations are from this edition.

24. Mary Loeffelholz, *Experimental Lives: Women and Literature, 1900–1945* (New York: Twayne, 1992), 23.

25. Richard Aldington, *Collected Poems* (London: Allen and Unwin, 1929), 32. Hereafter cited in the text as Aldington, *Collected.*

Chapter Two

1. Elizabeth Helsinger, *Rural Scenes and National Representation: Britain, 1815–1850* (Princeton: Princeton University Press, 1997), 190. Hereafter cited in the text.

2. Quoted in Malcolm Kelsall, *The Great Good Place: The Country House and English Literature* (New York: Columbia University Press, 1993), 159.

3. Quoted approvingly in Arthur Melville Clark, *The Realistic Revolt in Modern Poetry* (1921; rpt., New York: Haskell House, 1966), 33.

4. John Lucas, "The Sunlight on the Garden," in *Seeing Double: Revisioning Edwardian and Modernist Literature,* ed. Carola M. Kaplan and Anne B. Simpson (New York: St. Martin's Press, 1996), 64.

5. Louis Untermeyer, ed., *Modern British Poetry* (New York: Harcourt, Brace & World, 1962), 233. Hereafter cited in the text. For poets not reprinted in new editions, such as Monro, Untermeyer's anthology includes a generous selection of hard-to-find poetry.

6. Quoted in Andrew Motion, *The Poetry of Edward Thomas* (London: Routledge & Kegan Paul, 1980), 9. Motion hereafter cited in the text.

7. Wilfrid Gibson, *Hazards* (London: Macmillan, 1930), 48–49. Gibson's letter to Frost's official biographer, Lawrance Thompson, is in the Frost-Barrett Collection at the University of Virginia's Alderman Library.

8. Philip Larkin, ed., *The Oxford Book of Twentieth Century English Verse* (Oxford: Clarendon Press, 1973), 138. Hereafter cited in the text.

Notes

9. Quoted in Norman Page, *A. E. Housman: A Critical Biography* (New York: Shocken Books, 1983), 162.

10. *The Works of A. E. Housman* (Ware: Wordsworth, 1994), 11. Hereafter cited in the text as *Housman.*

11. Kenneth Millard, *Edwardian Poetry* (Oxford, Clarendon Press, 1991), 98. Hereafter cited in the text.

12. John Lucas, *Modern English Poetry from Hardy to Hughes* (London: B. T. Batsford, 1986), 68.

13. *The Complete Poems of W. H. Davies*, with an introduction by Osbert Sitwell (Middletown, Conn.: Wesleyan University Press, 1965), 215.

14. John Evangelist Walsh, *Into My Own: The English Years of Robert Frost* (New York: Grove, 1988), 186.

15. Quoted in Jan Marsh, *Edward Thomas: A Poet for His Country* (New York: Harper & Row, 1978), 143. Marsh hereafter cited in the text.

16. *The Works of Edward Thomas* (Ware: Wordsworth, 1994), 124–25. Hereafter cited in the text as *Works.*

Chapter Three

1. *The Poems of Wilfrid Owen*, ed. Jon Stallworthy (New York: Norton, 1985), 117. Hereafter cited in the text as *Owen.*

2. Miriam Cooke, *Women and the War Story* (Berkeley: University of California Press, 1996), 1–2.

3. E. B. Osborn, *The Muse in Arms* (London: John Murray, 1917), ix. Hereafter cited in the text.

4. Quoted in Peter Parker, *The Old Lie: The Great War and the Public School Ethos* (London: Constable, 1987), 26. Parker hereafter cited in the text.

5. Quoted in Tom Shone, "The Road to Crash," *The New Yorker*, 17 March 1997, 71.

6. Catherine W. Reilly, *English Poetry of the First World War: A Bibliography* (New York: St. Martin's Press, 1978).

7. Sam Keen, *Faces of the Enemy* (San Francisco: Harper, 1986), 76, 78.

8. Jessie Pope, *More War Poems* (London: Grant Richards, 1915), 47.

9. *The Best Loved Poems of the American People* (NY: Doubleday, 1936), 282. Printed here are also E. L. Thayer's "Casey At the Bat" and many inspirational poems, such as "A Smile": "Let others cheer the winning man,/There's one I hold worthwhile;/'Tis he who does the best he can,/ Then loses with a smile" (99). Later American take-offs on Rice's cliché show the greater distance of American society from these Edwardian attitudes, quips such as Leo Durocher's "nice guys finish last" or Vince Lombardi's "winning isn't everything, it's the only thing."

10. Basil Bunting, *Complete Poems*, ed. Richard Caddel (New York: Oxford University Press, 1994), 221. Further quotations are from this edition.

Notes

11. Herbert Asquith, "The Volunteer," in *Poems 1912–1933* (London: Sidgwick and Jackson, 1934), 69.

12. Charles Williams, *Poetry at Present* (1930; rpt., New York: Books for Libraries Press, 1969), 133.

13. Jon Silkin, *Out of Battle: The Poetry of the Great War* (London: Oxford University Press, 1972), 136. Hereafter cited in the text.

14. Siegfried Sassoon, *The War Poems* (London: Faber & Faber, 1983), 29. Hereafter cited in the text as *War*.

15. Siegfried Sassoon, *Collected Poems, 1908–1956* (London: Faber & Faber, 1984), 237. Hereafter cited in the text as Sassoon, *Collected*.

16. Quoted in Fred D. Crawford, *British Poets of the Great War* (London: Associated University Presses, 1988), 78. Crawford hereafter cited in the text.

17. M. H. Abrams, ed., *The Norton Anthology of English Literature*, 6th ed. (New York: Norton, 1993), 1837.

18. *The Collected Works of Isaac Rosenberg: Poetry, Prose, Letters, and Some Drawings*, ed. Gordon Bottomley and Denys Harding, with a foreword by Siegfried Sassoon (London: Chatto and Windus, 1937), 289–322. Further quotations are from this edition.

19. Alan Judd, *Ford Madox Ford* (London: Collins, 1990), 241.

20. John H. Johnston, *English Poetry of the First World War* (Princeton: Princeton University Press, 1964), 256.

21. Richard Aldington, *Life for Life's Sake: A Book of Reminiscences* (New York: Viking, 1941), 209.

22. Quoted in Paul Fussell, *The Great War and Modern Memory* (New York: Oxford University Press, 1975), 270. Fussell hereafter cited in the text.

23. Gregory Woods, *Articulate Flesh: Male Homo-Eroticism and Modern Poetry* (New Haven: Yale University Press, 1987), 59. Hereafter cited in the text.

Chapter Four

1. Charles Osborne, *W. H. Auden: The Life of a Poet* (1979; rpt., New York: M. Evans & Co, 1995), 44.

2. Garland Greever and Joseph M. Bachelor, eds., *The Soul of the City: An Urban Anthology* (New York: Houghton Mifflin, 1923), 227. For an extended discussion of this anthology and of the urban tradition, see John H. Johnston, *The Poet and the City: A Study in Urban Perspectives* (Athens: University of Georgia Press, 1984), 155–81.

3. Samuel Hynes, *A War Imagined: The First World War and English Culture* (New York: Atheneum, 1991), 254. Hereafter cited in the text as Hynes 1991.

4. Osbert Sitwell, *Collected Satires and Poems* (London: Duckworth, 1931), 36. Hereafter cited in the text as *Satires*.

5. Stanley Weintraub, *A Stillness Heard Round the World: The End of the Great War, November 1918* (New York: Dutton, 1985), 262–63.

Notes

6. Richard Perceval Graves, *Robert Graves: The Assault Heroic, 1895–1926* (New York: Viking, 1987), 43.

7. David Garnett reconstructs the conversation in *The Flowers of the Forest* (New York: Harcourt Brace, 1955), 190–91.

8. Victoria Glendinning, *Edith Sitwell: A Unicorn Among Lions* (New York: Knopf, 1981), 14–15. Hereafter cited in the text.

9. John Pearson, *Facades: Edith, Osbert, and Sacheverell Sitwell* (London: Macmillan, 1978), 116. Hereafter cited in the text.

10. John Press, *A Map of Modern English Verse* (London: Oxford University Press, 1969), 159.

11. Osbert Sitwell, *The Winstonburg Line* (London: Hendersons, 1919), 6–7.

12. Edith Sitwell, *The Collected Poems of Edith Sitwell* (New York: Vanguard, 1954), 12, 13, 21, 28, 30, 33. Hereafter cited in the text as *E. Sitwell*.

13. Susan Schweik, *A Gulf So Deeply Cut: American Women Poets and the Second World War* (Madison: University of Wisconsin Press, 1991), 99–101.

14. Richard Ellmann and Robert O'Clair, eds., *The Norton Anthology of Modern Poetry*, 2d ed. (New York: Norton, 1988), 380.

15. Eleanor Farjeon, *First and Second Love* (London: Michael Joseph, 1947), 56. Further quotations are from this edition.

16. Charlotte Mew, *Collected Poems and Prose* (London: Virago Press, 1981), 35–36. Further quotations are from this edition.

17. Robert Graves, *Fairies and Fusiliers* (London: Heineman, 1917), 26.

18. Robert Graves, *Whipperginny* (London: Heinemann, 1923), 38.

19. Robert Graves, *Mock Beggar Hill*, (London: Leonard & Virginia Woolf at the Hogarth Press, 1924), 16.

20. "Remembering Robert Graves," *The New Yorker* 71:26 (4 Sept. 1995), 73.

21. Deborah Baker, *In Extremis: The Life of Laura Riding* (New York: Grove Press, 1993), 202–3.

22. Martin Seymour-Smith, *Robert Graves: His Life and Works* (New York: Henry Holt, 1982), 190.

23. Michael Millgate, *Thomas Hardy: A Biography* (New York: Random House, 1982), 526.

24. D. N. G. Carter, *Robert Graves: The Lasting Poetic Achievement* (Totowa, N.J.: Barnes & Noble, 1989), 81. Hereafter cited in the text.

25. *Robert Browning: The Poems*, ed. John Pettigrew and Thomas J. Collins (New Haven: Yale University Press, 1981), 719.

26. Robert Graves, *Complete Poems*, 2 vols., ed. Beryl Graves and Dunstan Ward (Manchester, England: Carcanet, 1995–97), 2:237. Hereafter cited in the text as *Complete*.

27. Robert Graves, *Collected Poems* (New York: Doubleday, 1961), 350.

Notes

28. D. H. Lawrence, *The Complete Poems,* ed. Vivian de Sola Pinto and Warren Roberts (New York: Penguin, 1977), 191. Further quotations are from this edition.

29. Patricia Hagen, *Metaphor's Way of Knowing: The Poetry of D. H. Lawrence and the Church of Mechanism* (New York: Peter Lang, 1995), 47–48.

30. Neil Roberts, "Lawrence, Imagism and Beyond," in *British Poetry, 1900–1950: Aspects of Tradition,* ed. Gary Day and Brian Docherty (New York: St. Martin's, 1995), 92.

31. *The Works of G. K. Chesterton* (Ware: Wordsworth, 1995), 75.

32. Elaine Feinstein, *Lawrence and the Women* (New York: Harper Collins, 1993), 9.

33. *The Writings of Anna Wickham: Free Woman and Poet,* ed. R. D. Smith, (London: Virago, 1984), 355. Hereafter cited in the text as *Wickham.*

34. Sandra M. Gilbert and Susan Gubar, eds., *The Norton Anthology of Literature by Women,* 2d ed. (New York: Norton, 1996), 1382. Hereafter cited in the text as Gilbert and Gubar 1996.

35. Bonnie Kime Scott, *The Gender of Modernism* (Bloomington: Indiana University Press, 1990), 614.

36. Vivian de Sola Pinto, *The City That Shone* (New York: The John Day Co., 1969), 265.

Chapter Five

1. Samuel Hynes, *The Auden Generation: Literature and Politics in England in the 1930s* (New York: Viking, 1972). Hereafter cited in the text as Hynes 1972.

2. Ian Chilvers, Harold Osborne, and Dennis Farr, eds., *The Oxford Dictionary of Art* (Oxford: Oxford University Press, 1988), 483.

3. *The Poems of Dylan Thomas* (New York: New Directions, 1971), 120. Hereafter cited in the text as *D. Thomas.*

4. Sandra Gilbert and Susan Gubar, *No Man's Land: The Place of the Woman Writer in the Twentieth Century,* vol. 1, *The War of the Words.* (New Haven: Yale University Press, 1988), 165. Hereafter cited in the text as Gilbert and Gubar 1988.

5. Celeste Schenck, "Exiled by Genre," in *Women's Writing in Exile,* ed. Mary Lynn Broe and Angela Ingram (Chapel Hill: University of North Carolina Press, 1986), 228.

6. Stevie Smith, *Collected Poems* (New York: New Directions, 1983), 447–48. Further quotations are from this edition.

7. In Linda Hall, ed., *An Anthology of Poetry by Women* (London: Cassell, 1994), 50.

8. Ruth Pitter, *A Trophy of Arms* (London: Macmillan, 1936), 81.

9. Mary Webb, *Fifty-One Poems* (London: Jonathan Cape, 1946), 45. Further quotations are from this edition.

Notes

10. Ann Douglas, *Terrible Honesty: Mongrel Manhattan in the 1920s* (New York: Farrar, Strauss & Giroux, 1995), 533.

11. Robert Hewison, *Under Siege: Literary Life in London, 1939–1945* (New York: Oxford University Press, 1977), 96. Hereafter cited in the text.

12. *The English Auden: Poems, Essays, and Dramatic Writings, 1927–1939*, ed. Edward Mendelson (London: Faber & Faber, 1977), 242. Hereafter cited in the text as *English Auden*.

13. Bernard Bergonzi, *Wartime and Aftermath* (Oxford: Oxford University Press, 1993), 72.

14. Philip Larkin, *Collected Poems* (London: Faber & Faber, 1988), 21.

15. Kingsley Amis, ed., *The New Oxford Book of Light Verse* (1978; rpt., Oxford: Oxford University Press, 1992), 294.

16. Stan Smith, *W. H. Auden* (Oxford: Blackwell, 1985), 1. Hereafter cited in the text.

17. W. H. Auden, *Collected Poems*, ed. Edward Mendelson (New York: Vintage, 1976), 250.

18. Richard Davenport-Hines, *Auden* (New York: Pantheon, 1995), 128. Hereafter cited in the text.

19. W. H. Auden, *Juvenilia: Poems, 1922–1928*, ed. Katherine Bucknell (Princeton: Princeton University Press, 1994), 47. By the end of his life, Auden owned three copies of Hardy's poetry, all heavily marked (note, 96).

20. Stephen Spender, *Collected Poems, 1928–1953* (New York: Random House, 1955), 43. Further quotations are from this edition.

21. Adrian Caesar, *Dividing Lines: Poetry, Class, and Ideology in the 1930s* (Manchester: Manchester University Press, 1991), 1.

22. Harold Bloom, *The Anxiety of Influence* (New York: Oxford University Press, 1973).

23. Davenport-Hines, 132. See also Brian Conniff's review essay "Richard Davenport-Hines's *Auden* and the Problem of Auden Criticism," *Christianity and Literature* 46:2 (Winter 1997), 179–86.

24. "The German Auden: Six Early Poems," trans. David Constantine, in *W. H. Auden: "The Map of All My Youth*," ed. Katherine Bucknell and Nicholas Jenkins (Oxford: Clarendon Press, 1990), 6. Translation used here is my own.

25. The marriage of the sonnet, colloquial language, and homoerotic love does not appear so strongly again until Marilyn Hacker's sonnet sequence about lesbian love in 1985, *Love, Death, and the Changing of the Seasons*.

26. Frances Spalding, *Stevie Smith: A Biography* (New York: Norton, 1988), 80.

27. Elizabeth Daryush, *Collected Poems*, with an introduction by Donald Davie (Manchester, England: Carcanet, 1976), 127.

28. Louis MacNeice, *Collected Poems* (London: Faber & Faber, 1966), 41. Hereafter cited in the text as MacNeice, *Collected*.

29. *Collected Poems of Hugh MacDiarmid* (New York: Macmillan, 1962), 39. Hereafter cited in the text as *MacDiarmid*. Includes a glossary of Scots words.

30. Hugh MacDiarmid, *Lucky Poet* (Berkeley: University of California Press, 1972), 67.

31. *The Socialist Poems of Hugh MacDiarmid*, ed. T. S. Law and Thurso Berwick (London: Routledge & Kegan Paul, 1978), 30; ending quotation marks are omitted. Hereafter cited in the text as *Socialist*.

32. Edwin Muir, *An Autobiography* (London: The Hogarth Press, 1964), 63. Hereafter cited in the text as *Autobiography*.

33. Edwin Muir, *Collected Poems* (London: Faber & Faber, 1960), 144. Further quotations are from this edition.

34. *The Poetical Works of Andrew Young*, ed. Edward Lowbury and Alison Young (London: Secker & Warburg, 1985), 80.

35. Donald Davie, *Under Briggflatts: A History of Poetry in Great Britain, 1960–1988* (Chicago: University of Chicago Press, 1989), 158.

36. David Jones, *In Parenthesis*, with an introduction by T. S. Eliot (1937; rpt., London: Faber & Faber, 1961), vii. Further quotations are from this edition.

37. Glyn Jones, "Whose Flight is Toil," in *Vernon Watkins*, ed. Leslie Norris (London: Faber & Faber, 1970), 26. Norris hereafter cited in the text.

38. Vernon Watkins, *Ballad of the Mari Lwyd* (London: Faber & Faber, 1941), 41. Further quotations are from this edition.

39. George Tremlett, *Dylan Thomas: In the Mercy of His Means* (New York: St. Martin's Press, 1992), xii.

40. Roy Fuller, *Professors and Gods* (London: Andre Deutsch, 1973), 120. Hereafter cited in the text.

41. Jon Stallworthy, *Louis MacNeice* (New York: Norton, 1995), 248.

42. Linda Shires, *British Poetry of the Second World War* (New York: St. Martin's Press, 1985), 68. Hereafter cited in the text.

43. Jon Stallworthy, *The Anzac Sonata* (New York: Norton, 1986), 38–39.

· Selected Bibliography ·

Primary Sources

Aldington, Richard. *Collected Poems*. London: Allen & Unwin, 1929.
———. *Death of a Hero*. 1929. Rpt., London: Hogarth Press, 1984.
———. *Life for Life's Sake: A Book of Reminiscences*. New York: Viking, 1941.
———. *D. H. Lawrence: Portrait of a Genius But. . . .* 1950. Rpt., New York: Collier, 1967.
———. *Selected Critical Writings, 1928–1960*. Ed. Alister Kershaw. London: Feffer & Simons, 1970.
Asquith, Herbert. *Poems 1912–1933*. London: Sidgwick and Jackson, 1934.
Auden, Wystan Hugh. *The Dyer's Hand*. New York: Random House, 1962.
———. *The English Auden: Poems, Essays, and Dramatic Writings, 1927–1939*. Ed. Edward Mendelson. London: Faber & Faber, 1977.
———. *Collected Poems*. Ed. Edward Mendelson. New York: Vintage, 1991.
———. *Juvenilia: Poems, 1922–1928*. Ed. Katherine Bucknell. Princeton: Princeton University Press, 1994.
Austin, Alfred. *Lyrical Poems*. London: Macmillan, 1896.
Betjeman, John. *Slick But Not Streamlined: Poems and Short Pieces by John Betjeman*. Sel. and intro. by W. H. Auden. Garden City, N.Y.: Doubleday, 1947.
———. *John Betjeman's Collected Poems*. Sel. and intro. by The Earl of Birkenhead. Boston: Houghton Mifflin, 1959.
Brooke, Rupert. *The Works of Rupert Brooke*. Ware, England: Wordsworth, 1994.
Bunting, Basil. *Complete Poems*. Ed. Richard Caddel. New York: Oxford University Press, 1994.
Chesterton, Gilbert Keith. *The Works of G. K. Chesterton*. Ware, England: Wordsworth, 1995.
Clare, John. *The Works of John Clare*. Ware, England: Wordsworth, 1995.
Cornford, Frances. *Collected Poems*. London: Cresset, 1954.
———. *Selected Poems*. Ed. Jane Dowson. With a memoir by Hugh Cornford. London: Enitharmon, 1996.
Daryush, Elizabeth. *Collected Poems*. With an introduction by Donald Davie. Manchester, England: Carcanet, 1976.
Davies, William Henry. *The Complete Poems of W. H. Davies*. With an introduction by Osbert Sitwell. Middleton, Conn.: Wesleyan University Press, 1965.
Day Lewis, Cecil. *Collected Poems*. London: Jonathan Cape, 1954.
Doolittle, Hilda. *H. D., Collected Poems, 1912–1944*. Ed. Louis Martz. New York: New Directions, 1983.

Selected Bibliography

Douglas, Keith. *Keith Douglas: The Complete Poems.* Ed. Desmond Graham. Oxford: Oxford University Press, 1978.

Eliot, Thomas Stearns. *On Poetry and Poets.* New York: Farrar, Strauss & Giroux, 1961.

———. *Collected Poems, 1909–1962.* New York: Harcourt Brace, 1991.

Farjeon, Eleanor. *First & Second Love.* London: Michael Joseph, 1947.

———. *Edward Thomas: The Last Four Years.* Ed. Anne Harvey. 1958. Rpt., Phoenix Mill, Gloucestershire: Sutton, 1997.

Frost, Robert. *The Poetry of Robert Frost.* New York: Henry Holt, 1969.

Gibson, Wilfrid. *Hazards.* London: Macmillan, 1930.

Graves, Robert. *Over the Brazier.* London: The Poetry Bookshop, 1916.

———. *Fairies and Fusiliers.* London: Heinemann, 1917.

———. *Country Sentiment.* New York: Knopf, 1920.

———. *On English Poetry.* New York: Knopf, 1922.

———. *Whipperginny.* London: Heinemann, 1923.

———. *Mock Beggar Hall.* London: The Hogarth Press, 1924.

———. *Good-Bye to All That.* 1929. Rpt., New York: Doubleday, 1985.

———. *Collected Poems.* New York: Doubleday, 1961.

———. *Complete Poems.* 2 vols. Ed. Beryl Graves and Dunstan Ward. Manchester, England: Carcanet, 1995–97.

Graves, Robert and Laura Riding. *A Survey of Modernist Poetry.* 1927. Rpt., New York: Folcroft Library Editions, 1971.

Hardy, Thomas. *The Complete Poems of Thomas Hardy.* Ed. James Gibson. London: Macmillan, 1976.

Hopkins, Gerard Manley. *The Works of Gerard Manley Hopkins.* Ware, England: Wordsworth, 1994.

Housman, Alfred Edward. *The Works of A. E. Housman.* Ware, England: Wordsworth, 1994.

Jones, David. *In Parenthesis.* With an introduction by T. S. Eliot. 1937. Rpt., London: Faber & Faber, 1961.

———. *David Jones: Letters to Vernon Watkins.* Ed. Ruth Pryor. Cardiff: University of Wales Press, 1976.

Kipling, Rudyard. *The Works of Rudyard Kipling.* Ware: Wordsworth, 1994. Based on *Rudyard Kipling's Verse: Definitive Edition.* New York: Doubleday, 1940.

Larkin, Philip. *Collected Poems.* Ed. Anthony Thwaite. London: Faber & Faber, 1988.

Lawrence, David Herbert. *Complete Poems.* Ed. Vivian de Sola Pinto and Warren Roberts. London: Penguin, 1977.

Lawrence, T. E. *The Selected Letters.* Ed. Malcolm Brown. New York: Paragon House, 1992.

Lewis, Cecil Day. *Collected Poems of C. Day Lewis.* London: Jonathan Cape, 1954.

MacDiarmid, Hugh. *Collected Poems of Hugh MacDiarmid.* New York: Macmillan, 1962.

———. *Lucky Poet.* Berkeley: University of California Press, 1972.

———. *The Socialist Poems of Hugh MacDiarmid.* Ed. T. S. Law and Thurso Berwick. London: Routledge & Kegan Paul, 1978.

MacNeice, Louis. *Collected Poems.* London: Faber & Faber, 1966.

Mew, Charlotte. *Collected Poems of Charlotte Mew.* With a Memoir by Alida Monro. New York: Macmillan, 1954.

Muir, Edwin. *Collected Poems.* London: Faber & Faber, 1960.

———. *An Autobiography.* London: The Hogarth Press, 1964.

Osborne, John. *Look Back In Anger.* New York: S. G. Phillips, 1959.

Owen, Wilfrid. *The Poems of Wilfrid Owen.* Ed. Jon Stallworthy. New York: Norton, 1985.

Pinto, Vivian de Sola. *The City That Shone: An Autobiography (1895–1922).* New York: John Day, 1969.

Pitter, Ruth. *A Trophy of Arms: Poems, 1926–1935.* New York: Macmillan, 1936.

———. *Poems, 1926–1966.* London: Cresset, 1968.

Raine, Kathleen. *The Collected Poems of Kathleen Raine.* London: Hamish Hamilton, 1956.

———. *Farewell Happy Fields: Memories of Childhood.* London: Hamish Hamilton, 1973.

Sassoon, Siegfried. *Collected Poems, 1908–1956.* London: Faber & Faber, 1983.

———. *The War Poems.* London: Faber & Faber, 1983.

Sitwell, Edith. *The Collected Poems of Edith Sitwell.* New York: Vanguard, 1954.

———. *Taken Care Of: The Autobiography of Edith Sitwell.* New York: Atheneum, 1965.

Sitwell, Osbert. *Collected Satires and Poems.* London: Duckworth, 1931.

———. *Great Morning.* London: Macmillan, 1948.

Smith, Stevie. *Collected Poems.* New York: New Directions, 1983.

Spender, Stephen. *Collected Poems, 1928–1953.* New York: Random House, 1955.

———. *The Thirties and After: Poetry, Politics, People, 1933–1970.* New York: Random House, 1978.

Symons, Arthur. *Arthur Symons: Poetry and Prose.* Chatham, England: Fyfield/Carcanet Press, 1974.

Stallworthy, Jon. *The Anzac Sonata.* New York: Norton, 1986.

Thomas, Dylan. *Letters to Vernon Watkins.* Ed. Vernon Watkins. New York: New Directions, 1957.

———. *The Poems of Dylan Thomas.* Ed. Daniel Jones. New York: New Directions, 1971.

———. *On the Air with Dylan Thomas: The Broadcasts.* Ed. Ralph Maud. New York: New Directions, 1992.

Thomas, Edward. *Richard Jefferies*. London: Hutchinson, 1909.

———. *Letters to Gordon Bottomley*. Ed. R. George Thomas. London: Oxford University Press, 1968.

———. *Edward Thomas on the Countryside*. Ed. Roland Gant. London: Faber & Faber, 1977.

———. *A Language Not to be Betrayed: Selected Prose of Edward Thomas*. Ed. Edna Longley. New York: Persea Books, 1981.

———. *The Works of Edward Thomas*. Ware, England: Wordsworth, 1994.

Warner, Sylvia Townsend. *Collected Poems*. Ed. Claire Harman. Manchester, England: Carcanet New Press, 1982.

Warner, Sylvia Townsend, and Valentine Ackland. *Whether a Dove or Seagull*. London: Chatto & Windus, 1934.

Watkins, Vernon. *Ballad of the Mari Lwyd*. London: Faber & Faber, 1941.

Webb, Mary. *Fifty-One Poems*. London: Jonathan Cape, 1946.

Wickham, Anna. *The Writings of Anna Wickham: Free Woman and Poet*. Ed. R. D. Smith. London: Virago, 1984.

Young, Andrew. *The Poetical Works of Andrew Young*. Ed. Edward Lowbury and Alison Young. London: Secker & Warburg, 1985.

Anthologies

Abrams, M. H., ed. *The Norton Anthology of English Literature*. 6th ed. New York: Norton, 1993. Most widely used anthology in American universities.

Adcock, Arthur St. John, ed. *For Remembrance: Soldier Poets Who Have Fallen in the War*. 1918. Revised and enlarged, London: Hodder & Stoughton, 1920. An example of conflicted postwar attitudes.

Amis, Kingsley, ed. *The New Oxford Book of Light Verse*. 1978. Rpt., Oxford: Oxford University Press, 1992. Amis revises greatly the choices Auden made for the original *Oxford Book of Light Verse* (1938).

Dowson, Jane, ed. *Women's Poetry of the 1930s: A Critical Anthology*. London: Routledge, 1996. I discovered Dowson's important work too late to use its insights in this book. In the words of John Lucas, it brings to light "good poetry that has been carelessly buried under the heaped-up orthodoxies of literary history."

Ellmann, Richard, and Robert O'Clair, eds. *The Norton Anthology of Modern Poetry*. 2d ed. New York: Norton, 1988. Extensive coverage but shows a Modernist bias.

Gardner, Brian, ed. *The Terrible Rain: The War Poets, 1939–1945*. London: Methuen, 1966. Includes poems by poets of the 1930s: Auden, MacNeice, Barker, Treece, Day Lewis, Reed, Thomas.

Gilbert, Sandra M., and Susan Gubar, eds. *The Norton Anthology of Literature by Women*. 2d ed. New York: Norton, 1996. Establishes a women's tradition.

Selected Bibliography

Hall, Linda, ed. *An Anthology of Poetry by Women: Tracing the Tradition.* London: Cassell, 1994. Well-chosen selection of lesser-known women poets, mainly British.

Larkin, Philip, ed. *The Oxford Book of Twentieth Century English Verse.* Oxford: Oxford University Press, 1973. Larkin's attempt to reshape the canon selected by Yeats.

Marsh, Edward, ed. *Georgian Poetry, 1911–1912.* 1912. Rpt., London: The Poetry Bookshop, 1923. The influential first Georgian anthology.

Neuberger, Julia, ed. *The Things That Matter: An Anthology of Women's Spiritual Poetry.* New York: St. Martin's Press, 1992. Lesser-known British and American women poets, including large selections of Alice Meynell, Mary Coleridge, Edith Nesbit, and Vita Sackville-West.

Osborn, E. B., ed. *The Muse in Arms.* London: John Murray, 1917. Extraordinarily popular—and revealing—wartime anthology.

Reilly, Catherine W., ed. *Scars Upon My Heart: Women's Poetry and Verse of the First World War.* London: Virago, 1981. Often cited collection whose purpose is to rescue women's wartime writing; unfortunately, the poems are selected too uncritically, often supporting inadvertently the slurs made against women poets during the war.

Scott, Bonnie Kime, ed. *The Gender of Modernism: A Critical Anthology.* Bloomington: Indiana University Press, 1990. Small selections of 26 American and British (mostly female) writers; points to directions for new studies.

Silkin, Jon, ed. *The Penguin Book of First World War Poetry.* Harmondsworth, England: Penguin, 1979. International flavor, though heavily English.

Untermeyer, Louis, ed. *Modern British Poetry.* 1920. Revised, New York: Harcourt, Brace & World, 1962. A good source for harder-to-find poets whose reputations have waned since the first half of the century.

Yeats, William Butler, ed. *The Oxford Book of Modern Verse.* New York: Oxford University Press, 1936. The century's greatest poet makes his often politically motivated choices of the century's best verse.

Literary Histories

Perkins, David. *A History of Modern Poetry: From the 1890s to the High Modernist Mode.* Cambridge: Harvard University Press, 1976. A survey of both American and British poetry that is both broad and deep; extraordinarily ambitious—and successful.

———. *A History of Modern Poetry: Modernism and After.* Cambridge: Harvard University Press, 1987. The project completed, with consistency and balance.

Pinto, Vivian de Sola. *Crisis in English Poetry, 1880–1940.* London: Hutchinson University Library, 1951. A wide-ranging mind—editor, poet, translator, critic, and professor—examines the modern period through the lens of the Renaissance, seeing a crisis with the ending of a stable, rural, hierarchically based society.

Press, John. *A Map of Modern English Verse.* London: Oxford University Press, 1969. Useful for its historicity, reproducing book reviews, criticism, and poems as well as its opinions.

Thwaite, Anthony. *Twentieth-Century English Poetry.* London: Heinemann, 1978. An important English poet surveys the century.

Untermeyer, Louis. *Lives of the Poets: The Story of One Thousand Years of English and American Poetry.* New York: Simon and Schuster, 1959. Popular, readable, and short biographies.

Secondary Sources

Ackerman, John. *Dylan Thomas: His Life and Work.* New York: St. Martin's, 1996. Critical study emphasizing Thomas's Welsh background.

Baker, Deborah. *In Extremis: The Life of Laura Riding.* New York: Grove Press, 1993. Literary biography.

Bergonzi, Bernard. *Heroes' Twilight: A Study of the Literature of the Great War.* New York: Coward-McCann, 1966. One of the earliest studies, by an important critic, which slights, however, Edward Thomas.

———. *Reading the Thirties.* Pittsburgh: University of Pittsburgh Press, 1978. Examination of the thirties which, like Samuel Hynes's, virtually ignores that any women were writing then, but gives sound judgments of canonical writers.

Bloom, Harold. *The Anxiety of influence.* New York: Oxford University Press, 1973. Quirky but influential theoretical study of intertextuality.

Booth, Allyson. *Postcards from the Trenches: Negotiating the Space between Modernism and the First World War.* New York: Oxford University Press, 1996. An examination of material culture, from postcards to glass to architecture.

Brinnan, John Malcolm. *Dylan Thomas in America.* New York: Viking, 1957. Subtitled "An Intimate Journal," Brinnan's account of his chaperoning of Thomas during his four visits to America.

Broe, Mary Lynn, and Angela Ingram. *Women's Writing in Exile.* Chapel Hill: University of North Carolina Press, 1986. Essays on canonicity, H. D., Mary Coleridge, Sylvia Townsend Warner.

Bryan, Sharon. *Where We Stand: Women Poets on Literary Tradition.* New York: Norton, 1993. Essays on the meanings and uses of tradition by Anne Stevenson and Eavan Boland, among others.

Bucknell, Katherine, and Nicholas Jenkins, eds. *W. H. Auden: "The Map of All My Youth."* Auden Studies 1. Oxford: Clarendon Press, 1990. Auden's earliest works, friends, and influences, including his German poems from the Berlin years, with translations.

————. W. H. Auden: "The Language of Learning and the Language of Love." Auden Studies 2. Oxford: Clarendon Press, 1994. Uncollected writings, new interpretations, and a bibliography of interviews with Auden.

Caesar, Adrian. *Dividing Lines: Poetry, Class, and Ideology in the 1930s.* Manchester, England: Manchester University Press, 1991. Critique of Hynes's *The Auden Generation,* arguing against letting Auden stand as a representative for the 1930s.

————. *Taking It Like a Man: Suffering, Sexuality, and the War Poets.* Manchester, England: Manchester University Press, 1994. Provocative study advancing Fussell's arguments about war and the erotic.

Carey, John. *The Intellectuals and the Masses: Pride and Prejudice Among the Literary Intelligenstia, 1880–1939.* New York: St. Martin's, 1992. Issues of class, especially as they affect the Edwardians and Georgians.

Carter, D. N. G. *Robert Graves: The Lasting Poetic Achievement.* Totowa, N.J.: Barnes & Noble, 1989. Study devoted to the poetry but aware of the prose.

Clark, Arthur Melville. *The Realistic Revolt in Modern Poetry.* 1922. Rpt., New York: Haskell, 1966. Illustrates class attitudes Carey discusses.

Conniff, Brian. "Richard Davenport-Hine's *Auden* and the Problem of Auden Criticism." *Christianity and Literature* 46:2 (Winter 1997). A review essay wrestling with the problem of reconciling the early and late Auden, Marxist and then Christian.

Cooper, Helen M., Adrienne Auslander Munich, and Susan Merrill Squier, eds. *Arms and the Woman: War, Gender, and Literary Representation.* Chapel Hill: University of North Carolina Press, 1989. Essays toward establishing a tradition of war writing for women.

Crawford, Fred D. *British Poets of the Great War.* Selinsgrove, Penn.: Susquehanna University Press, 1988. Critical study admirable for its coverage and insightful readings.

Davenport-Hines, Richard. *Auden.* New York: Pantheon, 1995. Literary biography.

Davie, Donald. *Thomas Hardy and British Poetry.* London: Routledge & Kegan Paul, 1973. Seminal study looking to establish an "English" tradition issuing from Hardy rather than Yeats, Pound, or Eliot.

————. *Under Briggflatts: A History of Poetry in Great Britain, 1960–1988.* Chicago: University of Chicago Press, 1989. A collection of reviews woven together more carefully than such collections usually are, so that it does function as a history.

Day, Gary, and Brian Docherty, eds. *British Poetry, 1900–1950: Aspects of Tradition.* New York: St. Martin's, 1995. Brief but strong essays by Neil Roberts, Stan Smith, and Gary Day.

————. *British Poetry from the 1950s to the 1990s: Politics and Art.* London: Macmillan, 1997. More good essays, especially on female canon formation.

Selected Bibliography

Delany, Paul. *D. H. Lawrence's Nightmare*. New York: Basic Books, 1978. Study of Lawrence and his circle during the war years, including H. D.

——. *The Neo-Pagans: Rupert Brooke and the Ordeal of Youth*. New York: The Free Press, 1987. Study of Brooke and his circle, including Virginia Woolf and Frances (Darwin) Cornford.

Douglass, Ann. *Terrible Honesty: Mongrel Manhattan in the 1920s*. New York: Farrar, Strauss & Giroux, 1995. Jazz Age America's break with tradition, with New York as the center of the new Modernism.

Eates, Margot. *Paul Nash: The Master of the Image, 1889–1946*. London: J. Murray, 1973. Contains a detailed chronology of the life and the works, with 144 plates.

Eksteins, Modris. *Rites of Spring: The Great War and the Birth of the Modern Age*. 1989. Rpt., New York: Anchor, 1990. A cultural study of Modernism, focusing on ballet, arguing that the primitivism valued by the early Modernists is connected to the fascism of the 1930s.

Feinstein, Elaine. *Lawrence and the Women*. New York: Harper Collins, 1993. Subtitled "The Intimate Life of D. H. Lawrence," deals mostly with Lawrence's lovers but also includes information on H. D., Anna Wickham, and Katherine Mansfield.

Ford, Hugh D., ed. *A Poet's War: British Poets and the Spanish Civil War*. Philadelphia: University of Pennsylvannia Press, 1965. Study of the poetic and personal responses of Auden, Cunard, and John Cornford, among others.

——. *Nancy Cunard: Brave Poet, Indomitable Rebel, 1896–1965*. Philadelphia: Chilton, 1968. Poems, biography, and reminiscences by friends of Cunard.

Fuller, Roy. *Professors and Gods*. London: Andre Deutsch, 1973. Fuller's last lectures as Oxford Professor of Poetry.

Fussell, Paul. *The Great War and Modern Memory*. Oxford: Oxford University Press, 1975. Seminal study of the "literariness" of WWI.

Gaston, George, ed. *Critical Essays on Dylan Thomas*. Boston: G. K. Hall, 1989. Essays and reviews by fellow poets: Empson, Nemerov, Aiken, Berryman, Thwaite, Hall.

Gervais, David. *Literary Englands: Versions of "Englishness" in English Writing*. Cambridge: Cambridge University Press, 1994. Study of the construction of "Englishness."

Gilbert, Elliot L. *Kipling and the Critics*. New York: New York University Press, 1965. Essays by Orwell and Eliot.

Gilbert, Sandra, and Susan Gubar. *No Man's Land: The Place of the Woman Writer in the Twentieth Century*. Vol. I: "The War of the Words." New Haven, Conn.: Yale University Press, 1988. Exploration of the "affiliation complex" of Modernist women writers.

Glendinning, Victoria. *Edith Sitwell: A Unicorn Among Lions*. New York: Knopf, 1981. Biography.

Selected Bibliography

Goldman, Dorothy, with Jane Gledhill and Judith Hattaway. *Women Writers and the Great War*. New York: Twayne, 1995. Examines the connections between men's and women's war writing.

Graham, Desmond. *The Truth of War: Owen, Blunden, Rosenberg*. Manchester: Carcanet Press, 1984. Sympathetic study by the poet, biographer, and editor of Keith Douglas's poems.

Graves, Richard Perceval. *Robert Graves: The Assault Heroic, 1895–1926*. New York: Viking, 1987. Biographical study of Graves's early career by a family member.

Hagen, Patricia. *Metaphor's Way of Knowing: The Poetry of D. H. Lawrence and the Church of Mechanism*. New York: Peter Lang, 1995. A careful reading of Lawrence's "sequences," as well as a practical application of ground-breaking work in metaphor theory by Lakoff and Johnson.

Heaney, Seamus. *The Redress of Poetry*. New York: Farrar, Strauss & Giroux, 1995. The Nobel laureate on Larkin, MacDiarmid, and Dylan Thomas.

Helsinger, Elizabeth K. *Rural Scenes and National Representation: Britain, 1815–1850*. Princeton, N.J.: Princeton University Press, 1997. Theoretical work on the relationship between land and nation.

Herbert, Robert L. *Impressionism: Art, Leisure, and Parisian Society*. New Haven, Conn.: Yale University Press, 1988. Social history of Impressionism.

Hewison, Robert. *Under Siege: Literary Life in London, 1939–1945*. New York: Oxford University Press, 1977. Social history of the arts.

Hoffpauir, Richard. *The Art of Restraint*. London and Toronto: Associated University Presses, 1991. Traces Yeats-Hardy influence through modern British poetry.

Hughes, Glenn. *Imagism & The Imagists: A Study in Modern Poetry*. New York: Biblo and Tannen, 1972. Study of Pound, Hulme, and the Imagist movement.

Hughes, Ted. *Winter Pollen: Occasional Prose*. New York: Picador, 1994. Poet laureate's sometimes quirky, always thought-provoking takes on literature.

Hynes, Samuel. *Edwardian Occasions: Essays on English Writing in the Early Twentieth Century*. New York: Oxford University Press, 1972. Seminal essay on Edwardian England.

———. *The Auden Generation*. 1972. Rpt., New York: The Viking Press, 1977. A cultural history of England in the 1930s.

———. *A War Imagined: The First World War and English Culture*. New York: Atheneum, 1991. How the war transformed English culture and imaginations.

Johnston, John H. *English Poetry of the First World War*. Princeton, N.J.: Princeton University Press, 1964. First comprehensive study.

———. *The Poet and the City*. Athens: University of Georgia Press, 1984. Traces urban imagery from classical times through Eliot.

Judd, Alan. *Ford Madox Ford*. London: Collins, 1990. Literary biography.

Kelsall, Malcolm. *The Great Good Place: The Country House and English Literature*. New York: Columbia University Press, 1993. Establishes meaning and themes of the country-house tradition.

Khan, Nosheen. *Women's Poetry of the First World War*. Lexington: University Press of Kentucky, 1988. Well-researched and balanced assessment of women poets.

Laskowski, William E. *Rupert Brooke*. New York: Twayne, 1994. Biographical and historical criticism of the poetry.

Levy, Mervyn, ed. *Paintings of D. H. Lawrence*. London: Cory, Adams & Mackay, 1964. Color reproductions, with essays by Harry T. Moore, Jack Lindsay, and Herbert Read.

Longley, Edna. *Poetry in the Wars*. Newcastle upon Tyne, England: Bloodaxe Books, 1986. Essays on Edward Thomas, others.

Lucas, John. *Modern English Poetry from Hardy to Hughes*. London: B. T. Batsford, 1986. Very good writer on the "English" tradition in poetry.

———. "The Sunlight on the Garden," in *Seeing Double: Revisioning Edwardian and Modernist Literature*. Ed. Carola M. Kaplan and Anne B. Simpson. New York: St. Martin's Press, 1996. Lucas, in the best essay in the collection, examines concepts of "house" and "garden" in H. G. Wells and E. M. Forster.

Marsh, Jan. *Edward Thomas: A Poet for His Country*. New York: Harper & Row, 1978. Critical and biographical study.

Meyers, Jeffrey. *Robert Frost: A Biography*. Boston: Houghton Mifflin, 1996. Strong on Frost's connection to Thomas Hardy and the Georgians.

Millard, Kenneth. *Edwardian Poetry*. Oxford: Clarendon Press, 1991. Thoughtful treatments of Henry Newbolt and John Masefield, as well as of more respected Edwardians.

Montefiore, Jan. *Feminism and Poetry: Language, Experience, Identity in Women's Writing*. 1987. Rpt., London: Harper Collins, 1994. Wide-ranging and judicious examination of Gilbert and Gubar's theory of female tradition in comparison with other possibilities.

Moore, Harry T. *Poste Restante: A Lawrence Travel Calendar*. Berkeley: University of California Press, 1956. A detailed record of Lawrence's travels, with an introductory essay by Mark Schorer.

Motion, Andrew. *The Poetry of Edward Thomas*. London: Routledge & Kegan Paul, 1980. Psychological readings of Thomas's poems from an important poet and admirer.

Mulford, Wendy. *This Narrow Place: Sylvia Townsend Warner and Valentine Ackland: Life, Letters, and Politics, 1930–1951*. London: Pandora, 1988. Study of Warner's novels and Ackland's poetry in light of their relationship.

Norris, Leslie, ed. *Vernon Watkins, 1906–1967*. London: Faber & Faber, 1970. Commemorative essays by friends and fellow poets, including Glyn

Selected Bibliography

Jones, John Heath-Stubbs, Philip Larkin, R. S. Thomas, Kathleen Raine, Marianne Moore, Michael Hamburger, and George Barker.

O'Neil, Michael, and Gareth Reeves. *Auden, MacNeice, Spender: The Thirties Poetry.* New York: St. Martin's Press, 1992. Close readings of key poems by the three poets whom the authors regard as the major figures of the decade.

Osborne, Charles. *W. H. Auden: The Life of a Poet.* 1979. Rpt., New York: M. Evans, 1995. Biography.

Page, Norman. *A. E. Housman: A Critical Biography.* New York: Schocken Books, 1983. Biography.

Parfitt, George. *English Poetry of the First World War.* New York: Harvester Wheatsheaf, 1990. Chapters on noncommissioned voices and on Robert Graves's relatively unknown war poetry.

Parker, Peter. *The Old Lie: The Great War and the Public School Ethos.* London: Constable, 1987. Social history.

Pearson, John. *The Sitwells.* New York: Harcourt Brace Jovanovich, 1978. Biography of the three siblings, with important references to D. H. Lawrence.

Quinn, Patrick J. *The Great War and the Missing Muse.* Selinsgrove, Penn.: Susquehanna University Press, 1994. Study of the early work of Robert Graves and Siegfried Sassoon.

Rankin, Arthur C. *The Poetry of Stevie Smith: "Little Girl Lost."* Totowa, N.J.: Barnes & Noble, 1985. Reprints many of Smith's "doodlings."

Reck, Michael. *Ezra Pound: A Close-Up.* New York: McGraw-Hill, 1967. Memoir.

Reid, Alastair. "Remembering Robert Graves." *New Yorker.* 4 September 1995. 70–81. Memoir.

Ross, Robert H. *The Georgian Revolt, 1910–1922: Rise and Fall of a Poetic Ideal.* Carbondale: Southern Illinois University Press, 1965. First attempt to resuscitate Georgians.

Salmon, Arthur Edward. *Poets of the Apocalypse.* Boston: Twayne, 1983. Helpful study of a lesser-known movement.

Schmidt, Michael. *Fifty Modern British Poets: A Reader's Guide.* London: Heinemann, 1979. Fifty short essays.

Schweik, Susan. *A Gulf So Deeply Cut: American Women Poets and the Second World War.* Madison: University of Wisconsin Press, 1991. Chapter on lessons of WWI.

Seymour, Miranda. *Robert Graves: Life on the Edge.* New York: Henry Holt, 1995. Biography.

Seymour-Smith, Martin. *Robert Graves: His Life and Work.* London: Sphere Books, 1983. Biography.

Shires, Linda M. *British Poetry of the Second World War.* New York: St. Martin's Press, 1985. Chapter titled "Where Are the War Poets?" examines perennial question about the differences between the literatures of the two world wars.

Silkin, Jon. *Out of Battle: The Poetry of the Great War.* London: Oxford University Press, 1972. Argues with Johnston on canon and criteria.

Smith, Stan. *W. H. Auden.* London: Basil Blackwell, 1985. Argues Auden's ideology.

Spalding, Frances. *Stevie Smith.* New York: Norton, 1989. Biography.

Spender, Stephen, ed. *W. H. Auden: A Tribute.* New York: Macmillan, 1975. Recollections of friends, fellow poets, family, lovers, and critics such as John Bayley. Many photos, including Auden in his U.S. Army uniform.

Stallworthy, Jon. *Louis MacNeice.* New York: Norton, 1995. Critical and biographical study.

Sternlicht, Sanford. *Stevie Smith.* Boston: Twayne, 1990. Introduction to life and works.

———. *Stephen Spender.* New York: Twayne, 1992. Introduction to life and works.

Thurley, Geoffrey. *The Ironic Harvest: English Poetry in the Twentieth Century.* New York: St. Martin's Press, 1974. Chapters on Auden, Spender, Empson, Thomas, and Gascoyne.

Treece, Henry. *Dylan Thomas: "Dog Among the Fairies."* 1949. Rev., London: Ernest Benn, 1956. Close analysis of Thomas's technique by the *New Apocalypse* editor (who offended Thomas with this book by referring to him as "Dylan" rather than "Mr. Thomas").

Tremlett, George. *Dylan Thomas: In the Mercy of His Means.* New York: St. Martin's Press, 1992. Biography.

Walsh, John Evangelist. *Into My Own: The English Years of Robert Frost.* New York: Grove Weidenfeld, 1988. Details Frost's early publishing history and relationship with the Georgians.

Wilhelm, J. J. *Ezra Pound in London and Paris, 1908–1925.* University Park: Pennsylvania State University Press, 1990. Examines Pound's influence on literary life in these early years.

Williams, Charles. *Poetry at Present.* 1930. Rpt., Freeport, N.Y.: Books for Libraries Press, 1969. A poet, Oxford don, and friend of Tolkien and Lewis sums up the state of poetry in 1930.

Williams, Raymond. *The Country and the City.* Oxford: Oxford University Press, 1973. Seminal study.

Wilson, Angus. *The Strange Ride of Rudyard Kipling: His Life and Works.* 1977. Rpt., New York: Penguin, 1979. Biography.

Woods, Gregory. *Articulate Flesh: Male Homo-Eroticism and Modern Poetry.* New Haven, Conn.: Yale University Press, 1987. Argues that homoeroticism is a more encompassing term than homosexuality, which tends to shunt the homoerotic experience onto a sidetrack reserved only for a few gay poets or poems.

· *Index* ·

Index

Index

Index

Index

Ito, Michio, 81

Jacob, 114
Johnson, Samuel, 169
Jones-Bateman, Frank, 96
Jones, David, 161, 168–69; *In Parenthesis*, 168–69
Jones, Glyn, 161, 169
Joyce, James: "The Dead," 80; *Finnegan's Wake*, 168; *Ulysses*, 1
Jungianism, 88, 150–51

Keats, John, 37; "Ode to a Nightingale," 46; and Owen, 77, 79; and Sorley, 62
King James Bible, 127
Kipling, Rudyard: "A Charm," 41; and class, 64; and Empire, 4, 5; "The Glory of the Garden," 25; "Gods of the Copybook Headings," 6; and the Graves Commission, 50; "The King's Pilgrimage," 50; "The Land," 6; "The 'Mary Gloster'," 5; and the Nobel Prize, 93; and popular poetry, 13; "Recessional," 5
Koume, Tami, 81
Kunitz, Stanley, 132

Landseer, Edwin: "The Old Shepherd's Chief Mourner," 33
Larkin, Philip, 13, 140, 158; "An April Sunday Brings the Snow," 147–48; "Church Going," 141; "High Windows," 141; *The Oxford Book of Twentieth Century English Verse*, 28
laureateship: and the Auden generation, 134, 154; and Austin, 3; and Bridges, 13–14, 93; and Heaney, 160; and Masefield, 93; and Southey, 24; and Tennyson, 3; and Wordsworth, 3
Lautréamont, 138
Lawrence, D. H., 22, 65, 121–28; *Birds, Beasts and Flowers*, 121, 123–24; and death, 128; and David Garnett, 97; "Healing," 127; *Lady Chatterly's Lover*, 124, 128; *Last Poems*, 121; *Look! We Have Come Through!* 122–23; and mechanization, 124–26; *Pansies*, 124; *Poetry of the Present*, 126; "Pomegranate," 123; "Prayer," 128; *The Rainbow*, 54, 97; 128; "The Scientific

Doctor," 127–28; and sex, 128–29; status as a poet, 124–27; *Women in Love*, 54, 56
Lawrence, Frieda von Richthofen Weekley, 22, 97, 122, 128
Lawrence, T. E.: *Revolt in the Desert*, 93, 113
Leavis, F. R., 104, 149
Lehmann, John, 136
Lewis, Alun, 145; "All Day It Has Rained," 146–47
Lewis, C. S., 5, 158
Li Po, 106
Llalans, 161, 168
Lloyd-George, David, 1
Loeffelholz, Mary, 19
Loy, Mina, 129
Lucas, John, 25, 34

MacDiarmid, Hugh (C. M. Grieve), 138, 161–63; "And, Above All, My Poetry Is Marxist," 162; "Another Epitaph on an Army of Mercenaries," 161–62; "At the Cenotaph," 162; "British Leftist Poetry, 1930–1940," 161; "An English War Poet," 162; "Fascists, You Have Killed My Comrades," 162; and Llalans, 161; "Parley of the Beasts," 161; "Poetry and Propaganda," 163; "Royal Wedding Gifts," 162–63
MacNeice, Louis, 134, 160, 175–76; *Autumn Journal*, 175; "Cradle Song for Eleanor," 175–76
Madge, Charles, 138
magazines: *Blast*, 81–82, 100, 136; *The Little Review*, 136; *New Signatures*, 136; *New Verse*, 136; *New Writing*, 136; *Penguin New Writing*, 136; *Poetry*, 17, 26; *Poetry London*, 137; *Twentieth Century Verse*, 136–37; *Wheels*, 100, 101, 136
Majorca, 116
Manning, Frederic: *Her Privates We*, 93
Mansfield, Katherine, 128
Marne, 50
Mars, 89
Marsh, Edward: and Brooke, 14, 27; and the Georgian anthologies, 14, 22, 30, 93; and Rosenberg, 75–76; and Sassoon, 72

Index

Index

Index

Index

· *The Author* ·

James Persoon, after stints of farmwork and soldiering, has spent the past 20 years teaching at universities in England, Poland, and America. He is currently professor of English at Grand Valley State University, where he has directed several of its writing programs. He has published articles and notes on Arnold, Browning, Hardy, Shelley, Shakespeare, Milton, Orwell, Kipling, Beatrix Potter, and the Venerable Bede. His wife is the fiction writer Christl Reges. They live with their six children far from the cornfields of Iowa, in a resort town on Lake Michigan.